Y0-BVO-489

Quakers World Wide

An 'Interim Executive Committee' which met in London in September, 1946, to determine directions for FWCC after Second World War. Front row (l to r): Harry Silcock, Passmore Elkinton, Carl Heath, Anna Griscom Elkinton, Hans Albrecht, Barrow Cadbury. Back row: Maurice Webb, Errol Elliott, Bertram Pickard, Blanche Shaffer, Leslie Shaffer, Frederick Tritton.

A15043 751259

Quakers World Wide

A History of Friends World Committee for Consultation

Herbert M. Hadley

*BX
7605
.H33x
West*

FRIENDS WORLD COMMITTEE FOR CONSULTATION
DRAYTON HOUSE, 30 GORDON STREET, LONDON WC1H 0AX
in association with
WILLIAM SESSIONS LTD., YORK, ENGLAND

© Friends World Committee for Consultation 1991

ISBN 1 85072 078 9

The cover is by graphic designer, Helen Hadley, daughter of the author

Printed in 10/11 point Plantin Typeface
by William Sessions Limited
The Ebor Press
York, England

Contents

Illustrations

vi

Foreword

by Wilmer A. Cooper, Earlham School of Religion, Richmond, Indiana, USA

WE ARE ALL INDEBTED to Herbert Hadley for the painstaking research and writing he has done in preparing this history of the Friends World Committee for Consultation. Because of his personal involvement and commitment he has been able to tell the story from the inside, and yet he has demonstrated the kind of objectivity needed to make it a reliable account.

As the reader approaches this book it may be useful to reflect for a moment on the kind of world we have been living in during the 20th century, and what kind of forces have been at work during FWCC's developing years, 1920-1988.

Who can forget the dreadful two World Wars and the series of regional wars which have dominated this century? Coupled with this we have seen the rise and fall of ruthless dictatorships with the kind of disregard for human life that resulted in an unprecedented holocaust. We have also seen periods of serious economic depression and dislocation, the explosions of population attended by poverty, famine and starvation. All this has taken place in a century which has seen the most far-reaching development of scientific and technological advancements toward human betterment the world has ever known. A century which began with a sense of optimism based on a progress view of history has become a century in which human hopes and aspirations have been subdued, and in some cases dashed. A world which has been divided between east and west for half a century, now appears to be increasingly divided between the north and the south, between 'the haves' and 'the have nots'.

At the turn of the century the Society of Friends was undergoing an historic transformation from a century dominated by Christian evangelicalism in both England and America to an emerging Quaker liberalism in theology and social policy. Quaker faith and practice were undergoing a metamorphosis. Herbert Hadley has acknowledged this shift from a dominant evangelical leadership to a significant group of younger Friends in England and America of more liberal persuasion. They wanted to refashion Quakerism into a vital faith and practice which could speak to

viii

the youth of this scientific age, and at the same time give expression to the basic testimonies of Friends.

These same Friends also had a vision for a divided Society of Friends in which members would rediscover each other through a deepening of their religious faith and an application of it in service to others. FWCC was initiated by Friends who were also associated with the Quaker service agencies.

Even though liberal Quakerism was in the ascendency during the first half of the 20th century, it is well to remember that evangelical Quakerism was very much alive in some quarters, especially in the United States. It was largely Friends of this persuasion who inaugurated the missionary movement in Kenya, East Africa, and in many other parts of the world: Latin America, the Middle East, South Asia, and the Far East. These Christian missions spawned the development of Friends work in the Third World, now the fastest growing area of Quakerdom.

As we read the history of FWCC we need to ask to what extent its development was influenced by religious and social forces from outside the Society of Friends. One of the peculiarities of Quaker history is that Friends often have written about their own experiences in journals and histories but have made little, if any, reference to how the world around impacted them.

As Friends interfaced with the religious and social forces of the 20th century, what were some of the influences upon them? One can begin with the widespread involvement of Rufus Jones, and many like-minded Friends, with religious mysticism. So great was this influence that liberal Quakerism came to be identified with what Rufus Jones called 'affirmative' or 'practical' mysticism. This identification was scarcely mentioned by Friends prior to the rewriting of Quaker history by Rufus Jones and William Charles Braithwaite at the turn of the century. But it so impacted Quakerism early in this century that for some Friends mysticism and Quakerism became synonymous terms. In turn, this expression of Quaker faith has had a marked influence on the development of FWCC.

Although Friends were influenced at the turn of the century by the liberal spirit of Protestant Christianity, the reverse of this happened when Christian liberalism was overtaken by Neo-orthodoxy by the middle of the century. A remarkable thing here is that Friends, both liberal and evangelical, pretty much ignored this new interpretation of Christian faith. Some Friends even prided themselves that they were uninfluenced by these theological developments. Yet some young Friends who were trained in the mainline seminaries and universities during the middle years of the 20th century took these changes more seriously. Among their mentors were Karl

Barth, Emil Brunner, Reinhold and H. Richard Niebuhr, and Paul Tillich. If we were to update this list to the present it would include other prominent names, some Roman Catholics among them.

In the still wider world, some Friends were made aware of existentialist thought of men like Kierkegaard and, later, Karl Jaspers who influenced the Quaker Richard Ullmann and his writings. In the area of social policy many Friends were strongly drawn to the Gandhian philosophy of non-violence, and the non-violent direct action work of Martin Luther King. There has also been a spinoff influence from the Liberation theologians of Latin America, especially the shift in Friends emphasis on peace based on reconciliation of differences, to an emphasis on social justice as the basis of a sound peace.

A relatively new development among Friends, which has involved FWCC directly, has been the move toward 'Quaker Universalism'. The question here is whether Quakerism should leave aside its historical, biblical, and Christian origins in favor of welcoming all seekers after truth, regardless of their religious orientation and affiliation. There has always been an historic Quaker universalism within the context of Christian faith, as articulated by Robert Barclay in the 17th century, but to set aside that formulation in favor of Quakerism as a pathway to God devoid of its historic Christian roots, this poses a new approach which the majority of Friends is unable to accept. Those known as the Quaker Universalist Group 'believe that all religious experience points toward a source of truth greater than that enshrined in any one religion'. Thus a growing number of persons want to be joined with Friends in the unprogrammed tradition with this new understanding of the meaning of Quakerism. FWCC often finds itself at the center of this controversy even though it has not attempted to articulate a position pertaining thereto. As FWCC tries to serve as a bridge to unite Friends in the worldwide Quaker family, it inevitably feels the effects of new directions, such as this, in the Society of Friends.

Quakerism has survived nearly 350 years of testing, sometimes resulting in tragic separations. Although FWCC and other important efforts at reconciliation have been at work throughout this century, there is still more work to be done. Many of these efforts have been enumerated by Herbert Hadley in this volume. At the same time, all of us who call ourselves Friends need to be vigilant in our search for a common vision that will heal our differences and unite us in a common fellowship with a common history. And we must be careful not to sacrifice our Quaker vision of God's leading for the sake of gaining outward unity. The unity we seek must be unity 'in spirit and truth'. In short, that must be the driving force behind the work of FWCC to which this important book is dedicated.

Wilmer A. Cooper

Acknowledgements

MANY PERSONS HAVE ASSISTED ME in one way or another as I have delved into archives, organized the information gleaned, and then written and re-written the chapters which now appear in this history of the Friends World Committee for Consultation. I am grateful to all, including my colleagues of committee and staff during the 25 years we worked together and I learned through experience about the FWCC.

Most of the recorded information I have used is in one of two libraries – Friends House Library in London and the Friends Historical Library at Swarthmore College in Pennsylvania. Edward H. (Ted) Milligan, as Friends House Librarian during the time I worked there, helpfully suggested sources of information and, critically useful to me, arranged for the FWCC files on deposit to be loaned to the Library at Woodbrooke College in Birmingham, during my nine months' sojourn there. Josef Keith, also at Friends House Library, accommodated my every need for boxes of files to be brought from, or returned to, their subterranean storage.

And at the Friends Historical Library, Swarthmore College, where FWCC's Section of the Americas archives are deposited, J. William (Jerry) Frost, Director, and Assistant Director, Albert W. Fowler, followed by Mary Ellen Chijioke, made certain that my requirements were met. There, Nancy Spears, Ramsey Turberg (now deceased), Jane Thorson, and Claire Shetter cheerfully provided the day-to-day services I needed.

Woodbrooke College, in Birmingham, England, made me a 'Fellow' for the year 1982-83, providing time and opportunity for some of my earlier work on this FWCC history. Christina Lawson, Woodbrooke Librarian, cared for the FWCC files on loan and gave me well lighted space for research in those files.

When, after counsel from many friends, and much revising of text, I thought my best writing had been done, Patricia Daly Ireland, as 'Assisting Editor', has made interlinear and marginal notes on my manuscript, with results which readers will surely appreciate.

To meet expenses of travel for research and other expenses incidental to writing, generous support has been provided through the FWCC and its Section of the Americas by the Barrow and Geraldine S. Cadbury Trust and the Joseph Rowntree Charitable Trust in Britain and by the Thomas H. and Mary Williams Shoemaker Fund in Philadephia.

Now that this history of the FWCC is ready for publication, the Joseph Rowntree Charitable Trust is again providing assistance through an arrangement which makes this publication possible. The Sessions Book Trust, in York, England, has also given generous assistance. The Thomas H. and Mary Williams Shoemaker Fund has contributed again at this stage, and both the Bequest Committee and the Publications Committee of Philadelphia Yearly Meeting have given generous support. A number of individual Friends have also assisted this project. The Friends Historical Association in the United States has garnered this financial support from American sources and has helped to move this project forward in other ways.

Elsewhere, I have referred to an advisory group of three Friends appointed by the FWCC to advise and assist me in the whole process of writing and publishing the work which is now ready for the reader. To Lewis Waddilove of York, England, and to Margaret Hope Bacon and Edwin Bronner, both of Philadelphia, I give warm thanks for all their help on this long road.

My daughter, Helen Hadley Dana, produced the cover design and has helpfully advised me about photographs and their use.

To Ruthanna, my wife, I give special thanks for her help with my research, for proofreading of the manuscript, for urging me on when I sometimes lagged in production, and for her patience with me when I was not available for family responsibilities. She has played an important part in making ready this story of the Friends World Committee for Consultation.

Herbert M. Hadley,
Philadelphia

Introduction

BEFORE I RETIRED from the staff of Friends World Committee for Consultation I offered to undertake the writing of a history of the FWCC. The Interim Committee appointed an Advisory Group to watch over and assist my work. These three Friends – Margaret Hope Bacon and Edwin Bronner of Philadelphia, and Lewis Waddilove of York, England – have provided valuable advice and assistance.

My love for the FWCC began years before I became its General Secretary in 1955. The American Section held many of its annual meetings in Washington while I was Secretary of Friends Meetings there, beginning in 1947. I arranged hospitality for its members and attended the sessions. Baltimore Yearly Meeting made me one of their representatives to the Friends World Conference in 1952, at Oxford, England. My acquaintance with Friends was widening.

My six years as FWCC General Secretary (1956-62) gave our family (Ruthanna and our three children and me) the wonderful experience of living among British Friends. Travel as FWCC staff visitor extended my acquaintance to Friends in Africa, Asia and the West Pacific, and Europe. Then after nineteen years as Section of the Americas' Executive Secretary I could feel at home with Friends in North America and the Caribbean Area.

With the exception of Carl Heath, the FWCC's first chairman (1937-47), I have had personal acquaintance with the principal officers of the FWCC and its Sections during the committee's first half-century. To better understand the man whose vision helped to hold a fledgling FWCC together during the Second World War, I interviewed many Friends who knew Carl Heath intimately.

This rich experience of being a part of world Quakerism leaves me in debt to the FWCC. I hope that my offering this history of the committee's first fifty years is in some measure payment of that debt.

The first four chapters of this book tell the story of the FWCC's first quarter century in chronological order, from its prenatal period through a rather difficult birth; then through troubled infancy during the Second World War and a problem childhood under too strict parental control in the postwar years. In mid-adolescence the struggling FWCC organism felt a loosening of bonds with the major reorganization of 1955. The Friends World Committee for Consultation could develop its own identity and purpose in the next six years.

Early counsel from one of my advisers suggested my writing less about what the FWCC does and more about what it is. I found it difficult to separate the doing from the being. But once its identity and purpose were established, the peculiar characteristics of the FWCC could be recognized. From IV onward, chapter headings provide that recognition – Catalyst for Consultation, Sponsor of Spiritual Nurture, and on through the list. Activities identifying the characteristic described by a chapter title are recorded each in its own sequential order.

Chapter IX is somewhat an exception. It is an account of the Fourth World Conference of Friends in 1967, an event and an experience toward which the FWCC organism had grown. It is my thesis that with this world conference the FWCC came to maturity, and that all which it might achieve after 1967 would be the actions of a mature body.

The two words 'for consultation' were put into the FWCC name intentionally to prevent its exercise of authority over yearly meetings. A strict and limiting interpretation of 'consultation' gradually was loosened until, in the implementation of concerns articulated by the 1967 conference, the FWCC's sponsoring of communication about, and cooperative support for, projects was accepted as 'consultation'. Thus consultation was no longer a limiting weakness, but FWCC's strength.

Since by its very nature Quakerism encourages diversity and decentralization, Friends have used a multiplicity of committees and organizations to perform the tasks they wish to accomplish. Names of most of these bodies contain three or four or more words. The use of acronyms, such as FWCC, AFSC, and QPS, is frequent in this book. An 'Explanation of Acronyms' is provided on the very last pages of this book.

Some who have read this history in manuscript form feel uncomfortable with my use of the term 'Quaker leader' applied to persons whose contribution to the life of the Religious Society of Friends has had particular significance. My impression, after enquiries on this point, is that more British Friends than American are reluctant to admit that some among us may be leaders. A recent group discussion in an American Quaker setting led to the conclusion that some Friends give leadership 'in process' but that we do not set one person above others in a group. In some degree, usage of the word 'leader' by Friends is dated. There are leaders among Friends in all our groups today, but we do not often call them leaders nor have we since about 1960. *Quakers World Wide* tries to abide by that time frame.

It is hoped that readers of this history will gain greater familiarity with a world wide organization working to encourage and strengthen the spiritual life among Friends; to help Friends to gain a better understanding of the world-wide character of their Religious Society; to promote consultation among Friends of all cultures, countries, and languages; to promote understanding between Friends everywhere and members of other branches of the Christian church, and of other religious faiths; and to keep under review the Quaker contribution in world affairs and in the world Christian mission, facilitating the examination and the presentation of Quaker thinking and concern in these fields. This organization is the Friends World Committee for Consultation.

J. Passmore and Anna Griscom Elkinton (1944 photo).

CHAPTER I

Toward a New Awareness of One Another

THREE ROOMS AND A CUBBY HOLE in Drayton House, just off the big Euston Road in London, serve as the nerve center for a far flung network of Quakers around the world. Here is the headquarters office of the Friends World Committee for Consultation (FWCC), an international resource for the more than 200,000 Friends in the world today and one channel for expressing the concerns of Quakers world wide. Currently, FWCC is for Friends a catalyst for consultation, a sponsor of spiritual nurture, an actor on the ecumenical scene, a prompter of positive moves at the United Nations, and a supporter of international cooperation in Quaker mission and service.

Through such diverse activities the FWCC carries forward the global vision of the founders of the Society of Friends in the 17th century. Greatly diminished by the end of the 19th century, that global concept was vigorously revived in the early 20th century by a handful of bold Quakers from America and Europe. Their visionary efforts, galvanized by the horrors of World War I and the early Hitler regime, culminated in the founding of FWCC in 1937, on the eve of World War II.

A condition of separateness

The first generation of Friends expected their spiritual fellowship to be world-wide. Neither political boundaries nor broad ocean kept George Fox and other Quaker ministers from taking their message to the European Continent or to the North American mainland. Such zealous message-bearing nearly disappeared from the Society of Friends during the 18th century and well into the 19th century, but traveling ministers from both Britain and America bound the trans-Atlantic Quaker community together.

In North America, beginning in Philadelphia in 1827, a series of 'separations' bitterly divided several yearly meetings into Orthodox and Hicksite branches. Orthodox Friends were Biblically oriented with emphasis on the historic Christ, while Hicksites looked to the Light Within

1

as the core of a non-authoritarian religious faith. The separation which had occurred in Philadelphia spread to the west, with one difference. The Hicksite branch in the Midwest was in each case much smaller than the Orthodox. A later separation from the Orthodox left a third, Wilburite, branch which came to be known as the Conservative Friends.

An evangelical emphasis arose among some British Friends in the 19th century. One of its leaders, Joseph John Gurney, was a partner in a powerful bankinghouse, a philanthropist, Biblical theologian and Friends minister, prison reformer, and advocate for the abolition of slavery. During his extensive visit among Friends in America from 1837 to 1840, Gurney had greatest influence among Orthodox Friends in Ohio, Indiana, and North Carolina, to whom the label 'Gurneyite' became attached. Orthodox Friends in Philadelphia were less responsive to Gurney's message, feeling it was more of the mind and doctrine than of the Spirit.

Due in part to the influence of the Great Revival Movement in America, especially in the frontier communities, Orthodox Friends meetings in Ohio and further west often adopted a regular pastoral ministry and programmed worship.

London Yearly Meeting recognized the Orthodox branch, but refused to exchange visitors, or to communicate except sporadically beginning in 1908, with Hicksite yearly meetings. Full communication with the Hicksite yearly meetings began in 1923. The small Wilburite yearly meetings in New England, Ohio, Indiana, Iowa, Canada, for a short time in Kansas, and later in North Carolina, maintained communications among themselves but had little or no contact with other branches of the Society.

Late in the 19th century the Hicksite yearly meetings began to hold conferences in which they considered common concern for religious education or for social problems, and Orthodox yearly meetings sent delegates to other conferences with hope for agreement on a common declaration of faith. Two distinct strands of cooperative effort developed within American Quakerism. Illinois led the six other Hicksite yearly meetings to form Friends General Conference in 1900. Most of the Orthodox yearly meetings, but not Philadelphia, joined together to form the Five Years Meeting (later Friends United Meeting) in 1902. Between these two bodies of cooperating yearly meetings there was no official communication for many years.

New spirit and life in London Yearly Meeting

Meanwhile, in London Yearly Meeting new life was stirring. At the request of its Home Mission Committee more than a thousand Friends gathered in Manchester in 1895 to discuss Quaker life and work. The agenda covered the whole range of Quaker concern for roots, for organization, for outreach, and for social problems.

The enthusiasm generated by the Manchester Conference spilled over into a summer school movement. The first of the summer schools was held at Scarborough in 1897, led by Friends whose scholarship, social concern, and religious commitment were strong. Other summer schools followed, inspiring monthly and quarterly meetings to arrange lecture courses and study circles.

The American Friend Rufus Jones, scholar, teacher, writer, and lecturer, had a part in the leadership of the adult school movement. He formed a close friendship with a key figure in this period, John Wilhelm Rowntree of York. Only thirty years old at the time of the Manchester Conference, John Wilhelm had come through a time of agnosticism and doubt to a faith which enabled him to meet the personal tragedy of deafness and impending blindness with assurance and courage. Rufus and John Wilhelm quickly decided to collaborate on a multi-volumed, scholarly history of Friends. Such a history, written objectively yet sympathetically, would help Friends to understand their right mission in the world. Unfortunately, John Wilhelm Rowntree died in 1905, during a visit to America, leaving the history and other critical projects unfinished. Another British Friend, William Charles Braithwaite, collaborated with Rufus Jones to complete the important series of volumes of Quaker history.

Established, however, was Woodbrooke, the permanent Quaker school for adult study in Birmingham, which Rowntree had envisioned. Opening its doors first in 1903, Woodbrooke immediately attracted an international student group including a number of young American Friends. Soon young Friends in Britain and America were crossing the Atlantic Ocean for exchange visits.

Anglo-American Young Friends Movement

The burgeoning new life within London Yearly Meeting at the beginning of the 20th century gave birth to many lively gatherings of young Friends. In 1905 the first of the young Friends 'tramps' was arranged. More than 60 young men came together for outdoor camping. From their campsite, small groups traveled to hold meetings nearby, or to provide stimulation to needy meetings. In subsequent years, young Friends gained strength from mutual support given each other at tramps in different places. In 1909 young women Friends began to join the tramps; and in the same year two young men went to Australia and introduced the tramps idea to young Friends there.

The coming together of young Friends increased with 400 participants at a conference held at Swanwick in Derbyshire in 1911. A few Americans took part in that conference. In return, the next year eight young British Friends journeyed to the United States to join in conferences and other gatherings. One conference, at the Whittier Guest House in Hampton Falls, New Hampshire, included young Friends from the four branches (Conservative, Gurneyite, Hicksite, and Orthodox). Exchange visits by young Friends continued, and significantly strengthened a sense of community among those who would soon be leaders in yearly meetings on both sides of the Atlantic.

A challenge to peace witness

The strengthening of purpose and of conviction experienced by young Friends through such visiting helped many young Quaker men to meet the challenge posed by military conscription during the First World War (1914-1918). More than 1,000 young British and American Friends, including some young women, served in relief and reconstruction units in France and elsewhere in Europe. An additional number of British young men went into the Friends Ambulance Unit, working close to the battle lines.

Still, the challenge which the war had brought to their Peace Testimony caught Friends off guard, and many throughout the Society were concerned that this testimony should be strengthened and become more relevant to world conditions in the 20th century.

Friends World Conference on Peace

By early 1917 British Friends had decided to invite representatives of all yearly meetings to take part in a conference in London, knowing that such a conference could not take place until the war had ended. The first world gathering, in London in August, 1920, was prompted by the general recognition by Friends that their historic peace testimony was much in need of cultivation and strengthening.

'Friends and War', the principal document issued by the 1920 conference, declares that theologians and the church have subverted the Christian concept of love, and that true Christian practice allows no deviation from the way of love, making 'participation in war under any circumstances impossible'. Described as 'A New Statement of the Quaker Position', this message was published separately from the Conference Report.

Billed as an All Friends Conference, this event was intended to include Friends from all groups in the world. English-speaking attenders predominated, however, with 492 from Britain, 333 from the United States, and much smaller numbers from Ireland, Australia, New Zealand and South Africa. The only other representative from Africa was one British mission worker from Madagascar, and the Asian contingent included nine British or American mission workers. From the West Indies came one native Jamaican, and from Denmark 3, France 2, and Norway 5 representatives. Only 21 participants had other than English as their first language.

International Young Friends contacts

During the 1920s and early '30s, however, international contacts among young Friends flourished, auguring well for the future. An International Young Friends Conference, also in the 1920 summer, urged young Friends to give to the world a revelation of God through the way they lived their lives, and to make this commitment, in part, by going 'out into politics'.

Visits by individuals and groups, as well as small conferences, involved principally British, German, and American youth. About 50 young Friends from 15 countries came together in Brussels, Belgium, in 1928. Representatives from 10 countries came to a conference in Copenhagen, Denmark, in 1934. 'The Quest', an international young Friends journal, first published in 1931 in England, continued for at least three years.

Some separateness diminishes, some becomes greater

Although within London Yearly Meeting there have been differences over points of theological belief, such differences have not caused long term separations. In America, where both Hicksite and Orthodox were numerous and lived in near proximity to each other in Baltimore, New York, and Philadelphia Yearly Meetings, the walls of separation were not as high in the 1920s as at the beginning of the 20th century. Acquaintance with one another, mutual respect and acceptance were growing. In the great Midwest and Far West, where the Hicksites had been very few and their meetings far apart, some Orthodox-Gurneyite Friends tended to suspect the doctrinal soundness of a Friend bearing the Hicksite label. This suspicion was strongest in those whose Quaker faith had been bent toward fundamentalism.

Although there had been cooperation in the support of a peace witness during the World War, and for a time in relief service to those whose lives had been shattered by war and famine, the fundamentalist Friends did not long continue their support for the American Friends Service Committee. Their objection to the AFSC was in part based on the Service Committee's policy of serving human need without overt effort or open intent to make Christians, or Friends, of the persons whose physical needs were served.

In the decade of the 1920s the most strongly evangelical, fundamentalist Friends and meetings drew away from cooperation and communications with the yearly meetings and organizations which they felt unable to trust. First Oregon, then Kansas, Yearly Meeting withdrew from the Five Years Meeting. The Ohio Yearly Meeting (Gurneyite) continued in isolation from others. The Orthodox Yearly Meeting in Philadelphia and the Hicksite yearly meetings were not 'within the fold' so far as the fundamentalists were concerned. All claimed the name 'Friends'.

One man destined to make a difference

J. Passmore Elkinton (1887-1971), a Philadelphia Friend in the Orthodox Yearly Meeting, yearned for a loving and cooperative relationship among Friends of all the branches. Through most of his working career he was in the sales department of the Philadelphia Quartz Company, a family firm producing silicates which have a great binding quality, useful for many purposes in industry. In 1920 Passmore Elkinton became vice-president in charge of sales, and by his own estimate he traveled by railway an average of 20,000 miles each year. At the age of 66 he wrote that 'after finishing my sales work and over weekends when too far away to return home, I met and came to love many Friends of different yearly meetings'. He resolved to do what he could to help 'bind' Friends together with the 'silicates' of mutual trust and acceptance.

American Friends test each other in conference

At a meeting of the American Friends Service Committee in Indianapolis in 1924, Passmore Elkinton proposed that the AFSC issue a call for a conference representing all Friends in North America. The proposal was approved, and a sub-committee for conference planning was named with Passmore as its chairman.

The conference was held in Oskaloosa, Iowa, in early September, 1929. Never before had American Friends come together on such a broad basis of Friendly fellowship. There were more than 400 from 27 American states, 2 from Ireland and 3 from London Yearly Meeting. In the first conference session wide differences in theological viewpoints were evident as disagreement with the two opening addresses was expressed. The two speakers were leading members of fundamentalist evangelical groups on the Pacific Coast. In the days which followed, less controversial topics were considered – Quaker Education, Applying Quaker Principles, Pursuing the

Quest for Peace. The later conference topics again brought friction – Concerning Worship and Ministry, and Outreach of Quakerism in Foreign Fields. One participant reported the conference was 'as gusty as the winds that blew in Oskaloosa – a temperamental, theological, philosophical free-for-all'. The Oskaloosa experience made some feel that no unity would be achieved among American Friends. But Passmore Elkinton thought differently, determined to work harder.

More promising for unity was the General Conference of Young Friends held at Richmond, Indiana, preceding the gathering at Oskaloosa. Called the twentieth conference of young Friends in America, those responsible for it deliberately chose to have no planned program. The conference itself would build the program. A message sent to Friends closed with these words: 'Alone we feel inadequate to our task but with the clarifying power of the Inner Light we can see the road before us. The challenge to us is to live NOW in the Kingdom of God'. Some thirty young Friends went on from Richmond to take part in the All Friends Conference at Oskaloosa.

Carl Heath and 'linked Quaker Embassies'

Meanwhile, in Britain a man with great spirit and vision appeared among Friends. Brought up in the Congregational Church, Carl Heath had lived several years with his parents in Paris. After a period of social service among the poor in London, followed by a few years as teacher, he had been drawn to the peace movement. In 1909 he became secretary of the National Peace Council whose active chairman, Thomas P. Newlin, was a Friend. As World War began in 1914, Carl realized that Friends were among the few who continued to be true to a peace witness. In 1916, he and Effie Heath joined the Society of Friends; and in 1920 Carl became secretary of London Yearly Meeting's newly-formed Council for International Service. In 1927, the CIS was merged with the Friends Foreign Mission Association to form the Friends Service Council. Carl Heath and Harry T. Silcock, who had been secretary of the FFMA, became joint secretaries of the new FSC.

As early as 1917, Carl Heath had suggested that after the war Friends should establish 'Embassies of Quakerism' in every capital in Europe. Their function would not be merely humanitarian or philanthropic, but 'rooted in spiritual life which centers in Christ'. They would exist for service, and for social study and experiment. And, especially important, all these centers would be linked like ganglia in a nerve system.

Friends International Conferences in Europe

In implementing this vision of Quaker embassies, Carl Heath and his principal assistant in the Friends Service Council, Frederick J. Tritton, developed intimate acquaintance with Friends on the Continent of Europe. Together they planned a series of 'international conferences', the first and second in 1931 – at Elsinore in Denmark and at Paris, respectively. The first Quaker conference on the Continent of Europe focused on the topic 'Quakerism in Modern Life and Thought'.

Worsening economic conditions in Europe, and especially in Germany where political stability was threatened, made Friends feel that they ought to say something about such specific questions as finance, industry, and disarmament. At the conference in Paris in November, 1931, French, British, German, and American Friends shared their views on these matters, generating the 'unanimous feeling' of participants that this experiment in consultation between Friends of different countries must be continued. Several issues were suggested as urgently requiring collective thought.

Pursuing this concern, the International Conference at Paris called for a permanent committee to be established to manage future conferences of this kind. The FSC and the AFSC endorsed this proposal and proceeded to form a committee with members from Austria, Czechoslovakia, Denmark, France, Germany, Great Britain, the Netherlands, Norway, Sweden, Switzerland, and the USA. To guide this committee's deliberations Carl Heath was named 'International Secretary', but when he asked in 1935 to be relieved of detailed responsibility, the committee appointed Carl as chairman with Fred Tritton as secretary.

Such International Conferences were held annually in Europe through 1936 – in Amsterdam, 1932; in Geneva, 1933; near Prague in Czechoslovakia in 1934; near Paris in 1935; and at Old Jordans Hostel in Britain in 1936. At each conference the American participants represented the American Friends Service Committee.

At these conferences Friends were burdened over the troubled situation in Germany, with the growing dominance of Hitler. On one occasion they also considered the problems faced by Friends in China and Japan, along with the Japanese invasion of the Asian mainland. And for conference participants there was a growing sense of international character for the Society of Friends.

An international Society of Friends?

In the epistle from their yearly meeting in 1929, German Friends had asked, 'Does Quakerism consist only of individual Yearly Meetings, which independent of one another manage their own affairs in their own districts, or is it a great Society of Friends, reaching away over all boundaries and nations?' German Friends answered their own question:

We believe that the time has come to put all our common strength together where the great tasks lie . . . Let us go further along the road which leads from the limitation of our single yearly meetings to the community of a great Society of Friends.

Whether in response to the German Friends or not, the American Friends Service Committee keenly felt a need to arouse Friends everywhere to their world mission and responsibilities. The AFSC first appointed a 'Message Committee' to communicate this concern to Friends in the USA. The Message Committee was succeeded by a 'Fellowship Committee' which sponsored annual conferences in Washington during the 1930s, open to representatives of all groups of Friends. The chairman of the Fellowship Committee was Passmore Elkinton who continued as chairman when the AFSC expanded the role of this committee and called it the American Friends Fellowship Council (AFFC), with 65 members representative of Friends in the USA.

In 1932, the Fellowship Committee suggested to its parent body, the AFSC, that steps be taken to develop a world conference of Friends. The American yearly meetings were consulted and each was asked to appoint a representative to a Conference Committee. Many did make the appointment, and a World Conference Committee was formed with Passmore Elkinton as chairman.

Also in 1932, the AFSC addressed a letter to 200 selected Friends around the world, headed 'An International Society of Friends'. The letter described several functions that an international office, or information clearing house, might perform. Recipients of the inquiry were urged to comment in writing. While the responses were not universally favorable to an 'international Society of Friends', the large majority of responders supported some kind of international arrangement.

By far the most comprehensive and thoughtful reply came from Bertram Pickard. As a British young Friend he had been active in the 1920 international Young Friends Conference and was editor of the conference report. Soon after, he had become secretary of the Peace Committee of London Yearly Meeting, then was appointed secretary of the new International Friends Center in Geneva. He gained wide international experience in Geneva, headquarters of the League of Nations and of a variety of international non-governmental organizations. But he pointed out that his representing only one national Quaker body – London Yearly Meeting – limited his influence in the international community. Nor would it suffice, he argued, to involve only a small number of nationalities (or yearly meetings). The AFSC-envisioned 'International Society' must be the world community of Friends, '. . . an organic whole, the catholicity of which would be unquestioned but whose purpose would not be centralized authority but unity in diversity, and of loyalty through voluntary submission to the best good of the whole body'.

One of the documents distributed in advance of the 1933 International Conference in Europe was the AFSC's letter of inquiry entitled 'International Society of Friends'. It was agreed that this should be considered by the next conference in 1934, in Prague. To that conference Passmore Elkinton sent a letter asking whether the International Committee, responsible for planning the conferences in Europe, might be included in the committee for the next All Friends (World) Conference proposed for 1937. This was agreed. In this way a broadly representative group of European Friends became a part of the World Conference Committee, along with the representatives appointed by American yearly meetings.

Citing increasing business demands on his time, Passmore Elkinton resigned from chairmanship of the World Conference Committee in 1934. His wife, Anna Griscom Elkinton, who fully shared Passmore's concern for unity among Friends, became the new chairman.

Vigorous pursuit of World Conference plans

From the middle of 1934, Anna Griscom Elkinton was the very active chairman of the World Conference Committee. She traveled extensively in North America, to contact members of her committee and to encourage general interest in the forthcoming conference. In May and June of 1936 she visited Friends in Britain and Ireland, and in six countries on the European Continent, on a similar mission.

The World Conference Committee appointed commissions to prepare reports on subjects which reflected widely held concerns:

I The Spiritual Message of the Religious Society of Friends
II The Individual Christian and the State
III Methods of Achieving Economic, Racial, and Social Justice
IV Friends Contribution to Education
V International Cooperation of Friends

For Commission V Passmore Elkinton was chairman and Bertram Pickard vice-chairman.

Careful preparation of the Commission V proposal

At the end of the conference at Old Jordans in 1936, the International Committee in Europe considered a memorandum by Bertram Pickard on

Bertram Pickard (right) and Denis Barritt of Ireland Yearly Meeting
(1958 photo).

'International Cooperation of Friends'. The result of their discussion was sent to Passmore Elkinton with the title 'Next Steps in the International Cooperation of Friends'. The careful work done by Bertram Pickard and Carl Heath and the International Committee was recognized by Passmore and other members of Commission V in America. When the Commission Report was printed and circulated it included large portions of the 'Next Steps . . .' document without change.

Passmore Elkinton, Bertram Pickard, Carl Heath, and Clarence Pickett, the Executive Secretary of the AFSC, had worked with great concern toward some means by which world awareness among Friends could be more widely recognized, and through which cooperation on a large scale might be possible. They knew very well that many of their fellow Friends would be fearful of organization and of a superstructure which might encroach on local or yearly meeting sovereignty. It was the spirit of cooperation which they urged, however.

The Commission V document described a growing conviction that there was, at least potentially, a world Society of Friends which had not yet found expression in external forms. Organization must be kept subordinate to spirit and life. The Society of Friends had rightly feared overcentralization and everything approaching bureaucracy. Top-heavy centralization had been avoided precisely because the Quaker method could dispense with it. Nevertheless, organization had its place, since spirit without form is always in danger of dissipating itself. So ran the argument presented by the International Committee in Europe and adopted in its report by Commission V.

Representative character of conference, compared with 1920

The conference of 1,000 Friends, held at Swarthmore College near Philadelphia in early September, 1937, included Friends from eight countries not represented in London in 1920. They were Cuba and Mexico in the Western Hemisphere; and, in the European Continent, Austria, Czechoslovakia, Germany, the Netherlands, Sweden, and Switzerland. Altogether, 24 countries were represented compared with 16 in 1920. At least 23 of the 25 yearly meetings in the United States had representatives at the 1937 conference.

There were many more American participants than in 1920 at London, 774 compared with 333. Canadian participation moved up from 3 in 1920 to 18 in 1937. Due to distance and cost of travel, the number of London Yearly Meeting participants declined from 492 to 120, and of Ireland Yearly Meeting from 57 to 9. From other English-speaking countries – Australia, New Zealand, and South Africa – the 1920 number was 14, and 12 in 1937. The proportion for whom English was their first language, 93 percent in 1937, was about the same in both conferences.

Conference endorses Commission V proposal

On the third day of the conference the work of Commission V was presented by Bertram Pickard, and the minutes record that 'animated discussion followed'. In spite of the conservatism of some and the caution of others, and whatever active opposition there may have been, the conference called for a special session during an afternoon period three days later. At that session the matter of setting up a continuing international body would be discussed at length.

The special session was well attended and was widely representative. Paul D. Sturge, the young General Secretary of the British and Irish Friends Service Council, presided, and it was he who brought its proposals to the final session of the World Conference. He acknowledged that no organization could evoke, internationally, a spirit of cooperation and unity, but that the spirit must call the organization into being. Friends from all parts of the Quaker world had met in special session and 'felt it desirable that this conference should not disperse without making some provision for further promotion of contacts and cooperation among Friends'. Friends concerned in this matter 'believe that this will be best accomplished by providing for the setting up of a committee, the purpose of which would be to act in a consultative capacity to promote better understanding among Friends the world over, particularly by the encouragement of joint conferences and intervisitation, the collection and circulation of information about Quaker literature, the revision of the handbook (a first edition had been done by the AFSC in 1935), and other activities directed toward this end'.

Then, with minor changes in Commission V's proposals for implementation, the conference endorsed these recommendations:

1. The International Committee which had arranged the conferences in Europe would serve as nucleus of a permanent committee.

2. The Friends Service Council (London) would name five additional representatives for British and Irish Friends.

3. The AFSC would name ten or more American Friends to serve for a year, or until a substantial number of yearly meetings have appointed their own representatives. At the same time, the AFSC would invite all yearly meetings on the American Continent, plus Cuba and Jamaica, to appoint representatives to a permanent committee.

4. The committee thus formed would invite groups of Friends outside of Europe and America to name one representative each.

5. Carl Heath and Fred Tritton would serve temporarily as chairman and secretary, respectively, for the World Consultative Committee.

6. In due course, Carl Heath and Fred Tritton would convene, at a convenient place and time, accessible members of the committee who by then have been appointed.

7. The permanent committee, when created, would look toward establishing regional groups: one for Europe, a second for all of the Americas, and a third for the Orient.

Accepting these recommendations, the Friends World Conference, at Swarthmore in September, 1937, gave approval for the establishing of a world wide committee to promote international contacts and cooperation among Friends.

CHAPTER II

A Vision Blurred by Constraints

VOLCANOES OF HATRED AND VIOLENCE erupted around the globe, bringing division, destruction, and death in the Second World War. The fragile structure of the new World Consultative Committee withstood the strains and stress of these times because a few were determined that the vision of a network of Friends, caring and world wide, should not be lost. They flung skeletal bridges of love and mutual respect across the lava floods of hatred and violence which threatened to bury the world.

What role for the new Consultative Committee?

While Quaker periodicals of the day reported the conference held at Swarthmore, they gave little attention to conference action approving a World Consultative Committee. Among Friends who were aware that a world committee had been authorized, there was general agreement that it should promote consultation among Friends in different yearly meetings and of different nationalities. There was disagreement about its potential for arranging international action.

The action-oriented Passmore Elkinton hoped for a world Quaker body which would exercise influence in world affairs and provide international service. On this point he represented the view of many American Friends, especially those in the non-pastoral, unprogrammed meetings. But Bertram Pickard advocated the limited consultative role for any world Quaker body. This view reflected the position of most British Friends at that time.

Small, new yearly meetings, like most on the Continent of Europe, yearned for support from beyond their borders. Such yearning was expressed at the Swarthmore conference by a German Friend, Asta Brugelmann, pleading for realization of 'the extreme importance there is for a very close collaboration between (older, larger bodies) and the many small and newly founded yearly meetings and groups scattered all over the world . . . (They need) your love, your understanding, and your spiritual help. They stretch out their hands to you across the oceans, hoping that you will firmly grasp them'.

Two Friends who well understood this yearning by members of small groups were Carl Heath, Chairman, and Frederick Tritton, Secretary, of the new World Consultative Committee.

The early leadership

Carl Heath (1869-1950) was a person of vision, with a forward-looking mind and positive personality. But he did not have strong administrative skills. He needed to have at his side a colleague who would take care of detailed work required if vision were to become reality. Fred Tritton filled that need.

Frederick J. Tritton (1887-1968) was born into an English family of humble position. He had little formal education, but took a shorthand-typing course and obtained a job in London. With unusual ability to learn languages, he taught himself French, Spanish, and German. When wartime conscription came in 1916 he declared himself a conscientious objector and was ordered to do agricultural work.

After the war, strongly desiring international work, Fred took a routine job with the (Friends) Council for International Service. In 1920 he became a member of the Society of Friends, and met Carl Heath, recently appointed secretary of CIS. Fred was made assistant secretary.

So, in 1920, Carl and Fred, in many ways unequal and different, began a close working relationship. Their field of operations was inside Europe where both men came to be loved by workers in Quaker service, and especially by members of the small groups of European Friends. Carl attended larger gatherings and meetings to determine policy. Fred came to the same events, but he stayed for longer time and was known by nearly all of the Continental Friends as a visitor in their homes.

Fred had attended the World Conference at Swarthmore. Then for three weeks he visited Friends in Philadelphia and some parts of Midwest America. In his journal he wrote with kindness and appreciation of Friends he had met during his American visit, but he seems not to have felt 'at home' among them, especially in the pastoral, programmed meetings. Intellectually, and at a distance, Fred was becoming aware of the 'Quaker world', but at heart he remained a European.

FWCC's first meeting and early organization

Carl Heath had been unable, because of illness, to go to the conference at Swarthmore. But he quickly learned of the action authorizing a World Consultative Committee which he would serve as temporary chairman. As a first step he and Fred Tritton convened the old International Committee in early May, 1938, at Doorn, The Netherlands. Here, the name 'International Committee' was dropped and the gathered representatives became the European Section of a world body. They planned an Eighth Conference to be held at Vallekilde, Denmark, in September, but the conference would not be called 'international'. It would be European.

With the focus on 'The Christian Community in the Modern World', the conference at Vallekilde declared that widespread discrimination against Jews was '. . . not alone a challenge to the conscience of the whole Christian Church, but (it) calls for Christian repentance of the age-long persecution of the Jews before any lasting solution of the Jewish question can or will be found'. The conference forwarded the complete statement to the World Consultative Committee whose first meeting followed on September 12 and 13, 1938.

One year after the Swarthmore Conference, 32 yearly meetings and groups had appointed representatives, but unfortunately distance and cost of travel prevented many from attending this first meeting. 20 representatives were present, however, from 14 yearly meetings and groups.

After recording with approval the formation, already accomplished, of the American and the European Sections, the representatives present accepted for the committee the name which had been recommended by the two Sections – Friends World Committee for Consultation. Although without formal approval, this suggestion of purpose for the committee was noted:

> To promote a world-wide Society of Friends and to develop a sense of loyalty and interdependence; to seek continually, and to make better known, the spiritual values of Quakerism, and to enable Friends more effectively to work toward the healing of the world.

The committee continued Carl Heath and Fred Tritton in the offices of chairman and secretary, and Helen Peach (later Brooks) was appointed assistant secretary. It named Barrow Cadbury as treasurer. Recognizing that these offices, with primary functions, were filled with British Friends, the committee appointed Hans Albrecht, of Germany, as one vice-chairman, and left the second to be appointed by the American Section which named Anna Griscom Elkinton to this position at its annual meeting the following January. The headquarters office would continue to be at Friends House in London for one more year.

The FWCC authorized its staff to proceed with revision of the handbook of Friends around the world; then to look toward publishing an annual calendar of yearly meetings and some simple form of international journal.

Recognizing a need for 'extension of visitation amongst Friends', the committee asked yearly meetings to try to find ways this concern could be implemented.

The minute of concern for Jews, forwarded by the European conference which had just closed, was referred to yearly meetings to 'consider whether they might not approach the other Christian churches of their country with a view to a united demonstration of the sympathy of Christians of all communions with the Jews, and to promote large-scale measures of relief and of permanent rehabilitation'.

Writing to all members after the meeting, Chairman Carl Heath urged them to give 'thought, prayer and suggestion' to the work of FWCC, keeping close touch with the officers, and serving as links for two-way communication between local and yearly meetings on one hand and the World Committee on the other. This first meeting, he wrote, '. . . may one day be looked back to as a landmark in the history of the Quaker community . . . the beginning of a permanent effort to build up a cooperative life of Friends right around the world'.

The Sections – European and American

At the European Section's second meeting, held at Friends House in London on the 31st of May, 1939, Regnar Halfden-Nielsen of Denmark was named chairman, and as vice-chairmen, Isabel Grubb of Ireland, Jim Lieftinck of The Netherlands, and Bertram Pickard of the Geneva Friends Group. For secretary-treasurer the Section appointed Helen Peach who was already the full time office secretary and assistant to Fred Tritton who continued to carry a full time assignment with the Friends Service Council. Beyond formation of its structure of membership and officers, the principal achievement of the European Section at its first two meetings was to prepare two European conferences, in each of which there were some American participants – in Denmark in 1938 and at Geneva, Switzerland, in August 1939.

To initiate an American Section of the new World Committee, the concerned Friends might have attempted to build upon the already established American Friends Fellowship Council. Its role, from within the American Friends Service Committee, was to give encouragement to the new groups springing up in cities and towns across the USA, and to promote intervisitation among American Friends. Most of the small, new groups were in college and university towns, with members liberal in theological belief. Nearly all followed the unprogrammed way of worship. Such groups had sometimes arisen within the territory of yearly meetings whose practice was different, and questions of nurture, or even of acceptance, might result in strained relationships.

The AFFC did not have widely representative support among American Friends, especially with the more evangelical, pastoral and programmed yearly meetings. The American Section of the new Friends World Committee for Consultation needed to be inclusive of all yearly meetings, so far as this was possible.

Leslie Durand Shaffer (1901-1950) grew up among Friends of evangelical persuasion in a rural community in Illinois, where his strong religious faith developed. A graduate of Earlham College in Richmond, Indiana, and the Hartford Theological Seminary in Connecticutt, he was serving happily as pastor of the Eden Avenue Friends Meeting in Cincinnati when, in December, 1935, Clarence Pickett invited Leslie to be the secretary of the newly formed Fellowship Council. He accepted, and went to the post in Philadelphia the following month.

Leslie's duties with the AFFC did not require his full time. He soon had the further responsibility of secretary to the World Conference Committee, working with Chairman Anna Elkinton, leading up to the Swarthmore Conference in September, 1937. For Leslie, the beginning of many friendships came during that conference. One of these was very special – his meeting a young member of the Swiss delegation, Blanche Weber of Geneva, who later became his wife.

The FWCC American Section's first meeting was held in Washington, in January, 1938, in tandem with the annual meeting of the American Friends Fellowship Council, a frequent annual meeting arrangement until the two organizations were merged in 1954. There was discussion of the publication of literature as a responsibility of the World Committee; of an information service which would provide news and articles of Quaker interest; and of international study groups on topics of universal concern. The Section appointed Leslie Shaffer as secretary, and named other officers to serve only until the next meeting:

Chairman: Alvin T. Coate, of Western Yearly Meeting
Vice-Chairman: Anna Brinton, of Philadelphia Yearly Meeting
Assistant Secretary and Treasurer: Barbara Cary (later Curtis)

The second meeting in June, 1938, filled only part of an afternoon during the biennial Friends General Conference at Cape May, New Jersey. 15 persons, including Chairman Alvin T. Coate, were present. Temporary appointment of officers was continued, to allow time for other yearly meetings to name representatives. The officers were asked to explore the feasibility of holding an All American Friends Conference in 1943.

The annual meeting, held in Washington in January, 1939, named a new chairman, J. Hoge Ricks, of Baltimore Yearly Meeting (FYM). The American Section met next in Richmond, Indiana, in April. Members of the Executive Committee of the Five Years Meeting were in Richmond at the same time. With local Richmond Friends, they helped to make up an attendance of nearly 60 for the Section meeting. Although most were not representatives to the FWCC, Friends from 17 yearly meetings had this contact with the new World Committee.

Leslie D. Shaffer (1949 photo).

Leslie Shaffer had not been outside of North America, though his work with the 1937 World Conference had brought him many personal friends in Europe and elsewhere. With the encouragement of Clarence Pickett, he arranged to travel to Europe in the summer of 1939. When the European Section met in Friends House, London, on May 31st, Leslie had just arrived from Philadelphia and could report in person some of the actions of the American Section. He attended the sessions of London Yearly Meeting, then moved on to the European Continent and visits with a number of Friends groups and to Friends International Centers. Leslie's summer visit ended with his participation in the FWCC's second meeting, followed by the European Friends Conference, both held in Geneva. No doubt he found time, too, for visits with his Swiss friend, Blanche Weber.

The FWCC's Second Meeting, as war clouds gather

The second meeting of the FWCC was held on two days preceding the European Conference, August 9 and 10, then it reconvened on the 14th. 32 yearly meetings, and 10 other general meetings and groups, had named representatives, although only 24 official representatives from 15 yearly meetings and groups were present in Geneva. The same officers were continued for another year, and a committee (two Europeans and two Americans) was named to bring, the next year, recommendations about location of the office and guidelines for appointment of officers. The FWCC adopted a budget of £750.

Friends in the Ninth European Conference were under the weight of crisis in Europe. The general topic was 'The Task and Method of Quakerism'. On a sub-topic, 'Toward the Christian State', Carl Heath spoke movingly. The conference asked him to write down the address in brief form, which the FWCC gave wide distribution under the heading GOD REIGNS. Recalling the problems faced by Friends in the Far East and the Near East, and 'the tension and dread possessing Europe' the message, in brief excerpt, declares:

> The faithful life calls for grace, considerateness, knowledge, restraint and much courage in the face of crushing evil and pain. And we ask ourselves: who is sufficient for these things? We know with sorrow our great weakness in facing the tremendous demands of the courageous life – and in maintaining the calm and free spirit in front of dreadful ill. We cannot hide this weakness from ourselves. Yet we know that GOD REIGNS and it is our abiding strength that he, the source of power that is love and love that is power, gives himself to us as light and strength; and in this great communion his strength is made perfect in our weakness. Thus we can and must go straight on,

led by a creative vision and doing with joy every action this may lead us to.

Thus the members of the FWCC, and all Friends, were challenged by Carl Heath to face their special tasks.

Hitler's German forces invaded Poland on September 1st, scarcely more than two weeks after the close of the conference and the FWCC meeting in Geneva. The Second World War had begun in Europe.

Courage and strength to face dark times

The American Section invited Carl and Effie Heath to visit among Friends in the United States during the summer, 1940. By mid-April Carl wrote that he must decline. He could not come out of Europe in times like this, for 'claims on Friends like myself are very considerable and increasing'.

In the early months of the war, Carl took an active part in correspondence of the FWCC, exchanging letters with Leslie Shaffer and Anna Elkinton. Gradually that responsibility was passed more and more to Fred Tritton who had continued assistance from Helen Peach.

In the American Section, the new chairman, J. Hoge Ricks, who lived in Richmond, Virginia, was glad to accept Anna Elkinton's offer to keep close to day-to-day functions of the office, since she was near and could find it convenient. Anna's double role as vice-chairman of the FWCC and also of the American Section, coupled with her great interest in the purpose and function of the committee, provided support which Leslie valued. He was fortunate to acquire other support in the person of Hannah Stapler, a young Friend in the Philadelphia area, who became his assistant. She would serve the American Section for 40 years.

American Section takes on London office responsibilities

Leslie Shaffer wrote late in October, 1939, to Carl Heath, asking whether it might be desirable for the American Section to correspond with Friends in countries from which Britain was cut off due to the war. This offer was accepted. As months passed, it became more practical for publications to be handled by the American Section – first the Handbook in process of revision, then the annual Calendar of Yearly Meetings, and finally the periodical bulletin which, after two numbers in 1939, was first published as *Friends World News* in July, 1940.

On September 18, 1940, Fred Tritton and Helen Peach wrote a letter in which they questioned whether it was right for officers in Britain to continue to hold the main responsibility for World Committee affairs. They hoped that the American Section was giving much thought to matters of the World Committee as a whole, and 'that you would be prepared on our behalf to take any executive action that you might think necessary, communicating with us of course if possible'. To this letter Carl Heath attached his note of endorsement.

Although the neutrality of Switzerland had not been violated by the countries at war in Europe, Bertram and Irene Pickard decided to leave their post in the Friends Center in Geneva and to return to England, and then to go on to the United States. From early 1941 to the end of the war, they made their home in Washington. Bertram and Irene gave time and thought to the work of the American Section, attending its meetings when they could.

Also from Geneva, Blanche Weber arrived in Philadelphia in late summer, 1940. She and Leslie Shaffer were married on the 7th of September. Blanche and the Pickards brought a sense of international fellowship and participation into the work of the American Section in wartime.

Postwar service and building the peace

In December, 1939, Anna Elkinton sent a letter to at least one prominent Friend in several countries, describing an effort by selected Friends in the United States to study the possibility and potential for building a just and durable peace. She urged that, in each country, Friends seek out persons who would join in similar study. Such groups should use all their influence to persuade their respective governments to take steps toward a just peace. From Denmark, France, Ireland, The Netherlands, Norway, Sweden, and New Zealand came appreciative response.

At its annual meeting in January, 1940, the American Section appointed a small committee to consider plans for a future peace, with Anna Elkinton as its chairman. A major undertaking was the formation of a 'Peace Commission' of American Friends, with 35 members. In 1941, the Peace Commission produced a Peace Study Outline with the title *Problems of Applied Pacifism*, a pamphlet of 79 pages. With the suggestion that the study outline be used by individuals and by meetings, the American Section gave it wide distribution in North America and the Caribbean Area, and sent copies to Friends in other parts of the world.

To insure postwar cooperation by British and American Friends in planning relief services, it was necessary for certain Friends in responsible positions to travel between the United States and Britain. William Eves, III, Homer L. Morris, Clarence E. Pickett, E. Raymond Wilson, and

D. Robert Yarnall were among the Americans who traveled to Britain and to parts of the European Continent, while Roger C. Wilson came from Britain to America for conferring about postwar service. These Friends were careful to include the interests of the FWCC, taking and bringing back messages and helping to maintain contacts which reduced the feeling of isolation.

Meanwhile, a committee appointed by the American Section was already making plans for an All American Friends Conference in 1943, to include Friends from the Caribbean Area, Central and South America, Mexico, and Alaska, along with the United States and Canada. A radical change in conference planning followed the declaration of war by the United States on December 8, 1941. The Board of Directors of the AFSC, meeting later that month, urged that American Friends meet in conference as soon as possible, to consider their responsibilities in the changed situation. The American Section of the FWCC accepted that challenge and arranged for a conference of 250 Friends at Richmond, Indiana, in April, 1942. 25 of the 30 yearly meetings in the United States and Canada were represented.

In their message from the conference at Richmond, Friends declared that 'we have a duty to continue to uphold the rights of conscience, to withstand increasing encroachments upon civil liberties and the war-time trend toward regimentation, to maintain the sacredness of personality, and to relieve suffering'. They also urged the American Section to arrange a program of study and further conferring.

In response, the American Section's Executive Committee asked Raymond Wilson, of the AFSC staff, and Leslie Shaffer to make plans for another conference. More than 80 Friends took part in this Conference on Peace and Reconstruction, held in early September of the same year, 1942, at Wilmington, Ohio. The conference statement, published in a pamphlet with the title *Looking Toward the Postwar World*, includes a section on 'Relief and Reconstruction' foreshadowing the service done in Europe by Friends after the war and another 'Toward the Political Organization of Peace' which is relevant to later Quaker involvement with the United Nations Organization.

Effort to gather information from around the world

In the summer of 1942, Irene Pickard circulated a memorandum in which she suggested that information about other activities of Friends would be needed in preparation for postwar responsibilities. The Section in annual meeting, January, 1943, felt it would be unrealistic to try to form commissions for a number of concerns. Instead, one sincere and able Friend could begin to collect material on a particular subject. His or her efforts might draw others into cooperation.

With this working plan in view, the Section discontinued its Peace Commission. Bertram and Irene Pickard were named 'Consultants' on concerns for peace. In June, 1943, the Section appointed Consultants to pursue specific concerns for Spiritual Life, Organization, Social Order, Education, and Race Relations. These Consultants initiated much correspondence, but the gathered information which appears in print is limited to two reports by the Pickards and one by Thomas and Esther Jones on Race Relations, all in *Friends World News*.

Promoting communication among Friends in the Asia-Pacific area

Some Friends continued to hope for a Section of the FWCC in 'the Orient' as the World Conference in 1937 had proposed. A further proposal for the setting up of a Friends Center in Shanghai, China, had brought more prompt response. Harry T. Silcock and Herbert Hodgkin, appointed by the FSC in London, and Walter Borton for the AFSC, arrived in Shanghai in February, 1939, to join the small group of Friends in Shanghai in the establishing of a Center.

Harry T. Silcock (1882-1969) was educated at Oxford to be a university lecturer. When his own Congregationalist missionary society had no place for one with his training, he applied to the Friends Foreign Mission Association (FFMA) and was accepted. His service in Chengtu, Szechuan, began in 1907. From the time the West China Union University was established in 1911 by missions of several denominations, Harry Silcock was teacher and administrator, later becoming vice-president.

While on furlough in Britain in 1920, Harry was named secretary of the FFMA. When the FFMA and the Council for International Service were merged in 1927, he was appointed a Co-Secretary, along with Carl Heath, of the newly formed Friends Service Council. In 1932 he resigned from the FSC position to become the full time Secretary of the Universities China Committee, organized to provide friendship and assistance to Chinese students at universities in Britain. His accumulated experience proved a valuable asset for the Friends Center work which Harry undertook in Shanghai early in 1939.

The World Conference had suggested three offices for the World Consultative Committee, one in America, one in Europe, and one in the Orient. Harry Silcock assumed that the office for the Orient would be at the Shanghai Center, and that a primary function of the Center would be the organizing of a 'Far Eastern' representative gathering, at appropriate intervals, along with maintaining contacts with the American and European Sections.

In 1940, Donald and Erica Groom, British Friends recently arrived at the Friends Mission at Hoshangabad in India's Central Province, proposed that a plan be made for regular correspondence among the various groups in the Asia-Pacific area. Positive, but cautious, replies came from Harry Silcock in Shanghai, from William Sewell in West China, and from Friends in Australia and New Zealand. A follow-up letter from the Grooms, 20th March, 1941, reviewed the responses received and expressed hope for regular contacts in the future.

Fred Tritton, in London, received a copy of the letters from the Grooms and shared them with Leslie Shaffer in Philadelphia. Soon Leslie was writing to the Grooms, to Harry Silcock, and to Gilbert Bowles in Japan, proposing that the time had arrived for more definite thinking about a date and place for an Eastern conference, looking toward the establishing of a Pacific Area Section. Leaders among Friends in the different countries recognized a need for intergroup contacts, but the ordinary Friend in Asia and the Pacific Area had little idea of a regional conference or an organized section of FWCC.

Growing concern for the Asia-Pacific Area

Members of the staff at the Shanghai Center made visits to other meetings in China, and Harry Silcock visited Japanese Friends only eight months before the Japanese attack on United States naval ships in Pearl Harbor in the Hawaiian Islands. At the time of that attack, December 7, 1941, Harry was visiting the Friends in West China, and as Japanese forces immediately took control of Shanghai, he could not go back to the Center. He had expected to return to England after one or two years, but now he was in a different situation. Friends in Szechuan Yearly Meeting needed Harry's help and encouragement. And he played a part in opening a small Friends Center in Chungking.

By 1943, Friends in Australia and New Zealand were writing to Leslie Shaffer about their sense of isolation during the war. They hoped that a Friend familiar with Japan and China might spend time in each meeting in their two countries. Leslie remembered that Harry Silcock would return to Britain soon, so why not urge him to travel from Chungking to India, to Australia, to New Zealand, staying long enough with each group to minister in a caring way and to relieve their feelings of loneliness? Then, American Friends suggested, Harry could travel across the United States, sharing information about Friends in the countries visited and in Asia.

At first Harry objected. He had hoped before long to be at home with his family in England. But it was his nature to sacrifice his own interests if the needs of others could be served, and soon he agreed to make the journey and the visits suggested.

In December, 1943, Harry left Chungking by plane for Calcutta. He conferred with Friends at Centers in Calcutta and Delhi, and in the Mid-India Yearly Meeting. In February, he came on to Australia, visiting meetings in each of the state capitals, and was with Friends in New Zealand during April and May. After an ocean voyage from Australia, he arrived in San Francisco in mid-June, 1944. Passmore Elkinton was in the San Francisco area for business reasons, and Leslie and Blanche Shaffer were visiting there on behalf of the American Section. The four Friends conferred about prospects for Friends in Asia and the Pacific Area as they traveled together by train to Los Angeles.

California Friends met with Harry and the Shaffers on July 8th. This group was concerned that some Friends should travel in the ministry, with expressions of love to the groups in Shanghai and Tokyo, as soon as the war should end. To further this concern, a committee of West Coast Friends was appointed. Soon after, the annual meeting of the Pacific Coast Association of Friends (predecessor of Pacific Yearly Meeting) appointed a 'Committee on the Orient' to pursue the development of association among Friends in Asia and the Pacific Area.

Harry Silcock, moving on to the Eastern states, met with the Executive Committee of the American Section on July 20th. He reported again the experiences of recent years in Asia and his visits to Friends in India, Australia and New Zealand. He spoke of his discussions with Friends in California. While in Philadelphia, Harry put in writing his recommendations for steps to be taken toward nurture of Asian groups when hostilities should cease, and toward a Pacific Friends Regional Conference and the setting up of a Pacific Section of FWCC. The American Section gave hearty approval to these recommendations when it met in August, and appointed a committee to implement them, working in cooperation with the committee which had been appointed by Friends on the Pacific Coast.

Still more support for Asia-Pacific Area contacts

After five long years, Harry Silcock was again united with his family in England, but corresponding with Leslie Shaffer about measures to more closely link Friends in the Asia-Pacific Area. The small committee which had been named by the American Section was not idle. In October it asked the Section's Executive Committee to provide a more official status and a reconstituting of its membership. Passmore Elkinton became convenor of a sub-committee whose members included Gilbert Bowles and Esther Rhoads – Friends with long experience in Japan. The Section endorsed a suggestion that Harry Silcock be named to develop, by correspondence from England, the relationships deemed so important for Friends in the Pacific Area.

Late in 1944, the FWCC officers proposed that Harry Silcock should act provisionally as Associate Secretary of the World Committee, assisting Fred Tritton, and giving special attention to plans for a Pacific Conference and the formation of a section of the World Committee in the Pacific Area. On September 1, 1945, the FWCC made this a regular assignment.

Support given through Friendly visits

The Second World War ended in Europe in May, 1945, and in the Pacific Area in August. As postwar conditions in Asia came to be seen more realistically, the difficulties of bringing Friends together for a regional conference were more obvious. To send one or two well chosen Friends as visitors to the groups in China and Japan became a priority objective. From Britain, the Friends Service Council sent its General Secretary, Paul Sturge, on a staff visit to India and China in mid-1946; and their request for an American to go with him was met by the AFSC's sending Anna Brinton. Both Paul and Anna were members of the FWCC.

As the first postwar visitor to Japanese Friends, FWCC chose Gilbert Bowles who, after forty years of Quaker service in Japan, was living in Honolulu, Hawaii. Travel to Japan was restricted, and food supplies were limited. Permission to enter that country for other than official government reasons was difficult to obtain. Finally, Gilbert was allowed to enter Japan by ship in February, 1947. American bombing during the war had destroyed buildings of the Friends Girls School and also the Tokyo Friends Meeting House; Gilbert discussed with Japanese Friends their hopes for rebuilding. His intimate knowledge of the Friends Mission and of all Quaker work in Japan, and the high regard in which he was held by Japanese Friends, made Gilbert Bowles' visit a great encouragement to them.

Attention to Australia and New Zealand

Many Friends in Australia and New Zealand expressed deep apprecia-
tion for Harry Silcock's visit. As the war ended, still feeling the isolation and loneliness of the war years, they asked the FWCC if a Quaker couple might

visit all their meetings and in the homes of members, staying at least a year. Robert and Lyra Dann, members of the Pacific Coast Association living in Oregon, felt a concern to respond to this invitation.

From mid-August to late November, 1946, the Danns and their 'teen-age daughter, Dorothy, visited in the homes of New Zealand Friends and in their meetings. Crossing the Tasman Sea to Australia, they attended the General Meeting of Australian Friends held at Hobart. They visited each of the meetings in Australian state capitals, most meetings two times because the difficulty of arranging boat passage delayed their departure. On August 4th they sailed from Sydney, arriving at San Francisco in time to attend part of the 1947 meeting of their own Pacific Coast Association of Friends.

The American Section's Caribbean and Latin constituency

During the war years the American Section was able to make contacts with the Caribbean Area and Mexico more easily than with most other parts of the world. There was no Mexico City Friends Meeting until 1938 when Heberto Sein took the initiative to bring Friends together there. But the World Committee enjoyed a link with Friends in and near the northern state of Tamaulipas, with Ciudad Victoria as a center of the Mexican Friends' activities.

The missionary work of Friends in Mexico, Cuba, and Jamaica was under the care of the American Friends Board of Missions, a part of the program of the Five Years Meeting. Partly at the urging of Merle L. Davis of the AFBM and of the FWCC, the American Section held a Semi-Annual Meeting in Cuba – at Holguin, in Oriente Province, in April, 1941. Eight Friends from outside of Cuba were present. Some of these attended the Cuba Yearly Meeting which followed immediately after the FWCC meeting.

Passmore and Anna Elkinton and Robert E. Cope, who had attended the American Section meeting in Cuba, traveled on to Jamaica and were present at the organization of Jamaica Yearly Meeting on April 15, 1941. The next year, the American Section helped Logan Shannaman, chairman of the Young Friends Movement in Philadelphia, to attend the yearly meetings in both Cuba and Jamaica, and to visit young Friends and others in their local meetings. A similar visit in 1944 by Ruthanna Davis (later Hadley) was assisted by the American Section.

Early in 1945, A. Ward Applegate, an Ohio pastor and member of the FWCC since its beginning, visited Friends in Jamaica, with a proposal from the American Section for a conference of Friends from Honduras, Guatemala, Bolivia, Cuba, Mexico, and Jamaica. No conference, however, materialized at this time.

Summary

With the bare framework of organization, but with the bright vision of Carl Heath, the two Elkintons, Leslie Shaffer, Bertram Pickard and others, the newly born FWCC was caught in the maelstrom of world war. The war thwarted its primary purpose of fostering consultation through conferences and other ways of communication. The leadership and initiative handed to the American Section, when the office in London was unable to maintain world-wide contacts, created a tendency for that Section to hold onto initiative for a quarter century after the war ended.

Because the American Section could be in contact with Latin American and Caribbean Friends, communications with them were developed which, unfortunately, fell into decline when other contacts opened after the war. The strength of concern, on the part of a few, for Asia-Pacific Area Friends pushed against the barriers which made communication difficult among the small groups of Friends in that very large part of the world. But Friends there were strengthened by the visits and ministry of support provided from America and Britain.

The Quaker postwar service and contributions to building of peace were enhanced by the vision of a cooperating world family of Friends which the FWCC did much to maintain.

CHAPTER III

Wartime Restrictions End – Other Constraints Continue

As NATIONS ARDUOUSLY WORKED to rebuild ravaged cities and industries in Great Britain, Europe,. and Japan, stalwart Friends struggled to make FWCC the vehicle for communication and cooperation their concern desired it to be. During a time of challenges posed by need for postwar healing, by the ascendance of Communism, and by the founding of the United Nations, the separate, sometimes disparate, segments of Quakerism presented a challenge to the FWCC. Limited financial resource and the accompanying inability to function as a truly representative body almost overwhelmed the organization. Early death took Leslie Shaffer from the scene. But the patience and persistence of Friends who carried major responsibility for FWCC culminated in a successful world conference of 900 Friends in 1952 and, for the first time, appointment of a non-Anglo-Saxon Friend as Secretary, Ranjit Chetsingh.

Interim actions to reactivate the FWCC

The war in Europe ended in May, and in Asia in August, 1945. However, the officers of the FWCC soon realized that to hold a meeting of the committee as early as 1946 would not be possible. They also knew that their appointment as officers, in 1939, was made at a meeting when representation was limited. Any mandate they may have had to make policy decisions without benefit of committee action might now be questioned.

At the suggestion of Anna Elkinton, Carl Heath appointed an *ad hoc* Interim Executive Committee in the spring of 1946, with enough members to be representative but small enough to make practical the holding of occasional meetings. Still, the first meeting, on May 20, 1946, was predominently European. Leslie Shaffer was the only American present. He had obtained a leave of absence from his post with the American Section and, with Blanche Shaffer, was serving as Secretary of the Friends International Center in Paris. Regnar Halfden-Nielsen and Hans Albrecht came from the European Continent.

31

The officers carefully prepared for the second meeting of the Interim Executive Committee, held in London on August 30 and 31. Passmore and Anna Elkinton, Errol Elliott, and Leslie Shaffer were the American participants. Hans Albrecht was again present. Bertram Pickard was there; also Maurice Webb, a well known Friend from South Africa, who had been working with Friends Relief Service in Europe. The London officers and staff – Carl Heath, Barrow Cadbury, Fred Tritton, and Harry Silcock – rounded out the committee.

This committee agreed that the full FWCC should meet in the United States in 1947, probably in September, and that the office should continue in London. Since Fred Tritton would need to give full attention to his work with the Friends Service Council, Leslie Shaffer was appointed to succeed him in the position of secretary, and Fred was named a vice-chairman. The committee encouraged Harry Silcock to pursue his concern to visit again the countries in the Pacific Area.

The Interim Executive Committee drafted a memorandum to suggest the 'Main Lines of Development of the World Committee in the Next Five Years'. It encouraged short term and long term intervisitation and regional conferences, and proposed a world conference near the 300th anniversary of the founding of Quakerism, perhaps in 1949.

At the first postwar meeting of the European Section, in England in May, 1946, there was one representative each from Denmark, France, Germany, Ireland, the Netherlands, Norway, Sweden, and Switzerland, along with eight from Britain. In the meeting there was long discussion of 'the special message of Quakerism to this generation and (the means to) communicate it . . .' The first European conference after the war was held at Ommen in the Netherlands, April 4-7, 1947, with 68 Friends from 10 European countries and the United States, using the theme, 'The Spiritual Need of Europe and the Responsibility of Friends'.

Because of continued restrictions on trans-Atlantic travel and the need to make best use of available funds, the American Section and the AFSC set up a Joint Committee on Visitation. A Friend traveling on behalf of one organization would make contacts on behalf of the other. Friends coming to America from other parts of the world could be helpful to both.

Postwar American Section

William Orville Mendenhall (1879-1958) was the American Section Chairman during the year, 1946. His life work had been in Quaker education, and he had recently retired from the presidency of Whittier College in California. 'W.O.' was a useful visitor among Friends meetings in

Britain as the war ended. Ill health during 1946, and the long journey from California to much of the Section's activity, required his giving up the chairmanship.

To fill Leslie Shaffer's place during his leave of absence, the American Section employed J. Harold Hadley as Associate Secretary. He had grown up in Kansas Yearly Meeting, and was recently pastor of a meeting in North Carolina. While carrying the administrative role in the Section office, Harold was given the task of increasing the financial support for FWCC. With assistance from Thomas E. Jones (1888-1973) who had been American Section chairman from 1943 through 1945, Harold launched a successful campaign to provide three-fourths of FWCC's London office budget and to build up a fund for conferences and intervisitation. His one year with the Section was an interlude between pastoral service and further theological study, and by autumn of 1946 there was need to find a new secretary.

At its annual meeting in January, 1947, the American Section named D. Elton Trueblood (1900-   ) as its chairman. He was widely known among Friends in America and Britain, and in the larger Christian community, as a writer and lecturer. Recently he had come to the faculty of Earlham College after serving in a number of universities and other Quaker colleges. At the same time, Anna Elkinton asked to be relieved of the chairmanship of the Executive Committee. Her successor was William Eves, III.

The American Section appointed Allen J. White (1911-1989) as Executive Secretary. He had been an active young Friend in North Carolina, and had participated in AFSC youth programs. When appointed by the American Section, Allen was secretary of the Friends Meeting of Washington. He came to the Section office on January 1st, 1947, midst preparations for the FWCC's Third Meeting and for visiting by overseas Friends who would attend that meeting in Richmond, Indiana, September 5th to 15th.

FWCC meets again after eight years

Representation at the Third Meeting demonstrated the growing interest in FWCC. Seven yearly meetings on the Continent of Europe, so recently torn by war, sent representatives. Seven came from London Yearly Meeting and one from Ireland. Twenty yearly meetings of the United States and Canada had representatives, and members from Mexico and Jamaica rounded out the American Section participation.

Dr. J. Usang Ly of Shanghai represented the Szechuan Yearly Meeting of West China, along with their young members, Stephen and Ruth Yang, who were medical students at the University of Michigan. Gilbert and Minnie Bowles came from Hawaii to represent Japanese Friends since there were heavy restrictions on travel from Japan. Robert Dann represented Australia and Suzanne Adlam, New Zealand, recent visitors to Friends in those countries. Carl Heath, chairman of FWCC from its beginning, was in poor health and not able to come from England.

Sharing of information, country by country, about war-time experiences and postwar renewal efforts filled most of the first two days. Representatives agreed that the FWCC had provided useful and significant service to Friends, even under handicap, and that it should continue.

As FWCC chairman the Third Meeting appointed D. Elton Trueblood and gave Carl Heath the title Honorary Chairman. It also named five vice-chairmen – Norah Douglas (Ireland), Edmond Privat (Switzerland), Greta Stendahl (Sweden), Maurice Webb (South Africa), and Frederick Tritton who would carry special responsibility since he would be near the office in London. Barrow Cadbury was reappointed as treasurer. Other action provided for an executive committee, to include the officers just named, the chairman of each Section, a representative of the Pacific Area, and 'some Friends' from the area of the office location. Leslie Shaffer accepted appointment as secretary for a further two years.

The committee gave warm approval for holding another world conference, with 1952 now the more likely year. The conference would be in England, with the possibility that celebrations of the 300th anniversary of Quakerism would occur in the same year.

Relationship to UN and UNESCO

Also in its Third Meeting, the FWCC acted on a proposal urged upon it by the AFSC and presented on this occasion by Allen White, to apply for 'consultative status' with the Economic and Social Council (ECOSOC) of the United Nations. The UN Charter provided such standing for international non-governmental organizations (NGOs), and the AFSC offered to carry financial and administrative responsibilities required for a United Nations program under the name of the FWCC. The favorable decision did not come easily since to some FWCC members, especially to some from Britain, such action would take the FWCC into the political arena and beyond its agreed role of consultation among Friends.

The FWCC more easily accepted a similar relationship with the United Nations Educational, Scientific, and Cultural Organization (UNESCO) whose headquarters office was in Paris. During UNESCO's formative years its officers found interest in the principles of education generally upheld by

Friends, and in the Quaker experience with such 'out of school' means of education as work camps. Staff at the Friends International Center in Paris had given much attention to UNESCO, and both the FSC and the AFSC wanted a formal NGO relationship with it. So, in 1947 the FWCC recorded its desire for a link with UNESCO, and urged its executive committee to keep itself informed about UNESCO's work and to be associated with it so far as that might prove possible.

American Section – changing leadership, Leslie Shaffer's return

Like Leslie Shaffer and other staff who had served the American Section, Allen White was also part time secretary for the American Friends Fellowship Council. Most active members in each group were ready to merge the organizations. However, the AFFC had arisen in the mid-1930s to care for two concerns put forward by Rufus Jones, which were (1) the spiritual nurture of small new groups of Friends and of new meetings, and (2) care for the Wider Quaker Fellowship. As a member of the AFFC, Rufus was unwilling for that organization to be party to a merger which might result in decreasing attention to these responsibilities. Others felt that the overlap of function and the financial burden of maintaining both organizations were unnecessary; but action to merge was not taken while Rufus was there to oppose it. Allen White felt so strongly that simplification by merger was essential that he told members of both committees he could not continue as their secretary.

Allen stayed only six weeks more than a year in the post of Section secretary. During that year he helped to build the new FWCC relationship with the United Nations and the unofficial linkage between FWCC and the International Friends Centers administered by service bodies of American and British Friends. When he moved to the AFSC office in charge of International Centers, in February, 1948, Allen continued to provide strong support for FWCC involvement in Quaker international work.

Leslie and Blanche Shaffer had not felt comfortable with his role as secretary of the FWCC and its office in London. It seemed very clear to him that officers of London Yearly Meeting saw no reason for the existence of the FWCC. He had accepted further appointment at the Third Meeting, and return to the London office, with hesitation and with the understanding that he might reconsider his position at the end of one year.

By January, 1948, the Shaffers decided they should return to the United States. When they heard of Allen White's resignation, Leslie quickly offered to return to his former position with the American Section if that should be desired. The arrangement was made, and early in May Leslie and

Blanche were again in Philadelphia. Once more he was secretary of the American Section.

With Elton Trueblood's appointment by the Third Meeting as chairman for the world-wide FWCC, he relinquished the chairmanship of the American Section at the end of 1947. As his successor, the Section named Alexander C. Purdy (1890-1976) who was Professor of New Testament at the Hartford Theological Seminary in Connecticutt. He had previously taught courses in religion at Earlham College. Alex Purdy would serve as the American Section chairman for eight years. Until the merger with the AFFC in 1954, he was chairman of both organizations.

Alexander Purdy, Chairman of the American Section, 1947-1954.

Asia-Pacific Area – another Silcock visit

During the Third Meeting at Richmond, Japanese and Chinese representatives made a strong plea for Harry Silcock to visit their groups again. American Friends suggested that Harry stay on in the United States, visit meetings where an appeal might be made for travel money, first on the East Coast then on the West Coast, and proceed on to Asia. By mid-November the necessary funds were in hand, and on November 28th Harry sailed for Shanghai, arriving on the 16th of December.

From Shanghai, Harry visited Friends in Peiping, Nanking, Chungmou, and Kaifeng, then spent some time with members of Szechuan Yearly Meeting in West China. He carried their greetings to Friends in Japan where he arrived in mid-March, 1948. With the Friends Center in Tokyo as base, Harry visited meetings in Ibaraki Prefecture and in Odawara, Osaka, Nara, and Kyoto.

Leaving Japan on 30th of April he came to San Francisco on the 12th of May. Harry spoke to Friends at meetings arranged on the Pacific Coast from Los Angeles north to British Columbia, in Iowa and at Richmond, then on the East Coast. At home again in England late in June, he was frequently called upon to report his recent visits.

European Section – Elise Thomsen as secretary

Elise Thomsen (1901-   ) represented Denmark Yearly Meeting when FWCC met at Richmond. She remained to study at Pendle Hill near Philadelphia in the Autumn Term, and had opportunity for acquaintance with the American Section whose annual meeting she attended in January, 1948. By that time, European Section officers had tentatively decided to appoint Elise as their Section secretary. Returning to Copenhagen in February she began to serve part time.

Meeting in Birmingham, England, in July, the Section asked Elise to take up full time duties on the 1st of September, 1948. For the first time, a Friend from one of the Continental yearly meetings was serving on FWCC staff.

At the same meeting, William H. Marwick, of Edinburgh, Scotland, was named chairman of the European Section, succeeding Regnar Halfden-Nielsen who became treasurer. The American Section regularly sent money to support the European Section. Continental yearly meetings began to make small contributions, but most of them could not send money out of their countries. Instead, they held the money until it was needed for travel by FWCC staff, or for some meeting or conference, within the country.

Through visits, Elise became known to Friends in all the groups on the Continent. With special concern for German Friends in the postwar period, she gave several weeks to visiting and working with them. At the request of the Section, she helped to develop interest in an international young Friends movement. During the early postwar years in Europe a number of Friends from Britain and America provided a visiting ministry.

Strong concern for Pacific Area links – Friends there not ready

Tireless efforts of Passmore Elkinton and Harry Silcock as co-chairmen of the Pacific Area Sub-committee directed much of the concern of the FWCC toward Asia and the Pacific Area.

The first Friend to travel away from Japan after the war was Iwao Ayusawa, clerk of Japan Yearly Meeting. Before the war he had been Japan's representative at the International Labor Organization in Geneva. Now he could contact Friends while on government travel to America in 1948 and to Europe in 1949. From 1948 to 1950, Kiyoshi Ukaji, a younger Friend and writer on economic affairs, and Orie Shimazaki, principal of Friends Girls School in Tokyo, were students at Pendle Hill, and both were given opportunity to travel among Friends meetings.

William Oats, headmaster of the Friends School in Hobart, Tasmania, Australia, was for some months in Geneva, Switzerland. Through him links between European and Australian Friends were strengthened. Edward and Ruby Dowsett, of New Zealand, made very useful visits in the United States and Britain in 1948, with Ruby sharing her concern for production of a series of international Quaker letters for children.

Almost no contacts or communication had occurred between Friends in different countries of Asia and the Pacific Area. It was a great disappointment to both Chinese and Japanese Friends that S. H. Fong, President of West China Union University and a leader in Szechuan Yearly Meeting was not permitted, because of the political situation, to visit Japanese Friends again, as he had once done in the 1930s. Passmore Elkinton and Harry Silcock began to think of possibilities for Asia-Pacific Area Friends to meet and confer when they would travel toward Britain as representatives to the Friends World Conference to be held at Oxford, England, in 1952.

Financial and other restrictions for FWCC

In 1947 the American Section was unable to pay the full amount expected for support of the London office. In February, 1948, the financial picture was acknowledged to be less bright than was forecast at the Third Meeting. It was necessary to reduce expenses, already at minimum level.

Leslie Shaffer's leaving the London office in the spring of 1948, to return to the American Section, permitted some reduction of expense. The officers called on Fred Tritton, once more, for half-time service as secretary. The FWCC would give the Friends Service Council £200 toward Fred's salary during the rest of 1948. In May, the office was moved from cramped quarters in the Friends hostel for international students to a room made available in Friends House. It was on the top floor, 'much too cut off from everything else', according to Jean Thompson who had been Leslie Shaffer's assistant. In August, Mary Protheroe (later Eddington) became office secretary.

While the program of the American Section was lively, its financial and organizational affairs were at a low point. In 1948, contributions from individuals and meetings declined more than 20 percent. Only twelve members attended the annual meeting in January, 1949. Sixteen member yearly meetings were not represented at all.

The passing of Leslie Shaffer

In the spring of 1949, Leslie was ill and away from the office for a few weeks. He suffered from depression which seemed related to a strong distaste for the money-raising side of his work. Later in 1949 a continual weariness troubled him. His sister, Alice Shaffer, working in Central America for the United Nations Children's Fund, invited Leslie and Blanche to visit her for a month in Guatemala. Leaving Philadelphia on January 12, 1950, they enjoyed a month of vacation with Alice.

Leslie came back to his work feeling refreshed, but the weariness soon returned. Exploratory surgery late in March revealed widespread cancer of the lymph system. He died in a hospital on May 30th. The death of one who had been so much a part of the FWCC was deeply felt by Friends around the world.

Fresh beginnings in the American Section

It was necessary to find a new executive secretary to carry on the work of both the American Section and the Fellowship Council. When the committee found James F. Walker (1889-1978) he had recently retired after a 36-years' career at Westtown School, 25 of those years as principal. He gave leadership to the American Section for the next 12 years, during a time when program was expanding. His part time service continued still longer.

James Walker took up his new work with great interest. The big task was to help with preparation for the 1952 World Conference, which involved the raising of $30,000 as the American Section's share of conference expense and finding leaders for discussion and worship groups.

Blanche Shaffer continued to live in Philadelphia after Leslie's death. In September, 1950, she agreed to be editor of *Friends World News*. Soon she accepted further responsibility as 'publications secretary', working with the chairman of the Publications Committee, Dorothy Gilbert (later Thorne) of North Carolina. She undertook a new revision of the *Handbook of the Religious Society of Friends*, to be completed before the World Conference in 1952.

Carl Heath, forward looking until the end

As Honorary Chairman of the FWCC, Carl Heath met with the Executive Committee in London, who valued his wise counsel. On November 22, 1949, not long before his 80th birthday, Carl addressed a letter 'To Members of the FWCC', calling on Friends to form a world-wide 'Quaker Commission on Peace'. Such a commission, under the guidance of the Spirit, should prepare to offer to leaders in the secular world, solutions to problems, ways out of crises, paths to reconciliation and peace. Once more, Carl's vision challenged the best minds among Friends.

During the next three years officers of the FWCC sought to implement Carl's vision of an International Quaker Commission on Peace. Finally, it was agreed that the many peace committees, the Friends International Centers, and the representation of Friends at the United Nations and UNESCO were adequate organization, if coordinated, to bring the vision to reality. Meanwhile, death came to Carl Heath on March 4, 1950.

A more formal role for Harry Silcock

Harry Silcock was frequently in the FWCC office in London following his 1947-48 visit to Friends in China and Japan. It seemed logical that he should be responsible for FWCC's communications with Friends in the Asia-Pacific Area. Also it was useful for general purposes if Harry could be available during Fred Tritton's absences in Europe on behalf of FSC. From May, 1949, he had added responsibility as clerk of the Planning Committee for the 1952 Friends World Conference. The FWCC and the Conference Committee had adjoining offices, and Harry's involvement with the work in both offices increased.

The Fourth Meeting of the FWCC, at Oxford, in 1950, affirmed the value of current activities and moved forward the preparation for the World Conference to occur two years later. Soon after the Fourth Meeting, Harry Silcock accepted the invitation to serve as FWCC's secretary until the end of the conference in 1952.

Conferring after the 1950 FWCC Meeting in England (l to r): Frederick Tritton, D. Elton Trueblood, Elise Thomsen, Hannah Stapler.

Toward a Third World Conference

Meeting for Sufferings in London, in January, 1949, authorized an invitation which would be issued by the FWCC to yearly meetings, to send 1,000 representatives to England for a world conference at the end of July or beginning of August, 1952. London Yearly Meeting offered hospitality for the conference and the FWCC would plan the program.

When the Conference Committee met in July, 1950, just before the FWCC's Fourth Meeting, it was agreed that the conference should focus attention on 'Man's Condition and the Christian Answer', coupled with exploration of our 'Faith and Service', of our responsibility for 'Publishing Truth' and for a 'Ministry of Reconciliation'. FWCC Chairman Elton Trueblood stayed in England for a few weeks and produced Study Booklet Number One, 'The Vocation of Friends in the Modern World'. It emphasized the 'Role of the Reconciler' in different conflict situations:

'East and West' (i.e., the Communist and the non-Communist worlds), the 'Full and the Hungry', the 'Colored and White', and the 'Jew and Gentile'. The Second Study Booklet appeared a year later, in autumn 1951. It dealt with the conference themes more directly and in greater depth.

When 900 Friends from around the world met July 28 to August 6, 1952, they were housed and fed in the colleges of Oxford University, as the guests of London Yearly Meeting. Barrow Cadbury had made a personal gift of £30,000 to the yearly meeting for that purpose.

The conference experience

For many participants the conference was a new and unusual experience. To be in the same assembly with public Quakers whose names were familiar; to listen to addresses by many of those public Friends; to share discussion and worship-fellowship groups with Friends from yearly meetings and countries other than one's own; and to make friendships with those who shared the accommodations in the several colleges – these were experiences to be long remembered.

Some participants, however, were unhappy. Friends in the countries of Continental Europe, whose daily lives were affected by the East-West conflict, particularly felt that the pre-conference Study Booklets did not speak to the problems and the tensions they knew. Nor did the programmed addresses of the discussion sessions meet that need. A few of the Continental European representatives spoke out in the plenary sessions for discussion, calling on Friends to recognize the social ideal inherent in communism and to lift up the similar ideal in Christianity. They urged Friends to pursue a changed and a higher social order as a primary goal.

In summing up, the conference adopted two 'Messages'. One, addressed To All Friends, may be in essence expressed in these excerpts:.

> We believe the responsibility is laid on each individual Friend in our world family, to make a new 'holy experiment' in practical living. Our vocation may find its chief emphasis in our meetings for worship; in living a better family life; in re-thinking our personal standards of comforts and possessions; in working for peace in the political sphere or in the fields of economic or racial conflict; or in the day-to-day contacts of all of us. We must each begin just where we are . . . We pray that our Society may become a fellowship dedicated, in a spirit of confidence and of the love that overcomes fear, to holy adventure for God and His Kingdom.

And the brief 'Message to Men Everywhere' closes with this call:

Let us join together throughout the world to grow more food; to heal and prevent disease; to preserve and develop the resources of the good earth to the glory of God and the comfort of man's distress. These are among the tasks to which, in humility for our share in the world's shame, and in faith in the power of love, we call our own Society and all men and nations everywhere.

In addition to the printed Conference Report, with the title 'Friends Face Their Fourth Century', two more conference-related Study Booklets were produced. The Third Booklet was called 'The Life of the Meeting' and the Fourth, 'Practical Implications of Our Faith'.

A more mature FWCC . . . Ready for a new chapter in its life?

Held at Oxford, immediately following the World Conference, the Fifth Meeting of the FWCC was more widely representative than any previous meeting. Nearly 100 participants came from 38 yearly meetings and groups. From the Pacific Area, Japan and India, Australia and New Zealand were represented; but from Africa, only South Africa and Madagascar. Members of East Africa Yearly Meeting had attended the conference, but no representative was present at the FWCC meeting.

A statement of purpose, approved earlier by the Executive Committee, was now accepted for the FWCC:

1. To encourage and strengthen the spiritual life within the Society of Friends through such measures as the promotion of inter-visitation, study, conferences and a wide sharing of experience on the deepest spiritual level.

2. To help Friends to gain a better understanding of the world-wide character of the Society of Friends and its vocation in the world today.

3. To promote consultations amongst Friends of all cultures, countries, and languages. The Committee seeks to bring the different groups of Friends into intimate touch with one another on the basis of their common Quaker heritage, with a view to sharing experience and coming to some measure of agreement in regard to their attitude to modern world problems.

4. To keep under review the Quaker contribution in world affairs, and to facilitate both the examination and presentation of Quaker thinking and concern.

The FWCC was grateful for its consultative status with the United Nations and UNESCO, and for the services of its representatives in New

York, Geneva, and Paris. It approved continuation of this work and welcomed the relationship developed with the Quaker service bodies through their cooperation in it.

Friends from Africa who were at the World Conference had met together to discuss possibilities for exchange of information among yearly meetings and groups in that continent. Asia-Pacific Area Friends, meeting at Hampstead Meeting House in London preceding the World Conference, gave evidence of concern and initiative providing hope for future growth in relationships.

In the concluding minute of the Fifth Meeting, the FWCC looked at the five years since 1947 as a time of preparation for the right holding of the World Conference, and said, 'Now we go forward, believing that a new chapter in our lives may begin'.

To lead the FWCC into what might be a new era, the chairman would be Errol T. Elliott (1894-   ), General Secretary of the Five Years Meeting and editor of the *American Friend*. The appointment of Barrow Cadbury as Treasurer was continued. For Secretary, the Nominating Committee reported that they were considering several names and hoped to recommend one to the Executive Committee soon.

Somewhat unwillingly, Harry Silcock agreed to continue in the position of Secretary. He had been asked to take this post until the end of the World Conference. Now, at age 70, he would have liked to retire, but 20 months would pass before his successor was on the scene.

Need to make the Executive Committee more representative

In America and on the European Continent, members of the FWCC were increasingly troubled because attendance at meetings of the Executive Committee was not representative. Its members outside of Great Britain could not travel to meetings held in London on part of a single afternoon. London Yearly Meeting members predominated at committee meetings.

Hoping to keep in touch with new life engendered by the 1952 World Conference, the Executive Committee proposed to hold two or three weekend residential meetings a year. A few Friends from outside Britain would be invited each time. These longer, more representative meetings could better deal with FWCC business, and a small advisory group could meet in the interim as needed.

After the first weekend meeting, in January, 1953, the London area Friends were unwilling to leave interim business to an advisory group. The British dominated Executive Committee continued to function, therefore, as before. There was not readiness for the change in organizational structure, and accompanying financial cost, which would make possible the holding of regular meetings of a more representative committee.

FWCC struggling toward its potential

Too much of the energy of the officers, and of office staff, was spent on adequate efforts to make the Executive Committee a more appropriately representative body. Harry Silcock wrote that he was unable to work as rapidly as in former years, nor could he give full time to office duties. Mary Protheroe, who had done well as office supervisor for both the World Conference and the FWCC, resigned after the end of the conference. Her successor, Barbara Wigham, was soon carrying responsibility for more than office routines. FWCC was ready for change.

It was generally agreed that, if the office remained in England, the Secretary ought not to be British. Several Americans were considered as candidates. The FWCC's nominations committee, responsible for recommending a Friend as secretary, must have discussed the position with Ranjit M. Chetsingh (1902-1977) while all were at Oxford. Ranjit was an Indian Friend, educator, social worker, and one of two speakers at a conference session open to the public. But it seemed clear that he could not leave the Principalship of Baring Union Christian College in The Punjab until spring, 1954.

In July, 1953, the executive committee made Ranjit's appointment formal, realizing that this action represented a great stride forward in the growing internationalism of the work of FWCC. All rejoiced when Ranjit Chetsingh, Asian Friend, came into the office as secretary in mid-May, 1954!

CHAPTER IV

Gaining Identity Around the Quaker World

PHILOSOPHICAL AND ORGANIZATIONAL CHANGE transformed the FWCC between 1954 and 1960, from a loosely organized European-American body into an active, more international organization. Precipitated, in part, by Ranjit Chetsingh's unhappiness with the deference and the passive role expected of him by some Friends in London Yearly Meeting, the movement for change had the strong support of a few British Friends newly recruited to the Executive Committee which prepared proposals for reorganization of the FWCC.

With sweeping action in October, 1955, the Sixth Meeting of the FWCC in Germantown, Ohio, abolished the existing Executive Committee and gave the newly appointed 'General Secretary' more freedom to lead, with assistance from a four-person Advisory Committee. An Interim Committee with less than ten members, but with each region of the world represented, might be called together if needed.

Although the budget was still minimal, and two persons made up the complete staff of the world office, with the new structure in place the FWCC was able to make itself known and its services welcomed beyond its European and American constituencies, by Friends in Africa, Asia, Australia, and New Zealand.

Ranjit Chetsingh's disappointment

The FWCC announced Ranjit Chetsingh's appointment as Secretary to the Quaker press around the world. It welcomed 'the appointment of a Friend from Asia to this position as the beginning of a new chapter in the development of the international life of the Society'.

However, before even one day in the office, Ranjit began to feel the scope of his work would be limited. He attended a weekend meeting of the Executive Committee, May 14-16, 1954. There his assignment was described in specific terms. He should develop a news service for editors of Quaker journals. Also, he should promote intervisitation, with exchanges between countries.

Ranjit wanted to be personally involved. He felt that as Secretary of a world organization he must get out into the field, become acquainted with his constituency, talk with Friends about the purposes of their world committee. The Executive Committee told him he must first get acquainted with the office. And to make contacts within London Yearly Meeting he should consult with the Yearly Meeting's World Committee Affairs Committee whose Clerk was Stephen Thorne. Stephen was the principal staff officer of the Yearly Meeting; and perhaps the Friend most insistent that yearly meeting sovereignty should be observed. With wide experience and in vigorous health at age 52, Ranjit was unhappy with the restrictions placed upon him.

He tried to work within the situation, hoping it might improve. Before the end of 1954, however, Ranjit began saying to some Friends that he should return to India at the end of his two-year appointment. He talked frequently with Ralph Rose, an American Friend in residence at Woodbrooke College with his family. The American Section had an agreement with Ralph that he would become their Associate Secretary and open a new FWCC office in the Midwest on his return to the United States. Ranjit wrote to James Walker, Executive Secretary of the American Section, about his troubles and received sympathetic response. In letters, Errol Elliott, the Chairman of FWCC, also provided helpful advice and practical support.

Left to right: Errol T. Elliott, Ranjit M. Chetsingh, Isabel and Ralph Rose.

In addition, Ranjit received support from some British Friends, notably Paul Sturge, General Secretary of the Friends Service Council, and Fred Tritton, still Chairman of the Executive Committee. Fred was loyal to Ranjit, but did not have the strength of personality to withstand the insistent attitudes of Stephen Thorne and others who stood against the building up of the FWCC. At the time, moreover, FWCC had limited financial resources. Barrow Cadbury had been the beneficent Treasurer since FWCC's beginning, taking care of urgent financial needs through his own contributions. Little effort had been made to widen the base of financial support. So Ranjit could see no way to finance an imaginative program, or his own extensive travel which he felt would be essential.

Changed leadership in the European Section

The European Section again managed its affairs with part time staff when Archer Tongue succeeded Elise Thomsen in the Secretary's position in January, 1953. Immediately following his service as Secretary for the Friends World Conference at Oxford, Archer had assumed the directorship of the International Temperance Alliance, with an office in Lausanne, Switzerland. This was a full time position, requiring a great deal of travel; but Archer had permission to take time for short visits with Friends, giving encouragement and advice to small groups, during the course of his travels. Despite his other full time job, Archer arranged four annual meetings in four different countries from 1953 to 1956, with the help of Chairman Norah Douglas of Northern Ireland.

Many European Friends questioned the wisdom of joining in assemblies of the World Peace Movement whose headquarters were in the Soviet Union, knowing that resolutions would be passed and statements issued with little opportunity for democratic participation to influence such actions. The Section joined with the FSC and the Peace Committee of London Yearly Meeting to arrange a conference in Berlin during July, 1953, to consider this issue. Friends came from Austria, Britain, Finland, Germany (both East and West), Ireland, The Netherlands, Norway, Sweden, and Switzerland. While opinions were not radically changed, and no directive to yearly meetings was issued by the conference, differing viewpoints were better understood.

To deal with such questions, and others which might arise, the European Section decided in 1955 to form a small Executive Committee which could meet at least once between annual meetings. In 1956, Sigrid H. Lund (1892-1987) was named Chairman. Marguerite Czarnecki, of Paris, could not accept the Secretary role which was offered to her, and Sigrid

Lund agreed to undertake the duties of both Chairman and Secretary, with the title 'Executive Chairman'. The Section named Paul Sturge as Vice-Chairman and Dirk Meynen, of The Netherlands, Treasurer. These officers and Gerhard Schwersensky, of Berlin, became the Executive Committee, making it a much more 'European' body.

New office in the American Midwest

The American Section took a critical step foward with the opening of an office in Wilmington, Ohio, in September, 1954. Now, with an office as far west as southwestern Ohio, the Section held its Executive Committee meetings (four each year) alternately in the East and Midwest, insuring increased participation by Friends in the great middle area of the United States and some from the Far West.

In Ralph Rose the American Section chose an excellent Associate Secretary to initiate its work in the Midwest. His training and experience were in business and industry until 1949 when he began to work with the AFSC's Race Relations Program. To prepare for some future service, Ralph and Isabel, with their family, went to Woodbrooke College in England for the year 1953-54. During that year they became acquainted with British and European Friends. Ralph's European contacts, his warm personality, his energy and initiative, and his evident sense of divine guidance won the affection of many Friends throughout the Midwest, but especially in Ohio and nearby Indiana. He reported in 1955 that his travels averaged 2,000 miles per month.

James Walker traveled extensively, too, and not only on the eastern seaboard. He was present at a number of different yearly meetings each year, in many parts of North America. He visited small worship groups and new meetings springing up in many towns and cities, without affiliation with any yearly meeting.

Men of vision and courage, Ralph and James provided strong leadership, especially with regard to two issues greatly troubling Friends during this period – civil liberties and race relations.

A Conference on Friends and Civil Liberties

Created by a fierce hatred of Communism, an atmosphere of repression and fear pervaded much of the United States in the early 1950s. Led by Senator Joseph McCarthy, investigative committees in the Congress pressed their examinations on individuals and organizations accused of being tainted by Communism, seriously jeopardizing freedom of speech and the press. Several states passed laws requiring all public employees to sign statements or take oaths of loyalty to government and democracy. Many schools and some universities required teachers to take loyalty oaths. A citizen refusing to swear such loyalty was likely to forfeit employment; his or her right to travel outside of his or her country might be taken away by government.

The act and the manner of declaring loyalty to government, under legal requirement, was a sensitive subject, even among Friends when some looked upon refusal of the oath as a subversive act or, worse, a tacit admission of guilt. Because so many Friends were troubled by these matters in 1953, the AFSC asked FWCC's American Section to organize consideration of a religious approach to civil liberties. In the same year, Pacific Yearly Meeting urged the American Section to call a nation-wide conference of Friends on 'the problems of civil liberties in these times'.

To prepare for the conference, James Walker invited all monthly meetings in the United States to respond to a set of 15 questions about civil liberties and to describe restrictions of civil liberties placed against any Friend known to the meeting. A number of Friends had lost employment or had been denied passports for overseas travel because they refused to take the oath of loyalty. Eventually, at the call of FWCC's American Section, a National Conference of Friends on Civil Liberties was held at Scattergood School, in Iowa, April 2 to 4, 1954. There were 57 participants from 20 yearly meetings, the American Friends Service Committee, and the Friends Committee on National Legislation.

Regarding 'Religious Faith and Civil Liberties', the conference declared that God, not the state, is the source of truth; that 'any attempt on the part of government to determine what men may or may not believe, may or may not say, will be recognized as a perversion of government's function'.

The main part of the message issued by the conference was put in the form of 'A Query and Advices Addressed to Friends'. At the head of the message was the Query: 'Do Friends and Friends' meetings seek faithfully to uphold our civil and religious liberties, not only for ourselves but for all men?' Ten 'Advices' which followed encouraged Friends to live up to 'the ideal in the light given to us'. Although the message was prepared for distribution to Friends, more than 36,000 copies were circulated widely, largely through the efforts of the FCNL.

The forces in the United States Congress which had done so much to curtail civil liberties were put down before the end of the decade. But in the general society there remained groups which tried to exercise control over thought and expression. In 1962, the American Section appointed a 'Watching Committee' to gather information about such groups, of both the 'far right' and the 'far left'. As a result of the work of the Watching Committee, in 1964 the American Section published a small pamphlet, 'A Christian Response to Extremist Groups'. It was reprinted many times, and was much in demand by Friends and among other religious bodies.

Friends' own witness in Race Relations

At their mid-1954 gathering, executive secretaries from the national and regional offices of the AFSC noted with sadness that their efforts toward improving race relations were sometimes hindered because Friends were providing a poor example. The AFSC secretaries hoped that a national conference of Friends might consider this question, but were clear that a conference ought to be called by Friends themselves, or perhaps by the American Section of FWCC.

The Section received this concern with full sympathy, but hoped that a call to conference might come from one or more of the yearly meetings. Late in 1954, the Joint Social Order Committee of the two Baltimore Yearly Meetings communicated to the American Section their readiness to assist with planning a regional Friends conference, stating their expectation that a national conference would follow. The Section encouraged Baltimore and North Carolina Friends to proceed with plans for a conference of Southern Friends to consider responsibility in race relations.

The regional conference was held, June 25-26, 1955, at the small town of Woodland in rural eastern North Carolina. The one participant from outside the southern region was Ralph Rose from the Midwest Office of the American Section. Woodland was the focal point of the Conservative North Carolina Yearly Meeting. In 1955 the black population in this rural area was double the number of whites. Racial integration was scarcely given a thought by whites in the area, except by a few of the most concerned Friends. Sincere spiritual searching in this conference wrought a miracle of mutual understanding and acceptance among these rural Friends and their 'guests' from urban meetings.

The Baltimore Friends made good their promise to assist with follow-up of a regional conference. On April 3, 1956, David H. Scull of Baltimore's Joint Social Order Committee sent a call to a national conference to All Yearly Meetings in the United States, to Independent Meetings and Associations, to Friends' Organizations, Colleges, and Publications, and to Concerned Friends. To assure full participation by Friends from Southern states, Scull and his committee suggested that the conference take place in the South. Each yearly meeting and organization receiving this letter was urged to send one representative to a first meeting of a planning committee, in Richmond, Virginia, on April 29. The national conference to be planned should be held early in September.

When appointed representatives met as a planning committee David Scull was named its chairman. Errol Elliott, Clarence Pickett, and other well known Friends served on the committee. It was not possible to find a Quaker facility in the South large enough to accommodate 150 persons, some of whom would be black. So the first National Friends Conference on Race Relations was held at Wilmington, Ohio, August 31 to September 3, 1956. Ralph Rose, in the FWCC's Midwest Office there, was heavily involved in the arrangements.

At the conference there were 120 Friends, of whom more than 10 percent were blacks, from 16 yearly meetings and other Friends groups. 'Pastoral and non-pastoral, urban and rural, Negro and white,' these Friends had 'prayed together and spoken to one another honestly and in a spirit of love (and) have gained insight into one another's problems and have seen barriers fall . . . We earnestly pray that we can move under a sense of the urgency of world events from where we are to where God would have us be in race relations . . .' As a part of the conference statement eight Queries were addressed 'to each Friends Meeting and Church and to every individual Friend in America that we (may) tenderly and humbly consider them together. . .'

The conference named a committee to continue calling Friends to conscience on race relations. With David Scull as its chairman, the committee arranged for a Second National Conference on Race Relations at Westtown School near Philadelphia at the end of summer, 1958. From it came a request to the American Section to sponsor future race relations conferences in alternating years. A concerned Friend, Victor Paschkis, who had served as secretary for the conference at Westtown, traveled extensively among Friends meetings to encourage actions which would improve race relations.

Not all efforts wholly successful

Not all efforts by the American Section in the mid-1950s were so productive, however. It did not succeed, for instance, in establishing a formal relationship with the 'Evangelical' yearly meetings, although Kansas did continue an uneasy contact through this period. But when Everett Cattell, a most loving and statesman-like member of the evangelical Ohio Yearly Meeting, came to the Section's annual meeting in 1955 and urged that there be 'more clarity of thinking about Jesus Christ', the response was inadequate and more than a decade passed before the necessary dialogue was opened.

Fund-raising efforts equally faltered. FWCC officers had hoped that an office and secretary in the Midwest would soon pay for itself in terms of increased financial support from that area of American Quakerdom. This did not occur, in spite of strenuous efforts by Ralph Rose and Midwest Friends appointed to a Finance Committee. Despite two small gifts which permitted the establishment of a modest investment fund, the American Section's 1955 budget of $44,895, needed as much as $14,700 to come from new income sources.

A special meeting of the FWCC Executive Committee

Meanwhile, on the other side of the Atlantic, change was brewing. Late in the summer of 1954, Ranjit Chetsingh urged Errol Elliott to come to England for a special meeting of the Executive Committee. They agreed on the dates January 7 to 9, 1955. Errol knew that the committee must face Ranjit's dissatisfaction over the restrictions imposed on the secretary's role. He encouraged Ranjit to develop clear program proposals to be considered at the special meeting.

Errol arrived in London on December 27th. During the next 10 days he had long talks with Ranjit and with Paul Sturge; also with Stephen Thorne and others in Friends House. Errol went to Birmingham for the weekend, conferring at length there with Wilfred Littleboy, former Clerk, and with Harold Reed, Clerk, of Yearly Meeting. Returning to London, he was present at Meeting for Sufferings and the meeting of the Friends Service Council. This careful groundwork was blunted by a crisis in the Elliott family, although it bore significant fruit eventually.

The FWCC Executive Committee's special meeting began Friday evening in Friends House, but moved to Hampstead Meeting House in north London for Saturday and Sunday sessions. On Saturday morning a cablegram informed Errol that his wife had become seriously ill and was going to the hospital. With a quick change in travel plans, he was enroute home on Saturday evening, well before the end of the Executive Committee meeting.

Soon after the meeting Ranjit tendered his resignation, effective May, 1956, when he and his wife, Doris, had agreed they should return to India. He then turned his attention from effort to build a program for the FWCC to exploring means of changing the structure of the FWCC organization.

New officers for the Executive Committee

More than any action by the Executive Committee at its special meeting, it was the presence of Errol Elliott at Friends House in London, and at

*Howard Diamond (left) and Barrow Cadbury, second and first
FWCC Treasurers.*

events of Committee Week, and his concerned conferring with selected
'weighty Friends' which helped to clear the air for constructive steps to be
taken during the next few months. Most importantly, new people came
forward to assume leadership.

First, the Executive Committee named Paul Sturge as Vice-Chairman.
He worked quietly and unobtrusively to help Ranjit Chetsingh bring about
important changes.

At this time Barrow Cadbury, age ninety-two, indicated his readiness to
give up the treasurer's post, making way for the appointment of a Friend
who could increase financial support for the committee from a wider
constituency. Howard Diamond (1898-1974) was persuaded to accept the
post of Treasurer, successfully serving for 12 years.

To replace Fred Tritton who had served either as Secretary or as Chairman of the Executive Committee since the earliest days of the FWCC, Lewis Waddilove became the new Chairman for the Executive Committee. World War II service as a conscientious objector had introduced Lewis to the Society of Friends. Since the immediate postwar period, he had been Director of the Joseph Rowntree Memorial Trust. With a keen mind, a ready perception of problems within a situation, and a quick sense for constructive solutions, Lewis had gained the confidence of British Friends but was not yet burdened with many appointments. It was the right time to get his consent to serve the FWCC.

With Paul Sturge, Howard Diamond, and Ranjit Chetsingh, Lewis examined FWCC organization in order to bring a report to the Executive Committee when it would meet at Charney Manor on June 10 to 12, 1955.

Lewis E. Waddilove (left) with Ranjit Chetsingh.

Some radical changes proposed

The meeting at Charney Manor was not an easy one, but its achievements were significant for the FWCC. When it was first proposed that the Executive Committee be laid down to make way for a genuinely representative body, that seemed an impossible step. That proposal was finally made a recommendation, although specifics of reorganization had to wait for action by FWCC as a whole.

An important decision reached at Charney Manor was that the role of the FWCC Secretary must be redefined. Since in the foreseeable future there could not be money for an international executive body to meet regularly to direct the affairs of FWCC, the new Secretary would have to affect international consultation between meetings through extensive travel.

For Ranjit Chetsingh who had spent a difficult year in a small office in Friends House, feeling little freedom to take any constructive action, emotions ran high. He successfully pleaded that the FWCC office had to be moved from the immediate influence of London Yearly Meeting.

The Charney Manor meeting also prepared for the Sixth Meeting of the whole FWCC, to be held at Germantown, Ohio, at the end of October, 1955. During the weeks which followed, Lewis Waddilove led further reorganizational efforts, along with the search for candidates for the position of Secretary. When, finally, Friends came to the Sixth Meeting, it was evident that the Americans felt the action at Charney Manor had not been enough. An *ad hoc* committee on Reorganization, Secretarial Appointment, and Finance, led by Lewis Waddilove, labored in late night sessions at Germantown before they were ready to bring recommendations to the whole committee.

FWCC's Sixth Meeting

Friends in Southwestern Ohio and nearby Indiana, including the Richmond area, had worked well with Ralph Rose in the new Midwest Office at Wilmington. Together they found Camp Miami at Germantown, Ohio, about midway between Wilmington and Richmond, and prepared it to be used as the facility for the FWCC's Sixth Meeting.

At this meeting, world-wide representation increased. Among the 100 members attending, 65 came from 20 yearly meetings in the United States. Canada, Cuba, Jamaica, and Mexico accounted for nine representatives. Only five yearly meetings in the European Section were represented, with eight of the 15 members coming from London Yearly Meeting. East Africa, Australia, and New Zealand each had one representative, and Japan had two. Ranjit Chetsingh, of course, was from India but not a representative.

While reorganization was the major item on the agenda, the 1955 meeting conducted other business, including arrangements for providing regular information about the work at the United Nations and a determination to strengthen FWCC's links with Friends in Africa and Asia. Participants at the Germantown meeting identified arrangements for intervisitation among yearly meetings as a top priority task, and appointed these officers: Errol Elliott as Chairman for another three years, and six vice-chairmen – Elsa Cedergren (Sweden), Ranjit Chetsingh (India), Dirk Meynen (Netherlands), Benjamin Ngaira (East Africa), Miguel Tamayo (Cuba), and Lewis Waddilove (Britain).

New structure of FWCC is important

Reorganization, however, was the real achievement of the Sixth Meeting. First, it was agreed that the meetings held triennially must be truly representative, with assurance of attendance by Friends 'from the more distant groups'.

The existing Executive Committee was abolished. An Advisory Committee would assist and guide the Secretary as needed. It would consist of the FWCC Chairman, the Treasurer, and two other Friends, one of whom should be easily accessible to the office and the other appointed from members of the FWCC on the mainland of Europe. Friends who constituted the first Advisory Committee were Errol Elliott, Howard Diamond, Lewis Waddilove, and Elsa Cedergren.

If questions should arise with which the Advisory Committee felt unable to deal, it might call a meeting of an 'Interim Committee' composed of members of the Advisory Committee, the General Secretary, the Chairmen or Secretaries of the Sections, and a Friend from an area of the world with no formal section. This Interim Committee would have all the powers of an Executive Committee.

At Ranjit's insistence, the title 'General Secretary' was given to the principal staff position, in part to distinguish that office from secretarial positions in the Sections. The General Secretary should visit widely, and should promote and coordinate visits by others. He or she should have wide freedom to plan and administer the FWCC's affairs, subject to an established policy and predetermined budget. And for the next three years the office should be in Birmingham, England.

Appointment of General Secretary

The Sixth Meeting appointed me to the position of General Secretary. During the preceding eight years I had served as Secretary for the Friends

Meetings in Washington, and was familiar with the members and work of the American Section which frequently held its annual meetings in Washington. As a young child, I lived in Arctic Alaska where my parents served on the mission field of California Yearly Meeting. My further childhood and youth were within Kansas Yearly Meeting. During the Second World War, I did 'civilian service' in several parts of the United States, including Philadelphia. My marriage to Ruthanna Davis in 1946 brought me into the family of Merle Davis, Administrative Secretary of the Mission Board of the Five Years Meeting, and thus to acquaintance with individual Friends in East Africa, Palestine, Cuba, Jamaica, and Mexico. I had participated in the World Conference at Oxford in 1952.

Herbert M. Hadley.

Ranjit Chetsingh and the first African Friends Conference

On his return to London, Ranjit had less than six months to tie up loose ends in the office before his departure. Most significant of Ranjit's tasks in this period was preparation for the visit in East Africa he and Doris Chetsingh would include in their homeward journey. On 3rd May, 1956, they left England by ship, bound for Mombasa on the Kenya coast.

With the blessing of FWCC at its Sixth Meeting, Ranjit made the arrangements which brought together at Nairobi seven representatives from East Africa, two from Madagascar, and one from Pemba Yearly Meeting. This small group, along with the Chetsinghs, met at the Friends Ofafa Center in Nairobi on June 4 and 5, 1956, with no European or American Friends present.

Participants discovered there were similarities between East Africa and Madagascar, each yearly meeting serving tens of thousands of persons. Pemba is a small island, 42 miles long and 14 miles wide. Pemba Yearly Meeting, like East Africa and Madagascar, was the result of missionary work by Friends. In 1956 there were about 400 members, attenders, and children associated with three local meetings.

Few conferences achieve as much in two days as is evident in the 'Findings' recorded late in the second day at Nairobi. The conferees expressed gratitude for the missions organizations which had helped to bring these African groups thus far. But the 'necessity of training and fitting children of (our) soil for positions of growing responsibility is urgent and needs ever-increasing practical recognition'. Calling for great patience with the problems of African urbanization and of the upheaval in social codes, attenders declared the conference 'has given us a vision of our place in the world family of Friends, and we record our deep gratitude to the FWCC for bringing us together'.

The visit of Ranjit and Doris Chetsingh in Kenya from May 24 to July 2 was helpful to Friends and to Quaker work in a variety of ways. For two weeks they were with Benjamin Ngaira and other leaders of East Africa Yearly Meeting, and with workers in the Friends Africa Mission. The Chetsinghs gave some time to visiting the workers in the Friends Service Council projects in and near Nairobi, encouraging their efforts to bring social and economic stability into Kenya which, not long before, had experienced the disquiet and violence of the Mau Mau uprising. A wise American observer reported that the Chetsinghs' visit was 'an unqualified success'.

A different office and new staff for FWCC

Lewis Waddilove had taken the lead in making arrangements at Birmingham for the FWCC office to be set up at Woodbrooke College. Late in April, the office files and furniture arrived from London. Barbara

Wigham, the office secretary in London since late in 1952, also moved from London to Birmingham. Meanwhile, Ruthanna Hadley and I and our three children had arrived in Birmingham at mid-April, to a warm welcome from Birmingham Friends and the Woodbrooke staff. With new quarters and staff, and with radical change in organization, the FWCC entered a new phase in its history on the 1st of May, 1956.

Hadley's guidelines for program

I proposed three general areas for program emphasis. First, intervisitation by Friends would be encouraged, assisted, and in some cases sponsored, by the World Committee, as a primary means of achieving FWCC's purposes. For some time, the General Secretary's visiting would have first claim on resources available to support visitation, and the degree of support given to other visitors would be determined on a case by case basis.

Second, the relationship to the United Nations and to the UN Specialized Agencies should receive more attention by the FWCC. It should be participatory and active, although the Friends service bodies would continue to carry responsibility for administering and financing this work.

Third, it was necessary for Friends to look deeply into certain subjects about which there were strong and differing opinions among them, learning to understand and respect one another, and in this process gaining greater knowledge of truth.

A fourth point frequently emphasized during my tenure as General Secretary was the importance of a 'world-view' in tasks undertaken by the FWCC. While regional activities, even regional emphasis, might sometimes be necessary for convenience, FWCC personnel ought always to see their work in a world-wide context. Particularly, regional rivalry should be avoided.

Quite early, I decided I needed to travel first to Friends in Britain, Ireland, and the Continent of Europe, my 'home base'. Capitalizing on these contacts, we set the next world-wide meeting for Germany, in 1958.

To build relationships with, and among, Friends in Africa, Asia and the Pacific Area had high priority. Since valuable contact with African Friends had recently been made by Ranjit and Doris Chetsingh, I decided to travel to Asia and the Pacific Area before Africa. Although it was not foreseen at this early period, an intensive relationship with Friends in Africa would come with the planning of FWCC's Eighth Meeting held at Kaimosi, Kenya, in 1961.

New FWCC structure put to use

The new 'machinery' of the FWCC was particularly useful. As Secretary, I was able to administer affairs with the help of members of the Advisory Committee. In addition, I could always share my thinking with this group, particularly regarding funding for travel and other programs. The Advisory Committee set the first meeting of the larger Interim Committee, a more international group, for July 19 to 22, 1957.

As the Friend from an area outside the two organized Sections to take part in this meeting, we invited Benjamin Ngaira, Administrative Secretary of East Africa Yearly Meeting and a Vice-Chairman of the FWCC. Other participants in this first Interim Committee meeting were Elsa Cedergren, Howard Diamond, Errol Elliott, Herbert Hadley, Dorothy Gilbert Thorne (the new American Section Chairman), Lewis Waddilove, and Ilse Schwersensky of Germany, substituting for Sigrid Lund.

In the summer of 1957, Ellen Atkins (later Arnold) succeeded Barbara Wigham in the position of Office Assistant. For the next nine years, until illness and surgery early in 1966 left her paralyzed, Ellen served as a most dependable and helpful assistant, single-handedly running the office during most of my travel on business for the FWCC.

Taking FWCC through Europe and the Near East

While I traveled to France and Switzerland and Northern Europe several times in 1956-57, I visited Central and Southern Europe and the Near East at some length in the spring of 1958, attending yearly meetings and the European Section's annual meeting, visiting Quaker workers and isolated, lonely small groups and individual Friends, in Lebanon and Jordan, Israel, Greece, and Yugoslavia, then Italy, Germany, Switzerland, and France. My absences for journeys as long as this one made home life difficult for Ruthanna and our children; in this particular period a lively French young woman, Evelyne Armengau, was a great help as she lived with our family on an *au pair* basis.

Consultation at FWCC's Seventh Meeting

German Friends welcomed the proposal that the FWCC should meet in 1958 at Bad Pyrmont, making use of the only property which they owned corporately and the place where Germany Yearly Meeting was regularly held.

More than 100 Friends came to Bad Pyrmont for this week-long meeting, September 23 to 29, 1958. They came from 18 yearly meetings in the American Section and from 12 European groups; also from East Africa and Madagascar, Australia, New Zealand, India, and Japan. Because his wife was ill, Errol Elliott, the FWCC Chairman, was not able to be present, so Vice-Chairman Lewis Waddilove presided at business sessions.

Less burdened with matters of organization than the FWCC had been three years earlier, the Seventh Meeting was made a vehicle for important consultation. Friends in different parts of the world contributed to a 'symposium' of the written word under the general heading 'Sharing Our Faith', with these parts: Friends and Evangelism, Friends and Christian Missions, Friends and the Ecumenical Movement, and Friends and World Religions. A primary paper on each sub-topic, with comments by other Friends in different countries, was distributed in advance to members. For wider use, the papers were later published by the FWCC, with the title *Sharing Our Quaker Faith*.

A second subject for discussion at the Seventh Meeting was significant for Friends gathered near the line between East and West in Europe – 'The Contribution of the Quaker Faith to the Healing of a Divided World'. The scope of this theme was defined by introductory presentations. Horst Bruckner, from East Germany, spoke on 'Our Responsibility in Deep Political Divisions' and David Scull, of Baltimore Yearly Meeting, on 'Our Responsibility in Race Relations'. Copies of 'The Attitude of Christians in Tensions between East and West', an address given elsewhere by Margarethe Lachmund, a Berlin Friend, were distributed at the meeting, and Margarethe spoke briefly about her experiences of building understanding and reconciliation.

At the meeting, Elsa Cedergren, of Sweden, succeeded Errol Elliott as Chairman of the FWCC. Also, the Seventh Meeting accepted the invitation given by Jotham Standa of East Africa Yearly Meeting for the Eighth Meeting to be held in Kenya in 1961. This decision was difficult. While it seemed right to encourage African Friends by holding a representative world gathering in their region, most Friends at Bad Pyrmont felt that the FWCC would have to be satisfied with a small, less representative gathering three years hence at Kaimosi.

A vigorous Midwest Committee

The notable success of a 1957 All-America Friends Conference at Wilmington, Ohio, reflected rising interest of Midwest Friends in the FWCC. The 'texture' of Quakerism in Ohio and Eastern Indiana made participation in the Midwest Committee an exhilirating experience. Participants had to share, and to grow in mutual respect for, their differences. The Wilmington and Indiana (FYM) Yearly Meetings were made up of programmed, pastoral meetings. Indiana (FGC) Yearly Meeting was unprogrammed and liberal in tradition, while the Ohio Yearly Meeting with its center at Barnesville was unprogrammed and conservative in many of its practices. FWCC members from these four yearly meetings, who made up the Midwest Committee, faithfully attended meetings each month, usually held in their different homes in turn, preceded by a potluck meal together.

The Midwest Committee made arrangements for Friends visiting in their area, encouraged visitation from meeting to meeting in the Midwest, and appointed visitors to 'new meetings' in cooperation with the American Section's New Meetings Committee. It provided continual encouragement and support for the Associate Secretary and the Midwest Office.

Ralph Rose resigns . . . Marshall Sutton appointed

After three years, Ralph Rose resigned from his position with the FWCC, leaving in September, 1957, to return to the business world as partner in a Quaker printing firm. A succession of part time persons, members of the Midwest Committee, cared for the office for a year. Finally, the American Section appointed Marshall O. Sutton as the new Associate Secretary. A CO civilian worker during the Second World War, and later participant in an AFSC group working with Arab refugees in the Middle East, Marshall was the Executive Secretary of Baltimore Yearly Meeting (FGC) at the time of his appointment by the FWCC, and took part in the Seventh Meeting just prior to his going to the Midwest Office.

American Section's activities increase

During the decade, the American Section's activities grew considerably. Its work with new meetings required a great deal of attention during the second half of the 1950s. Annual gifts from Clement and Grace Biddle, of New York Meeting, for a Quaker Leadership Grants Program, made it possible to arrange Summer Study Tours to include individual members of new meetings. The first Quaker Youth Pilgrimage came in 1959, with 'teen-age Friends from the American Section joining a 'teen-age group from Europe in Northwest England where Quakerism began. James Walker and Hannah Stapler in the Philadelphia office were involved with all these programs, while Emma Cadbury was the busy correspondent with members of the Wider Quaker Fellowship.

The Quaker United Nations Office in New York employed a staff member who organized two- or three-day 'seminars' for groups sent by Friends organizations or schools, to learn about the United Nations and the work undertaken there in the name of the FWCC. The American Section and its Midwest Office, beginning in the 1950s, brought together such groups, largely made up of pastors of Friends meetings in the Midwest. One or two of these United Nations Seminars in New York were sponsored each year by the Midwest Office. Later, one-day conferences about the United Nations were held in different towns in the Midwest.

European Section program grows

Like the American Section, the European Section also grew in scope. As Executive Chairman of the Section, Sigrid Lund carried on the work of her office from her home in Oslo. She gave time to visiting meetings and groups, and in 1957 she and Margaret Gibbins, of Scotland, began a series of visits made jointly to, among other places, Vienna, Prague, and a number of locations in Germany.

Another of Barrow Cadbury's generous gifts made it possible to invite representatives of all yearly meetings in Europe to a conference. Held in Woodbrooke and other Selly Oak Colleges, in Birmingham, in the summer of 1957, the conference provided stimulus for increasing contacts by Friends from one country to another. Although there had been a few earlier small conferences of Friends who lived in adjacent countries, and who shared a common language, the number of such 'border conferences' now increased. The European Section encouraged these arrangements.

The Section gave care to groups in countries where there was no yearly meeting, sometimes where new interest was arising and no group had been previously. New groups and isolated individuals in Spain and Italy received concerned support from the Section.

For the production of Quaker literature the European Section encouraged the yearly meetings to take initiatives for literature in their languages. Sometimes the Section could give financial support to that initiative. It cooperated with Switzerland Yearly Meeting in publishing a pamphlet in Italian. Agreements were made between the European and American Sections about publication and distribution of literature in Spanish.

The Friends on the Continent of Europe felt a religious motivation for service, in the tradition of British and American Friends whose work was well known. A few Continental Friends had worked alongside the FSC and AFSC representatives, but European Friends yearned for a service program of their own. In the later 1950s, there began to be discussion of a possible service organization of Continental European Friends.

Benjamin N'gaira, first Administrative Secretary of EAYM, and a Vice-Chairman of FWCC.

Active follow-up of the Nairobi Conference

Following on the Chetsingh visit in Kenya and African Friends Conference at Nairobi in June, 1956, Benjamin Ngaira visited Malagasy Friends in October, at the time of the 75th Anniversary of Madagascar Yearly Meeting. Exchanges of visits were arranged between East Africa and Pemba Yearly Meetings, including women and men from both groups. When the People's Republic of Zanzibar (of which Pemba Island is a part) denied entry to British and American applicants, it was always possible for Kenyan Friends to travel there.

Since the great Island of Madagascar had been a French colony, young Malagasy Friends sometimes went to France for university study. At different times, the FWCC joined in arrangements for Malagasy Friends studying in France and Kenyan Friends studying in Britain to attend an annual meeting of the European Section.

In 1958, the Quaker UN Program and the FWCC joined forces to bring East Africa Yearly Meeting's representative to FWCC's Seventh Meeting, Jotham Standa, to the UN, along with his wife, Rhoda. Jotham served as a member of the 'Quaker Team' during the UN General Assembly.

Human Rights Seminars, sessions of the United Nations Economic Commission for Africa, and other UN sponsored events in Africa gave opportunity for other participation by African Friends as observers with credentials provided by the FWCC.

To Jamaica and Castro's Cuba

As I neared the end of my first three-year appointment, Ruthanna and I began our scheduled home leave in the United States, in December, 1958. We planned to travel to Cuba on January 1st, and a few days later on to Jamaica, to give encouragement and support to Friends in those island countries.

However, history intervened. On January 1, 1959, Fidel Castro's revolutionary forces took Havana and closed its airport on the very day we were to arrive. With a quick decision to visit Jamaica first, we then found we could get a plane from Jamaica to Cuba on the 11th of January. Ruthanna had lived in Cuba until age nine, while her father was the head of the Friends School in Holguin, and she had later visited there as a young Friend. The first Friends to arrive after the Castro coup, we spent five days with very welcoming Cuban Friends before returning to the United States and the annual meeting of the American Section. From there, I began my long journey to the East, while my family stayed at Ruthanna's parental home in Richmond, Indiana.

Asia-Pacific Area journey

The first stop on my Asian visit was at Dacca, East Pakistan (now Bangladesh), with Friends Service Council workers. Then, during 25 days in India, I visited the multi-national Friends group in Calcutta; AFSC workers in a village development project in the state of Orissa; the Bundelkhand Friends and Ohio Evangelical Friends Mission at Chhatarpur; the Mid-India Yearly Meeting, the Friends Schools, and the FSC project workers at Rasulia, all in the Itarsi area. I attended a two-days meeting of workers from the various Quaker projects in India, and was a few days with staff at the Delhi Friends Center. This recitation of Friends groups and Quaker work in India in 1959 indicates the variety and scope of activity – spiritual nurture, rural community development, and education for youth and adults – undertaken by Friends of Indian and other nationality, but in the huge land mass of India, and in the face of great poverty and social need of India's people, the Quaker contribution was small.

Traveling in Japan for three weeks, I visited the three meetings in Tokyo, the Friends Girls School there, and the meetings in Ibaraki Prefecture and in Osaka further south. Several members of Japan Yearly Meeting, both men and women, held responsible posts in universities and were influential in the rebuilding of educational and social structures in postwar Japan. Others were involved with Friends Girls School in Tokyo, or in kindergarten education in rural Ibaraki Prefecture.

I traveled the length of Australia during four weeks of April, visiting Friends in each state capital – Perth, Adelaide, Melbourne, Hobart, Sydney, and Brisbane – and in Canberra, the newly built national capital city. In New Zealand I attended yearly meeting at Palmerston North, and visited eight meetings in the North and South Islands. In both countries, Friends felt growing concern for the native peoples, the aborigines in Australia and the Maoris in New Zealand, against whom the white European populations discriminated in many ways. At the same time, they welcomed some weakening of traditional 'exclusion policies' as their universities began to admit students of color from Asian countries.

Asia-Pacific Area Friends not ready for regional association

In an article written for Quaker periodicals during these travels, I asked if Friends in Asia and the West Pacific were ready to form a regional arrangement for regular contacts and fellowship. While I had found seeds of an interest in regional contacts, there were many obstacles. Friends in India said they could not think of themselves as part of a 'Pacific Rim' group, for the Pacific Ocean was far from any Indian shore. The two Indian Friends groups, Mid-India and Bundelkhand, were not strong and gave little thought to relationships with Friends beyond their own areas. While postwar recovery in different aspects of Japanese life was well advanced in 1959, there was still work to do, and Japanese Friends felt unable to muster energy for building ties with other Friends in the Asia-West Pacific region. In both Australia and New Zealand Friends found the pull at their heartstrings was still from Britain and Europe, and they were reluctant to make any commitment to a regional arrangement with Asian Friends.

I concluded that relationships among Asia-Pacific Area Friends might be encouraged, but not urged unduly as may have been done by the FWCC and some American Friends in the past.

Before completing this round-the-world journey, I met with Friends in Hawaii and in six locations in California. Late in May I rejoined my family, weary from travel and 20 pounds heavier from the bountiful meals served on the tables of Friends in Australia and New Zealand. I attended at least parts of nine yearly meetings in the Midwest and Eastern United States, and conferred with American Section staff and with Friends engaged in United Nations work in New York. In early September our family returned by ship to England.

Preparing for the Eighth Meeting in Kenya

At its Seventh Meeting in 1958, the FWCC had appointed Elsa Cedergren as its Chairman. Before joining Friends, she had traveled from her home in Sweden to many parts of the world as an officer of the International YWCA. Devoted to the people of developing countries and newly independent nations, Elsa visited both Pemba and Kenya in April, 1959.

Norah Douglas, of Ireland Yearly Meeting (left), Chairman of European Section (1953-1955), and Elsa Cedegren, FWCC Chairman (1959-1961).

The FWCC's Eighth Meeting was to be held at Kaimosi in August, 1961. During her visit in Kenya, Elsa Cedergren had preliminary talks about plans for that meeting with officers of East Africa Yearly Meeting. Solomon Adagala, a Kenyan Friend, met with the Planning Committee in Birmingham in August, 1960; and a South African Friend, Hubert Malherbe, took part in the committee meeting in December.

I visited Friends in Africa during two months, August 19 to October 18, 1960. I attended the whole of East Africa Yearly Meeting at Shamberere, then went to Southern Rhodesia (now Zimbabwe) for visits with Friends in Salisbury (now Harare) and Bulawayo. In Johannesburg I met with the Southern Africa Yearly Meeting's 'Committee', one representative from each monthly meeting. I then visited Pemba for three days, followed by two weeks in Madagascar. Returning to Kenya, I spent a week with Friends in Nairobi and Kaimosi, working out arrangements for the FWCC Meeting nearly a year later.

CHAPTER V

Catalyst for Consultation

OUT OF CONFERENCE the Friends World Committee was born. No Friend questions the validity of conference as one of the functions of the FWCC. Following the Third World Conference of Friends, at Oxford in 1952, produced with strong support from London Yearly Meeting, Friends in many parts of the world became more aware of the work of FWCC, and more eager to come together in conferences. As a result, conference sponsorship proliferated, with European Friends adding family gatherings to their roster, Americans emphasizing more single issue conferences on controversial topics, and Africans becoming much more involved.

Conferences of African Friends

With Friends who were native peoples of Africa, though, that awareness was barely a flicker. Until 1956 when Ranjit and Doris Chetsingh came to Kenya to take part in the first African Friends Conference, not ten members of East Africa, Pemba, and Madagascar yearly meetings had any personal knowledge of the FWCC. The Nairobi Conference made it possible for indigenous Africans and Malagasy to take a first step in the household of the world family of Friends.

In 1969 the second African Friends Conference was held in Tananarive, capital city of Madagascar, under sponsorship of the FWCC. Representatives came from Kenya, Malawi, Rhodesia, South Africa, and Zambia, to meet with former Friends who had recently become part of the United Church of Jesus Christ of Madagascar. Participants of African and European origin considered together the church's responsibility to relieve poverty and hunger, and to speak to the many problems of society and the world.

European Friends Conference, 1957

In the month after the first African Friends Conference, a committee representing yearly meetings of the European Section met in Paris to plan for a conference to be held in 1957 at the Selly Oak Colleges, in

Birmingham. At that conference, July 22 to 29, a gift from Barrow Cadbury permitted ample representation from the Continental yearly meetings (9 to 12 from most, and 29 from Germany) in addition to 131 from Great Britain and Ireland. Focusing on the theme, 'Through Fellowship to Action', participants drew close to each other as they shared experiences of personal service performed in the various yearly meetings, and listened to Elsa Cedergren's description of Quaker work at the United Nations.

Each of the three Co-Chairmen of the conference – Sigrid Lund and Margaret Gibbins, along with Henri Schultz of France Yearly Meeting – spoke the three languages of the conference sessions, English, French, and German. To emphasize the world-wide character of the Quaker family, the conference committee invited other Friends – one each from Australia, East Africa, and South Africa, and seven from the American Section.

European conferences at six-year intervals

Pleased with the success of the 1957 conference, the 94-year-old Barrow Cadbury made a further gift. The income which this gift provided would make possible similar European conferences at six-year intervals for some time into the future. So, at the invitation of London Yearly Meeting which received the Cadbury gift, the European Section arranged two more conferences at the Selly Oak Colleges in 1963 and 1969, respectively.

At the 1963 gathering, the 250 Friends 'consulting' one another on subtopics of the theme, 'God and Man – A Quaker Approach', came from the nine yearly meetings of the European Section, along with one Friend each from Greece, Italy, Jordan, Lebanon, and Spain, and two from Poland. In the conference week many words were spoken, in the different languages, and Friends 'struggled with differences of belief and temperament, but we came through them too', declares the Letter of Greeting issued by the conference. 'We can hardly find the fresh words we need to express what we have found, and really speak to the hidden God in the hearts of men. Lacking words, we long that our lives may speak and serve.'

In keeping with the times, participants at the 1969 conference focused on a more action-oriented theme, 'Spiritual Strength for Responsible Living'. Study topics and Discussion Groups put forward some new concerns: Violence or Non-Violence in a Just Revolution, Spiritual Roots in a Secular Age, and The Stranger in Our Midst. The latter topic dealt with the needs of 'foreign workers' who had been attracted to Western European countries by a booming economy. To stimulate concern for 'Right Sharing of the World's Resources' the conference urged Friends individually to give one percent of income for projects to help the world's poorest nations.

Six years later, in 1975, with the turbulence of the 1960s subsided, the European Section conference in The Netherlands introduced new discussion topics appropriate to the time and conditions: Responsibilities in Prosperity, and Learning to Live with Anxiety. About 220 Friends took part in this conference, and many of them visited in local meetings on the Continent, as arranged by the FWCC.

Family camps and family conferences in Europe

As part of assistance to the small Continental yearly meetings in their work with children, the European Section sponsored an 'International Family Camp' in The Netherlands in 1971, with about 50 participants. This was followed by a larger Family Camp, 80 participants from Ireland and 70 from elsewhere in Europe at the Newtown School, Waterford, Ireland, in 1978.

To introduce the kind of conference which would include children, the Section brought together some 200 Quaker adults and children at the Reformierte Heimstatte, Gwatt, Switzerland, for a week at the end of July, 1981. With a great variety of creative activities for all ages, including daily worship and Bible study, the participants learned about 'Living Creatively in an Insecure World'. Another European Friends Family Gathering, with nearly 300 participants, was held at Waterford, Ireland, in 1986.

All-Friends Conference in American Section, 1957

Conference organization multiplied in the American Section during the 1950s. After the Oxford Conference of 1952, demands for conferences – topical, regional, or continent-wide – came from so many sources that the American Section formed a special 'Conference Committee' to sort out the suggestions and make appropriate recommendations.

Fearful that regional conferences might prove divisive rather than unifying, this committee advised against them. Instead, the Section decided to hold a conference of all American Friends in 1957. The Section's new Midwest office would soon open at Wilmington, Ohio, and an invitation to hold the conference at Wilmington College was quickly accepted.

Writing to all monthly meetings in December, 1954, Alexander Purdy, the American Section Chairman, announced: 'When we gather in 1957 at Wilmington . . . we expect, not to be inspired by great speeches, nor yet to have in hand a formula which will solve the problems of the world. We hope to gather together for a *time of discovery*'. A questionnaire accompanying that letter asked for suggestions for the forthcoming conference.

With responses from many meetings in hand, the Planning Committee arranged for only two addresses at the conference, by Douglas Steere of Philadelphia and Kathleen Lonsdale of London Yearly Meeting. Mornings were used for Worship-Fellowship Groups and for Discussion Groups with a variety of topics.

Because of limits of space at Wilmington College, it was possible to accommodate only 600 adult Friends at the conference, and quotas within this total were assigned to the different yearly meetings and groups. Canada, Costa Rica, Cuba, Jamaica, and Mexico were included along with yearly meetings in the USA. There were special programs for children of different ages, with junior and senior high school children accommodated at Wilmington Yearly Meeting's Camp Quaker Knoll ten miles away. To dramatize the world-wide character of the 'Quaker family', Ralph Rose prepared a 'Visual Epistle' of photo slides and accompanying voices recorded on tape, provided by Friends in Britain, France, Germany, Japan, Kenya, Madagascar, The Netherlands, New Zealand, Rhodesia, South Africa, and Sweden.

In addition to this large gathering, the American Section sponsored specially focused conferences on topics of much concern to American Friends during this period – civil liberties and race relations. Also, the Section provided focus on another critical issue, the penal system and criminal justice.

The American Section moves forward on race relations

In January, 1959, the American Section agreed to sponsor future conferences of Friends on race relations, held approximately every two years. Its role was conceived of 'as facilitating Friends across the country to share and consult on this testimony, and not (as) an action committee promoting the testimony'.

To assume responsibility for these conferences, in March, 1959, the Section appointed a Race Relations Conference Committee consisting of David Scull as Convenor, Ralph Rose, Victor Paschkis, and five other Friends. Authorized to enlist others to help, this committee recruited nearly 50 additional members, 10 or more of them Afro-American Friends.

Frank Loescher, a Philadelphia Friend, was the chairman of the committee during most of its planning for the next Friends Conference on Race Relations in 1961, and also chairman of the conference itself. James Walker was present at all meetings of the planning committee, wrote its minutes, and handled most of its correspondence.

Held at Earlham College, Richmond, Indiana, June 19-24, with 125 Friends from 60 local meetings in attendance, this was a working conference, with workshops on fair housing, voting rights, fair employment, and schools desegregation. As follow-up, the American Section and the Five Years Meeting's Board on Peace and Social Concerns jointly published a booklet 'In Whose Shoes?', designed to put readers in the shoes of persons of the minority group experiencing discrimination, then to relate this to action which a Friends meeting or individual Quaker might take.

After the 1961 conference, the American Section renewed its sponsorship, specifically for a Fourth Conference to be held in 1963, with the understanding that the 'continuing committee' would take care of all details of planning and correspondence. Victor Paschkis became the chairman of the Race Relations Conference Committee. He gave considerable time to visiting of meetings, in the Midwest and in New York and New England.

The Fourth National Conference was held at Oakwood School in Poughkeepsie, New York, in June, 1963. It sent a letter to Friends schools, expressing concern that so few Afro-American students were enrolled, with some schools having no students of a minority race. Searching questions were put to Friends meetings, asking about their attitudes and actions in situations where the civil rights of members of minority groups were infringed.

Leadership for the continuing committee was passed to Friends in the Midwest. The Section appointed as Co-Chairmen Herbert Huffman, Secretary of the Board on Peace and Social Concerns of the Five Years Meeting, and George Sawyer, an Afro-American Friend and lawyer in Richmond, Indiana. Cooperating with the continuing committee, I sent from the Section office to Clerks of yearly meetings a collection of statements by four Friends organizations and the National Council of Churches, on civil and human rights applicable to persons of minority groups. An accompanying letter suggested that the yearly meeting consider its right action in matters addressed by the documents, then report to the American Section 'within the next few weeks' what action the yearly meeting was taking.

The 1965 Race Relations Conference was held again at Earlham College, June 18-21. Its theme was 'THE FIVE-FOLD REVOLUTION: Race, Nuclear Weapons, Population, Automation-Poverty, and the Required Moral Revolution'. Once more, a letter was addressed to Friends schools and colleges. Attenders expressed strong desire that the next conference should be held in the South. John Yungblut was named the chairman for the next period, with Victor Paschkis as Coordinator. While formal sponsorship by the American Section continued, contacts between the Section and the continuing committee for the Race Relations Conference decreased. The continuing committee was inactive until early in 1967.

More intensive examination of Friends' attitudes on race

Among Afro-Americans in the United States a revolution of rising expectations was in progress. New laws and court decisions gave promise of better times, but progress toward equal rights and justice was slow. The non-violent movement led by Dr. Martin Luther King, Jr., however, was gaining strength. Afro-Americans, with a new self awareness, affirmed that 'black is beautiful'. As individuals and as a race, they chose to be called 'blacks'. When the term 'black power' came into use, many whites feared that it meant violence. Their fears were reinforced by the racial riots in many American cities in the summer of 1967.

The planning committee for the next Race Relations Conference, noting that a great part of the Society of Friends suffers from 'middle class bias', proceeded to define that bias in these terms: (1) Middle class people concentrate on change of individuals rather than on structural change in society. (2) Middle class people are afraid of conflict. (3) Middle class people are distrustful of power. The Sixth National Conference of Friends on Race Relations, at Black Mountain, North Carolina, July 6-9, 1967, urged Friends to strictly examine themselves and their motives in the life styles they maintained.

'Black Power – White Power – Shared Power' was the title which headed the 'message to Friends' sent from the conference at Black Mountain. It declared, '. . . we see at least that future action must be based on a willingness to work for social changes much more far-reaching than we had supposed the correction of racial injustice would require. (Our) existing social-economic-political-legal-military system – the framework within which the white establishment operates – simply cannot be patched up in such a way as to end exploitation and degradation. We must be prepared to discover how much we ourselves, sharing in and profiting from the operation of the system, are contributing to the power which maintains the very practices we are fighting against'.

At Black Mountain, the Race Relations Conference appointed Marian Fuson of Nashville, Tennessee, as chairman of the continuing committee. When the American Section's Executive Committee met at Nashville in February, 1968, Marian gave an oral report on the conference. In May,

1969, the Section's Executive Committee, concerned because so few blacks were Section members, asked its staff to keep good contact with the continuing committee for the Race Relations Conference.

Allowing a three-year interval between conferences, the continuing committee planned a different kind of event for 1970. It proposed that 20 young Friends go to Washington for a 'project', working with as many black and white individuals and groups as possible during a six-weeks period. 'Seeking to learn, think, feel (and) create change . . . participants will attempt to expand their knowledge of racism and how it affects people . . . (They) will read, attend Congressional hearings, court sessions, meetings – seeking always to gather together as much emotional and intellectual understanding as possible . . . The participants will also look at Quakerism and its relationship to what they are studying. (They will try) to understand all kinds of institutional and individual responses to the problem of racism . . . (and will) travel to various Quaker institutions where the question of race has arisen and has been or is being discussed among Friends.'

Then 200 to 300 Friends, from all parts of American Quakerdom, would gather in Washington with the 20 young Friends. During the five-days 'gathering' the experiences, insights, and feelings of the participating young Friends would, hopefully, be transmitted to the larger number who would 'learn new ways to talk about race, new ways to share what they feel and have learned, once they leave the gathering'.

Friends for Human Justice

Friends came to the 1970 'gathering' in much smaller numbers than the continuing committee had projected. Among those who were there the response was mixed. The few highly committed Friends who decided to carry on proposed to work under a new label, 'Friends for Human Justice'. As Co-Chairmen they named George Sawyer and Caroline Estes, the latter a Pacific Coast Friend living temporarily in Philadelphia. This group sought, and were given, sponsorship by the American Section. At the Section's Executive Committee meeting in Atlanta, in February, 1971, George Sawyer gave an address with the impassioned plea that 'problems exclusively black must be solved by blacks. White America must concern itself with the total eradication of racism in America. The burden is now on white America to purge itself'.

The small group which had formed Friends for Human Justice did not receive from Friends generally the support they hoped for. Each year they renewed their request to the American Section for sponsorship. In 1974 new officers for FHJ affirmed their desire to continue the concern but, at the same time, described their weakness and failure. Too few of the yearly meeting appointees to their committee attended meetings, and financial support from Friends, which was contributed through the American Section, was not sufficient for the program FHJ officers wanted to carry on.

To evaluate the organization and work of Friends for Human Justice, the Section proposed a joint *ad hoc* committee which recommended that FHJ and sponsorship by the American Section be continued. But in another year, it was clear that the time had come for that sponsorship to cease. In February, 1977, the Section's Executive Committee noted that committees in several yearly meetings, and the AFSC, were actively involved in the field of race relations and the broader concern of human justice. It expressed appreciation for the efforts of those who had worked with FHJ and in the National Friends Conferences on Race Relations, concluding that 'Friends in many regions are more sensitive in matters of race'.

A Conference on Crime and the Treatment of Offenders

Concern for the abolition of capital punishment had come before the American Section early in the 1950s, largely on the initiative of a representative of Baltimore Yearly Meeting, Emily Parker Simon. She had gathered information about action on this issue from American, and some other, yearly meetings, which she brought to the FWCC's Sixth Meeting in 1955. Her concern was referred to yearly meetings for 'sympathetic consideration' of ways they might work to abolish capital punishment.

Friends in New Jersey, Pennsylvania, and Maryland, deeply troubled about capital punishment and other penal questions, urged the American Section to call a conference in 1959. The Five Years Meeting and the Friends General Conference supported that request. The Section's Executive Committee appointed six Friends to explore the interest of yearly meetings in a consultative conference, and to proceed with plans if sufficient interest should be found. Chaired by Edmund Goerke of New York Yearly Meeting, a Conference on Crime and the Treatment of Offenders, with 80 Friends from the United States and Canada, was held at Camp Miami, Germantown, Ohio, November 12 to 15, 1959.

The conference message called on Friends 'to reaffirm our testimony regarding the abolition of capital punishment and to renew efforts to improve the penal system as it relates to probation and parole, the treatment of youthful offenders and the rehabilitation of jails'. The conference also urged Friends to increase their visiting of prisoners. It named a 'continuation committee' which sent a quarterly newsletter to about 400 Friends.

The continuation committee also produced a pamphlet 'What Do the Churches Say about Capital Punishment?', a compilation of official statements from 14 churches, church councils, and other religious groups. A special edition of this pamphlet was prepared, printed in India, and distributed to all delegates at the Third Assembly of the World Council of Churches at New Delhi, in November, 1961. As a result of such efforts, several American states adopted legislation abolishing capital punishment during the next few years. Becoming inactive, the continuation committee was disbanded in 1968.

The world-wide FWCC meets in Kenya, 1961

In 1958, when the FWCC accepted East Africa Yearly Meeting's invitation to meet in Kenya, even the committee's officers feared that attendance would be small. Time and history proved this fear unfounded. In three years' time Africa burst into the attention of the whole world. One after another, colonial territories gained independent nation status. Kenya was not yet independent in 1961, but the timetable for independence had been fixed and the people were caught up in the political process. National independence would come in 1963. Friends everywhere wanted to see Africa and the East Africa Yearly Meeting at first hand.

So, with 150 participants, 40 of them from yearly meetings in Africa, the Eighth Meeting was larger than any before it. It was held at Kaimosi, the mission station established by the Five Years Meeting in 1902 and now the headquarters of the EAYM. Elsa Cedergren was unable to chair because her husband's illness kept her in Sweden. So, once more, Lewis Waddilove served as acting chairman, assisted by Vice-Chairman Benjamin Ngaira.

The Program Committee did not envision a single theme for the Eighth Meeting; they arranged, therefore, for advance study papers on two topics. About the topic, 'Beyond Diversities to a Common Experience of God', Errol Elliott wrote that Friends' divergencies may reflect differing needs for expression of inward experiences which have much in common, and that the culture, faith, and practice of African Friends could bring in additional elements helpful to all of us. An address by Douglas Steere preceded two Group Discussion sessions on this topic. One group concluded that 'We must keep open, be humble, and realize that our main job is to earn the right in each generation to call ourselves Friends'.

Ranjit Chetsingh was scheduled to give an address on the second topic, 'The Application of Quaker Principles in Situations of Tension', but illness prevented his coming from India. Instead, five Friends familiar with developments in Kenya – Solomon Adagala, Thomas Lung'aho, Walter

Martin, Benjamin Ngaira, and Fred Reeve – responded to questions about the political and economic situation in that country. In two Discussion Group sessions, it was noted that Friends were at work in a variety of situations with tension, that not all result of tension is negative, and that Quaker testimonies, traditions, and practice can help Friends to handle tensions in creative ways.

For the next triennial period, the Eighth Meeting appointed James Walker as chairman. He would retire from the post of Executive Secretary of the American Section in September, 1962. With the increased burden of work in the office at Birmingham, an Associate Secretary would be found to

James F. Walker (left), Madelaine Jequier, Heinrich Carstens.

assist the new General Secretary, Blanche Shaffer, soon after she should arrive at that post. At Kaimosi, the FWCC accepted the invitation of Ireland Yearly Meeting to hold the Ninth Meeting in Ireland in 1964.

World Conference in 1967 to be held in North Carolina

As instructed at the Seventh Meeting in 1958, the staff had queried yearly meetings about their interest in a possible world conference in 1967, with favorable replies. Invitations were received from Earlham College in Indiana, from Whittier College in California, and from North Carolina Yearly Meeting which proposed that the conference should be in the town of Greensboro. Clyde Milner, President of Guilford College and a representative of North Carolina Yearly Meeting, urged that the conference be held at Guilford which was in the edge of Greensboro. The American Section had endorsed the invitation from North Carolina, further supporting a proposal that Guilford College in Greensboro should be the conference site.

During discussion at the Eighth Meeting, Sigrid Lund expressed hesitation about holding the conference at Guilford College, a Quaker institution in which the American Negro was not welcomed as a student. Benjamin Ngaira said it would be difficult for Africans and Asians to feel at home at Guilford College, knowing that American Negroes could not be students there.

When it was made clear that North Carolina Yearly Meeting viewed Women's College in Greensboro, which admitted both black and white students, as the site for the conference, James Walker said that the American Section, supporting Guilford as the conference site, hoped the college would be racially integrated by 1967. The Eighth Meeting accepted the invitation to hold the conference at Greensboro, but deferred consideration of the proposal to use Guilford College until the Ninth Meeting in 1964. The College Board did, indeed, change the policy and the way was cleared for the 1967 world conference to be held there.

The important contacts with Africa and African Friends

The high point of the Eighth Meeting for many of its participants was their contact with Africa and with African Friends. In travels to and from Kaimosi, FWCC members visited Friends in Pemba and Madagascar, in South Africa and Southern Rhodesia, in Kenya and Uganda, and in Ghana, Nigeria, and Ethiopia. On the two Sundays during the meeting, participants went by bus or car to 11 different African meetings, ranging from 10 to 81 miles in distance from Kaimosi. On four days, Kenyan

Friends who were not official representatives were welcomed to sessions where addresses were given, with consecutive interpretation from English to Luragoli.

A number of events were planned to follow the gathering at Kaimosi. In Nairobi on September 5th the Christian Council of Kenya hosted a morning coffee reception for members of the FWCC. In the late afternoon of the same day, the FWCC gave a tea reception in the Nairobi City Hall courtyard for 80 government and civic leaders. Using a Conference Center of the Christian Council of Kenya, at Limuru, the Five Years Meeting, the Friends Service Council, and the AFSC arranged consultation on Friends work in Africa, in which officers and other representatives of the African yearly meetings and Friends groups participated.

Quaker witness as Kenya moved toward independence

Preceding the Eighth Meeting, the FWCC recruited several of its members to join Kenyan Friends for a two-days 'Conference on the Friends Peace Testimony and its Application in Kenya'. In this conference at Kamusinga, 47 Friends from six nationalities took part. As a result, among Kenyan Friends there arose a concern for effective witness for right government as the independence of Kenya neared reality.

To follow up this concern, the FWCC arranged for Raymond Wilson, who had long experience working with government in Washington as Executive Secretary of the Friends Committee on National Legislation, to stop off in Kenya ten days in mid-December, 1961. Raymond was returning from India where he was a delegate to the Assembly of the World Council of Churches.

After many consultations with Friends and others, both in Nairobi and in Western Kenya, Raymond recommended that Kenyan Friends talk with elected members of the Legislative Assembly, who would soon travel to London to participate in the formulation of Kenya's constitution of government. He urged Friends to emphasize provisions for rights of women and for religious liberty in the constitution, and to make strong points for a Kenyan role for peace and in discussions on disarmament at the United Nations.

Some goals attained

For a variety of personal and family reasons, Ruthanna and I felt we must return to the United States at the end of my second three-years term in the FWCC office at Woodbrooke. From the American Section came information that James Walker was ready to retire at whatever time a successor might be named. I agreed to become the Executive Secretary of the American Section at the end of summer, 1962. Leaving the General Secretary position at the end of April, I felt satisfied that program goals for strengthening relationships with and among Friends in Africa, Asia, and the Pacific Area had been achieved. The Friends World Committee had gained an identity of its own in Friends groups around the world.

On June 1st, Blanche Shaffer came to the office at Woodbrooke as General Secretary. Swiss-born and a naturalized citizen of the United States, she had acquired an intimate knowledge of the FWCC in its early years while her husband, Leslie Shaffer, had been a principal member of staff. She was serving as Secretary of the Friends International Center in Geneva when she received the FWCC appointment. Blanche would carry established work still further, significantly expanding little developed aspects of FWCC program during the next nine years.

Blanche Weber Shaffer.

CHAPTER VI

Sponsor of Spiritual Nurture

THROUGH A VARIETY OF WAYS the spiritual life of the Society of Friends is nurtured through the Friends World Committee for Consultation. Intervisitation, sometimes called 'travel in the ministry', has been central to the committee's work from its earliest period. In certain situations, the FWCC has been called upon to give care to new groups of Friends whose growth is dependent on spiritual nurture. Friends isolated geographically needed contacts. To nurture the spiritual lives of younger Friends the FWCC has helped young people from many regions connect with each other and has devised pilgrimages and other programs for Quaker youth and children. In addition, when groups whose differing thought and practice took steps toward better understanding of each other, the FWCC was present to help.

Intervisitation, 'life-blood' of FWCC's mission

It has been said that in no other religious body are its leaders personally known by so many members as in the Religious Society of Friends. Indeed, the members of the Society have enjoyed intimate contact with Quaker leaders through the practice of visiting among meetings, or intervisitation. Friendly visitors have often traveled great distances to individual meetings, to speak publicly or simply to visit in members' homes.

There are many kinds of ministry, and the valued Friends visitor is one who travels 'under religious concern'. However the concerned Friend may feel led to share him/herself, or whatever message he or she may be concerned to share with others, the concern ought first to be tested by presenting it to the would-be traveler's monthly meeting. If the concern is endorsed, the monthly meeting will provide a minute, or letter, commending their member to those who may be visited. If the projected travel is beyond the limits of the traveler's yearly meeting, the appropriate body within the yearly meeting should add its endorsement to the travel minute.

When the Friend who would travel is well and favorably known by the FWCC or one of its organized Sections, the FWCC or the appropriate Section may provide further commendation for the Friend who feels led to visit other Friends. In special cases, the traveling Friend with his or her concern may be sponsored by the FWCC or one Section. Sponsorship usually implies that the sponsor will pay some part of the expense for the visiting journey.

When endorsement or sponsorship of a visitor with religious concern has been determined, the FWCC or Section notifies the yearly meeting and Section within which the expected visit will be carried out, so that preparation for the visit can be made. Friends in the meeting or area to be visited can help by arranging for a group, or groups, to meet with the visitor, or for visits to homes of member families. It is long tradition that a Friend who travels in the ministry will be given home hospitality by the members of the meeting which is visited.

Selected examples of intervisitation

The following examples of visitation under religious concern demonstrate how FWCC strives to provide spiritual nurture by sponsoring visitors back and forth across the globe. Frederick Tritton provided such ministry in FWCC's early years with his frequent visits to the small Friends groups on the Continent of Europe, where his quiet explanation of Quaker principle and practice was welcomed, with his wise counsel of individuals.

During the Second World War, and immediately after, both the American Friends Service Committee and the FWCC American Section felt it was their urgent duty to keep contact with Friends in Britain and on the Continent of Europe through Friendly visits so far as this was possible. At first, most of the visitors were American. Errol Elliott traveled in Europe in 1940, having brief contacts with Friends in Switzerland and France, and more time with British Friends. Then in 1946 he made visits to Friends in Ireland, Britain, The Netherlands, Denmark, Norway, Finland, and Germany, helping to relieve the feeling of isolation which was so much a part of their wartime experience.

In the spring and summer of 1946, D. Elton Trueblood stayed in Britain, working with British Friends in a variety of ways. On returning to America, he spent August attending yearly meetings and interpreting to American Friends the postwar situation for Friends in Britain and Europe.

To share the difficult experiences of war years with sympathetic listeners, and to receive encouragement for renewal of spirit and rebuilding of community at home, British and European Quakers visited American

Friends during the early postwar period. Among these visitors were Carl and Eva Hermann and Emil Fuchs of Germany, Marguerite Czarnecki of France, and Henry and Lucy Gillett of England. Continental European Friends were, in ways other than geographical, closer to British than to American Friends. Henri van Etten of France, Edmond and Yvonne Privat of Switzerland, and Regnar Halfden-Nielsen of Denmark made early postwar visits to Friends in Britain.

The chairmen of the FWCC have done much 'Friendly' visiting, not only to promote support for the organization but also to nurture spiritual life world-wide. Elsa Cedergren, for instance, traveled to Kenya and Pemba while she was chairman (1959-1962), and also among meetings across North America. Well known to Friends in Europe through his prior chairing of the European and Near East Section, Heinrich Carstens traveled extensively to visit meetings in America in 1971.

Edwin Bronner was well acquainted with Quakerism in North America and Britain before he became FWCC Chairman in 1974. Then, in 1978, accompanied by Anne Bronner, he made a six-months round-the-world journey with visits to Friends in Asia, Australia and New Zealand, Africa, the Middle East, and Europe. When Joseph Haughton became Chairman in 1980 he already knew Friends in many areas from his long service with FWCC as Interim Committee Chairman and in other capacities. During 1980-1985, as chairman, his travels included America and Japan. Simeon Shitemi, whose tenure began in 1986, had previously visited Friends in South Africa and was acquainted with Friends in parts of North America.

No Friend in modern times, perhaps in all time, has traveled in the ministry more extensively than Douglas Steere, accompanied in most of his travels by Dorothy Steere. Prior to 1965 when his six-years chairing of the FWCC began, Douglas was familiar with Friends in Britain and Europe, and in Africa, as well as in his own North America. During his tenure as chairman, his travels extended to India and Japan.

Historically, there has been a strong relationship between London Yearly Meeting and Friends in Australia and New Zealand. British Friends with concern to visit those countries have not felt need for endorsement by the FWCC. American Friends, however, have felt differently. Following long service as pastor of the Wilmington, Ohio, Friends Meeting, Ward Applegate and his wife, Lena, for instance, turned to the American Section and the FWCC to express their concern to visit Friends in New Zealand and Australia. Their six-months traveling ministry, in 1959-60, was well received. Ward Applegate then was chairman of the American Section from 1961 to 1967.

Among Friendly visitors whose service stands out with value are two British Friends: Margaret S. Gibbins of Scotland and Elfrida Vipont Foulds, British author and Quaker historian knowledgeable about the beginnings of Quakerism in her home area of Northwest England. In Elfrida's first visit to America, in 1950, she was a featured speaker at the 1950 Five Years Meeting. She made several later visits, with FWCC's American Section making part of the arrangements, and was an especially welcome visitor to Friends schools.

Margaret Gibbins' first visit in America in 1953, planned by the American Section, was primarily to Friends in the Southwest and Far West. Although she sometimes spoke at meetings, her ability to listen to individual Friends and to enter with sympathy into their concerns was particularly helpful. Early in 1955 she visited Friends in Norway where she again found warm response. Already fluent in the French and German languages, she was determined to learn Norwegian. As she visited Norway and learned the language, Margaret became close friends with Sigrid Lund. The two new friends then traveled in the ministry together on the European Continent and in the United States. When Margaret became Executive

Margaret S. Gibbins (left) and Sigrid H. Lund.

Secretary of the European Section in 1964, her travel within that Section increased. She had a special relationship with Friends in Lebanon and at Ramallah in the old Palestine.

The American Section made an unusual visitation arrangement with British Friend, George Boobyer. An internationally known New Testament scholar, George Boobyer offered to meet Friends as he traveled eastward across the United States following conferences he would attend in California in the summer of 1972. The Section found Quaker colleges delighted to tap George's expert knowledge for seven-to-ten-day periods, and to allow time for him to share his Biblical knowledge with meetings in each college vicinity. Similar visiting arrangements were made when George Boobyer was in the United States in 1975 and again in 1980.

FWCC sponsored intervisitation provided lifelines of spiritual nurture and connection to the struggling Friends groups in East Germany, South Africa, and Cuba during the long hard years of the Cold War, a completely unbending apartheid, and the isolation imposed on Cuba by the United States. Especially because of the political division between East and West in Europe which divided Germany, the European Section strove to maintain contacts with Friends in the German Democratic Republic. Visits to Friends in East Germany were sponsored by that Section, sometimes when permission to travel there was difficult to obtain. Fortunately, restrictions on travel became somewhat relaxed, and some East German Friends were permitted to visit parts of Western Europe, Britain, and the United States. Heinrich Bruckner, an East German Friend and pediatrician, contacted Friends in Cuba when he was invited to that country on the publication there of a Spanish language edition of his books on family life. Since 1959, several American Friends and a few British Friends have broken through the isolation of Castro's Cuba to visit Quakers there. Some young Cuban Friends, in turn, have joined in the activities of young Friends in Europe.

In other Latin American countries Friends have welcomed visits arranged by the American Section. In the late 1950s Friends in two areas of Mexico began to meet together for General Meetings at 18-months intervals. They asked each time for a visiting Friend to attend that gathering and to give an address. Among the visitors whom the American Section helped to provide on those occasions were Anna Brinton, Co-Director of Pendle Hill; Domingo Ricart, scholar and philosopher who emigrated from Spain to the United States; and Hiram Hilty, for several years a Friends missionary in Cuba, who had become chairman of the Modern Languages Department at Guilford College.

Retired early from United States consular service in several Latin American countries, Bainbridge Davis gave volunteer service in the

American Section office and was especially useful in contacts with Latin American Friends. In addition, he personally visited Friends in Cuba, Mexico, and Colombia. Heberto and Suzanne Sein, Mexican Friends, gave encouragement and spiritual nurture to Friends in many parts of the world, since Heberto's work as a language interpreter at international conferences made frequent travel possible for them.

After Gordon Browne became Executive Secretary of the American Section in 1981, his travel among Friends in nearly all the Latin American groups helped to nurture the growth of spirit and life in those meetings. (Note that in 1974 the name 'Section of the Americas' was adopted as more appropriate and inclusive of North, Central, and South America and the Caribbean Area.)

At the invitation of the Section of the Americas in 1983, the Clerk of the German Democratic Republic Yearly Meeting, Ines Ebert, and Helga Bruckner, also from the GDR, met with Friends in New York, Philadelphia, Washington, Richmond, Chicago, Denver, and Los Angeles, sharing their concern for building peace through mutual understanding.

In Southern Africa the number of Friends has always been small, never more than a few hundred. In the American Section, Friends felt led to send an American Quaker couple to South Africa for an extended visit, so that they could both minister to spiritual needs and strengthen the will to struggle against the evils of apartheid. In April, 1966, the Section sent John and June Yungblut, Directors of the Friends Center in Atlanta, Georgia, to Johannesburg. During more than three months, they visited all of the principal groups in South Africa, Rhodesia, and Zambia. Again, in 1973, John and June visited Friends in South Africa and shared their ministry at South Africa General Meeting in April. Following June's death, and his remarriage, John and Penelope Yungblut journeyed to minister to Southern African Friends in late 1983 and early 1984.

As further help to South African Friends and to Friends visited in the United States, the Section of the Americas, with cooperation from the AFSC, organized an exchange of group visits between 1978 and 1980. Still later, during 1987, Jennifer Kinghorn of Johannesburg and Joyce Mtshazo of Soweto visited in the United States at the invitation of the Section of the Americas.

The recounting above of visits made includes only a small fraction of the number of visits under religious concern to which the FWCC has given varying degrees of support. Some mistakes have been made and endorsement given when the expression of concern by a would-be visitor was not wisely assessed. The number of unfortunate encounters becomes small, however, alongside the hundreds of spiritually nurturing visits in the ministry which the Friends World Committee has supported during 50 years.

There was agreement at the 1979 FWCC Triennial Meeting that more careful study should be given to the basis of, and procedures for, travel under religious concern. A committee was appointed with 12 members from 10 yearly meetings and 9 different nationalities, and with George Watson of New England Yearly Meeting as its convenor. At the 1985 Triennial Meeting the committee presented the draft of a handbook on 'Traveling under Religious Concern', inviting comments and suggestions on which might be based a final draft for approval in 1988.

Two points of emphasis in the draft are noted here. First is the importance of preparation for visits to be made under religious concern, preparation by both the visitor and by the Friends to be visited. Second, the development of life in Friends meetings in economically deprived countries makes it possible for some members of those groups to travel in the ministry to groups elsewhere. Whereas, formerly, Friends from developing areas might travel among other Friends groups to learn, or to give information about their own group, they may now provide a ministry of spiritual nurture. A few examples will illustrate.

Paulina Titus, a member of Mid-India Yearly Meeting, was one of the missions area representatives at the early 1976 Mission and Service Conference in Maryland, USA, sponsored by the FWCC. For a brief period after the conference she visited Friends in the Eastern United States. Her spiritual sensitivity and the deep concern she carried for strengthening the life of the spirit in her own yearly meeting were inspiration to Friends whom she met. Furthermore, from the small meeting in Seoul, Korea, two members have traveled widely and their ministry has been helpful. Yoon Gu Lee has moved among Friends with a spirit of enthusiasm and optimism which lifts the spirit in others. Ham Sok Hon has imparted courage to those who struggle against discrimination and oppression because his struggle for freedom and democracy in his own country, motivated by spiritual not political concern, is well known. A Kenyan Friend, Joseph Kisia, has been a true traveler in the ministry in Australia and America.

Nurturing new Meetings

When the American Friends Fellowship Council and the American Section of FWCC were merged early in 1954, the care of new local groups and the recognition of such groups as monthly meetings when they had reached a stage of readiness were a program of the AFFC, developed over 16 years. More than 100 groups across the United States had come under its care; 38 of these had been given monthly meeting status. 15 of the monthly meetings had affiliated with an appropriate yearly meeting and two had been laid down. 21 of the meetings were still reporting to the Fellowship Council. 70 worship groups, of varying size and strength, were receiving attention from the AFFC.

With the merger of the American Section and the AFFC, arrangement for nurturing worship groups and new meetings changed very little. As Executive Secretary, James Walker wrote an occasional letter, with news from the Quaker world, which went to each group and meeting. He also provided printed material about the message and work of Friends. More important, he made several trips each year, in different directions, visiting a number of groups on each trip. When he retired from the Executive Secretary post in 1962, James continued to serve part time as 'Correspondent for New Meetings', for ten more years. More than any other Friend in this period, he was known by members of the new groups and was looked upon as their mentor.

Other Friends also undertook the responsibility of visiting the new groups, providing counsel and pastoral care or merely assurance of continued interest in the welfare of the group. Some, like Ferner Nuhn of Pacific Yearly Meeting in 1954, might give such service to 20 or more groups while traveling across America by auto. Others might go to only one group which was in need of counsel, like the new unprogrammed group in Denver visited by Harold Chance and Homer Coppock in 1956 when relationships with a pastoral, programmed meeting in the same city were at a low ebb. As the American Section's Midwest office began to function in 1954, the nurture of new groups in Ohio and Indiana and nearby states was accepted as a responsibility.

When a worship group began to indicate its desire for status as a monthly meeting, the New Meetings Committee first made certain that any yearly meeting (sometimes more than one) near enough for convenient affiliation was fully aware of the group. If, after sufficient time, it became evident that affiliation with a yearly meeting was not developing, the worship group would be given a set of questions which, when answered, would provide the group's own assessment of its readiness for responsibilities a meeting should carry. Two Friends appointed by the New Meetings Committee would then visit the group and its member families, usually on a weekend. On the basis of a report by these visitors, the New Meetings Committee might recommend to the Section's Executive Committee that approval be given for status as a monthly meeting. If the Executive Committee's action was positive, two or more representatives would be asked to confer with the group and to determine a date for the formal establishment of a monthly meeting at which the Section's appointed representatives would be present.

The practice of recognizing the official status of a monthly meeting was controversial even among members of the American Section. First, precedent among Friends held that this action should be taken by quarterly and yearly meetings. Second, most members of the new groups wanted unprogrammed worship without use of a pastor. When such a group developed within the area of a yearly meeting where programmed worship with a pastor was the norm, and especially if theological views were decidedly different, that yearly meeting might be very critical of FWCC support of the new group.

The American Section did not intend that the monthly meetings established under its care should always remain in that relationship, but that an affiliation with a yearly meeting should be made as soon as this became possible. Many affiliations with existing yearly meetings were made. However, where several of the new worship groups and monthly meetings were in a geographical region, they felt a need to meet together and regional conferences or associations developed.

The Lake Erie Association of Friends began with a regional gathering in the Cleveland, Ohio, area in 1939, and held a first annual session in 1945. In 1963 they formed a combined Lake Erie Association and Yearly Meeting. An All Florida Friends Conference met annually from 1950 onward, becoming Southeastern Yearly Meeting in 1962. A Southwest Conference of Friends held annual conferences beginning in 1953, then formed South Central Yearly Meeting in 1961. Another group of meetings held regular conferences from 1940 to 1947, then resumed annual gatherings in 1959; in 1970 they formed Southern Appalachian Yearly Meeting and Association. New meetings in Iowa, Kansas, Missouri, and Nebraska began to meet together in 1950 and formed the Missouri Valley Friends Conference in 1955; some of these meetings have joined nearby yearly meetings.

While in parts of North America there were still great distances between local meetings, by 1970 there was hardly any area which could not be considered territory of some yearly meeting. It seemed time to assume that new groups of Friends could find sponsorship and nurture by the nearest yearly meeting. The rise of new groups was less frequent. Furthermore, the Friends General Conference was better prepared to provide for the needs of new groups and declared its readiness to do so.

After conferring with the groups and meetings still under its care, and with Friends General Conference, Friends United Meeting, Evangelical

Friends Alliance, and Conservative Friends; with independent yearly meetings, and with the annual conference of Yearly Meeting Superintendents and Secretaries, the Section of the Americas discharged its New Meetings Committee in 1975.

Aware that no other Friends organization was prepared to assist new or isolated groups in Central and South America and the Caribbean Area, the Section of the Americas retained that responsibility. At various times it has nurtured informal groups whose members were mostly North American or European. One such group in Bogota, Colombia, began to have regular meetings for worship in 1964. Gradually, a few Colombians became interested, and in 1978 the Bogota group asked the Section of the Americas for monthly meeting status which was granted. The meeting remains small, but it participates with yearly meetings and groups in the Comite Organizador de Los Amigos Latinoamericanos.

New and isolated groups in Europe

The usual arrangement of Friends organization in Europe makes the geographical limits of a yearly meeting coincide with a national boundary. There are exceptions – Friends in Austria are a part of the Pyrmont Yearly Meeting in Germany; Friends in Sweden and Finland are one yearly meeting; the group in Barcelona, Spain, is a part of France Yearly Meeting; and Friends in Northern Ireland and the Irish Republic are one Ireland Yearly Meeting. There has been no well defined procedure for the European Section when a new group interested in Quakerism appears in a country with no yearly meeting.

Italy. Beginning in 1951 there were annual conferences of friends of Friends in Italy. The European Section provided modest financial support and asked Swiss Friends to keep in touch with developments. Two Italians, Maria Comberti of Florence and Guido Graziani of Rome, were the principal organizers of the conferences, assisted later by Mario and Ruth Tassoni of Bergamo.

After 17 years, it was evident that a number of Italians enjoyed these conferences but were not interested in taking responsibility for continuing organization. In 1968, Maria Comberti and the Tassonis decided to drop the conferences, but to try to maintain centers of Quaker interest in their respective cities, Florence and Bergamo. New interest has arisen since the mid-1980s, with groups meeting as Friends in three locations.

Spain. The Catholic Church, with support by the state, maintained rigid control of religious activity and worship in Spain. On the Island of Majorca, during the 1950s, a group under the leadership of Cayetano Marti began to meet for Quaker worship as they understood it. Archer Tongue, on behalf of the European Section, visited the group twice. A British Friend, Alfred Tucker, made several pastoral visits with financial assistance from the European Section and other Quaker sources. Without legal standing, the group met in some secrecy. Its members were poor and hardly literate, and Cayetano Marti had an unstable personality. He formally returned to the Catholic Church in 1960, and the Majorca group ceased to exist.

The story of a Friends group in Barcelona is different. In 1958, Alfred Tucker first visited a few persons in Barcelona whose names were on his list of independent thinkers in Spain, and found among them an interest in Quakerism. Contacts with French Friends were arranged, and in 1961 France Yearly Meeting agreed to accept the Barcelona Friends as a 'recognised group'.

Gerard and Nancy Negelspach, a young American Friends couple, were leaders of an international Quaker work camp in Spain. Since Gerry was an artist, the Negelspachs returned to Spain where he could paint for a few months. They visited the group in Barcelona and met Alfred Tucker there during his 1961 visit. Back in Philadelphia, a concern grew in them to live amongst the Friends in Barcelona and to help in the life of that meeting.

Early in 1964, the group asked that self-supporting Friends come to live in Barcelona, saying their preference would be for the Negelspachs. Arrangements were made for support, shared by their monthly, quarterly, and yearly meetings in Philadelphia, the Friends Service Council in London, the FWCC and its European and American Sections. Gerry and Nancy and their daughter, Kristin, arrived in Barcelona in February, 1965. They found a fourth floor apartment adequate for their needs and large enough for meetings of the group. Gerry taught English to adults in evening school and, from time to time, Nancy worked as an office secretary. They skillfully supplemented the activity of the group without assuming responsibility its members should carry. The newly open attitude of the Catholic Church, under the influence of Vatican Council II, gave opportunity for relationships with some priests and nuns. Nancy edited a Friends 'Circular' which was distributed to a few hundred Protestants and some Catholics throughout Spain. After two years, all agreed that the Negelspachs should stay for a longer time. Regular financial support to the Negelspachs from FWCC, however, ended in 1966, and their monthly meeting in Philadelphia continued to provide funds when needed.

Belgium. In 1963, the European Section noted that there were a few Friends scattered around Belgium. The Section asked the yearly meetings in France and The Netherlands to undertake nurture of Friends in parts of

Belgium nearest them. Between 1963 and 1969, a British Friend, Eunice Rees, 11 times made the round of visits to Belgian Friends in their homes. When she could not continue, Kenneth and Dorothy Clay made similar visits.

With the establishing of offices of the European Economic Community in Brussels, an active Friends group with international membership developed. The European Section gave it the official status of a monthly meeting in 1975. It, in turn, felt some responsibility for a group in Antwerp. A Quaker Council for European Affairs was developing through the 1970s, and its Governing Council was formed in 1979, based on a new Quaker House in Brussels, also the meeting place for local Friends.

Nurturing a Meeting in Korea

When Quaker service following the Korean War took the form of hospital administration and medical service in the town of Kunsan in South Korea, Korean assistants joined the American and British Quaker workers in group worship. After the Friends Service Unit closed and the overseas workers had left Korea, some former assistants and other Koreans held a first meeting in Seoul, in February, 1958.

Soon they found two Friends, Arthur Mitchell of Honolulu Meeting and Reginald Price of Washington, DC, both working at the International Cooperation Administration and living in Seoul with their families. Immediately, these Friends became trusted advisers for the new group, and meetings were held alternately in the Mitchell and Price homes.

Very early, the FWCC encouraged Seoul Friends to build relationships with Japan Yearly Meeting or with Honolulu Monthly Meeting. Two of the Koreans, Yoon Gu Lee and Shin Ai Cha, applied for, and were granted, membership in the Honolulu Meeting which, soon after, took this couple's marriage under its care. Japanese Friends welcomed the prospect for some association with Koreans, but political relations between the two countries made any formal arrangement a problem. It was difficult for a Japanese citizen to visit Korea at that time.

Study at Pendle Hill near Philadelphia, or at Woodbrooke in England, and contacts with Friends, seemed appropriate for the nurturing of leaders in the Korean group, and, through them, nurture for the group. Yoon Gu Lee was the first to come to Pendle Hill, then to travel home through Britain and Europe where FWCC arranged Friendly contacts. A similar plan was made for Ham Sok Hon, an independent religious figure in Korea and a non-violent fighter for democracy and human rights. More recently, a young man, Booh Gil Man, studied at Woodbrooke. He took part in the

World Gathering of Young Friends in North Carolina and in the FWCC Triennial Meeting in Mexico, both in 1985, before returning to Seoul.

Some Koreans who came to Pendle Hill have remained to pursue further study and eventually remained in the United States, with resulting loss to the Seoul Friends group. However, one of these, Haeng Woo Lee, has maintained contact with the Seoul Meeting and has been helpful to the FWCC and Friends interested in Korea.

In 1961, FWCC began sponsoring a series of visitors and 'resident Friends' in Korea. Former FWCC chairman, Errol Elliott, enroute to Kenya for the Triennial Meeting in that year, visited the group in Seoul for several days. When he brought to FWCC the Seoul Friends' request for 'direct and official relationship', FWCC instructed its 'Central Office (to) keep in touch with the group at Seoul, help to nourish its spiritual life, and to encourage it to strengthen its links with Pacific Yearly Meeting and with Japan Yearly Meeting'.

While individual British Friends who had worked in the Service Unit at Kunsan had active interest in the development of a Quaker group in Korea, among Friends in the United States the interest and concern were more widespread. The Lake Erie Yearly Meeting and the Ohio (Conservative) Yearly Meeting formed a 'Joint Committee on Korea'. A 'Committee on Friend in the Orient' promoted interest in Korea for Friends in Pacific Yearly Meeting. The Japan Committee of Philadelphia Yearly Meeting began to realize that interest in Korea was a natural extension of their work. The situation required the American Section to coordinate the various kinds of support for Korean Friends.

Herbert Bowles of the Honolulu Meeting had been involved with the postwar medical work at Kunsan, and he had a lifelong relationship with Japanese Friends through the 40-years' service of his parents in Japan. Visiting Korean and Japanese Friends in the spring of 1964, he and Gertrude Bowles nurtured relationships between Friends in the two countries.

Partly on the basis of Herbert Bowles' reports, in 1964 the FWCC granted Seoul Friends' request for official monthly Meeting status. The American Section had received a gift of $3,000 for purchase of a house to serve as a meeting place for the Seoul group; but until it was clear that Friends in Seoul wanted their own property and the responsibility for caring for it, the money was not sent. Blanche Shaffer visited Seoul late in 1964 as part of a staff visit to Friends in Asia. After careful consideration of the matter with Korean Friends, she sent a cable authorizing the American Section to transmit the money, and a house was immediately purchased.

With easing of restrictions against the entry of Japanese visitors to Korea, more Friends came from Japan to visit the Seoul Meeting, including Janice Clevenger, an American Friend who was teaching in the Friends Girls School in Tokyo. She soon felt a leading to live in Seoul and to assist the Korean Friends in further development and growth of their meeting.

Late in March, 1970, Janice arrived in Seoul as 'Friend in Residence', sponsored by FWCC with background support from the Japan Committee in Philadelphia. She taught English at the Hankuk University of Foreign Studies, with salary adequate for living expenses. During the next four years, Janice served as adviser, teacher, and helper for Korean Friends.

The Committee on Friend in the Orient, of Pacific and North Pacific Yearly Meetings, continued its concern for Friends in Korea. It sent Lloyd and Mary Margaret Bailey of New York Yearly Meeting to be 'Resident Friends' for most of a year, 1983-84.

An International Membership Committee formed

In the early 1970s, while pursuing a concern of Douglas Steere for communication with isolated Friends, the FWCC maintained contact with Hetty Budgen of the Friends Service Council staff. The FSC, as a part of London Yearly Meeting, had served as 'monthly meeting' for Friends living outside of the British Isles and away from any yearly meeting, and Hetty was Correspondent with the Overseas Members.

Informal discussions between FWCC and FSC led to the conclusion that persons who were 'overseas members' of London Yearly Meeting would more appropriately belong to an 'international membership' under the aegis of the FWCC; so at its Triennial Meeting in 1979, the FWCC agreed to this responsibility and appointed an International Membership Committee to care for this new function.

Since Hetty Budgen was ready to retire from her work with Friends Service Council, she joined the FWCC staff part time to continue nurturing the persons, groups, and meetings which became the 'international membership'. When she retired from this service at the end of 1982, Grace Hunter, of London Yearly Meeting, was appointed to it.

At the end of 1988, the International Membership included 68 Friends in Africa, Asia, the Americas, Europe, and the Indian Ocean Islands. A few were single, isolated Friends; but most were in very small worship groups in Bahrain, Cairo, Gaza, Hong Kong, Madrid, Managua, Lagos, Papua New Guinea, San Jose (Costa Rica), Singapore, and Rome. In addition, three recognized meetings handled their own membership matters: the

General Conference of Friends in India; Hill House Meeting in Accra, Ghana; and Seoul Monthly Meeting in Korea.

Relationships with young Friends

Reference to 'young Friends' in this history of the Friends World Committee for Consultation is, generally, to persons whose ages are from 18 to about 30 years. Their group activities – whether national, international, or world-wide – have usually been arranged independently, although their world-wide conferences have often been held near the same time and place as conferences arranged by the FWCC. In most times, the FWCC and its Sections have advised, provided financial or other assistance, or have invited Young Friends to send representatives to their meetings.

The American Young Friends Fellowship became 'affiliated' with the American Friends Fellowship Council in 1943. It arranged an American Young Friends Conference in 1947, at Earlham College, with 10 British, Irish, and French young Friends as invited guests. With increasing interest in international contacts, the AYFF in 1949 asked that its affiliation be changed from the Fellowship Council to the American Section of the FWCC, and in 1950 the name was changed to American Young Friends Committee.

In the late 1940s the European Section asked its Secretary, Elise Thomsen, to edit and circulate a European Young Friends Newsletter. The Young Friends Central Committee in Britain was very active in the early 1950s, and international contacts among young Friends flourished.

The American Young Friends Committee decided to disband in 1951, asking the American Section to appoint a temporary sub-committee for young Friends. The sub-committee arranged American participation at an International Young Friends Conference at Reading, England, in advance of the 1952 World Conference of Friends at Oxford. In 1953, there was another American Young Friends Conference, at Greensboro, North Carolina, with visitors invited from London, Ireland, and Germany Yearly Meetings. In 1954, the Young Friends Committee of North America was formed, to include Canadian Young Friends.

From 1960 to 1963, international intervisitation again flourished, involving especially American, British, and German young Friends. A small conference site was prepared by German Young Friends at Udenhausen, and a representative conference was held there in 1963. Blanche Shaffer, FWCC General Secretary, particularly encouraged British and German young Friends at this period. European Young Friends regularly sent reports to annual meetings of the European and Near East

Section. An International Conference was held in Norway in 1965, with both Blanche Shaffer and Margaret Gibbins in touch with the young Friends' conference committee.

Young Friends met in international conference at Westtown School, near Philadelphia, preceding the Friends World Conference at Greensboro, North Carolina, in 1967. Invited by Peter Eccles, Clerk of Young Friends Central Committee in Britain, Blanche Shaffer sent Monica Southall to speak with young Friends about FWCC affairs.

During the late 1960s and 1970s the American Friends Service Committee, for logical reasons, reduced its program of work camps and other types of volunteer service for youth. As a result, adult Friends made frequent complaints that young Friends no longer had opportunity for stimulating and inspiring experiences which once had been offered through volunteer service.

The American Section sent young Friend, Jay Thatcher, of North Pacific Yearly Meeting, traveling across the continent during the 1978 summer, visiting Friends gatherings and yearly meetings to provide information about available activities for young people and to talk with young Friends about their concept of need for volunteer service programs. His report, and further exploration by a special committee appointed by the American Section in 1981, indicated that, with changing times, concerns which challenged young Friends were different and that types of earlier volunteer service offered little attraction for them.

After a lapse of interest in international contacts among young Friends on both sides of the Atlantic during the mid-1970s, the Young Friends Central Committee in Britain was again in touch with Margaret Gibbins in 1978. Subsequently, the European and Near East Section provided financial help for international visits by young Friends. Urged by the Section of the Americas, some yearly meetings included young Friends among their representatives to the FWCC Triennial Meeting in Kenya in 1982. At that meeting a concern arose for a World Gathering of Young Friends.

Planning for the World Gathering was in the hands of young Friends, but offices of the FWCC gave support and cooperation. Initiative for the planning was given to British and European young Friends, with Simon Lamb of Ireland Yearly Meeting as clerk of their committee. Also, a strong committee was formed in America, with Jonathan Vogel of Pacific Yearly Meeting as clerk.

The Gathering held at Guilford College in Greensboro, North Carolina, July 19-26, 1985, was more representative of all groups of Friends than any world conference has been. Young Friends gained the response of yearly meetings in Africa, Asia, and Central and South America, and raised the funds required for travel by their representatives. More than 300 young Friends, from 34 countries and 57 yearly meetings, participated in this World Gathering. Some 25 of these went on to Oaxtepec, Mexico, taking with them the deep spiritual experience and sense of Friendly unity gained at the Gathering, to take part in FWCC's Triennial Meeting.

Since the World Gathering, the number of young Friends participating regularly in the Section of the Americas has increased. European and Near East Young Friends are officially associated with the European and Near East Section. The Young Quakers Association of FWCC, Africa Section, has been formed. Its newsletter is edited by the Africa Section Executive Secretary, Zablon Malenge, who also helped to organize an international work camp for young Friends from Philadelphia Yearly Meeting and the yearly meeting in Kenya, in August, 1987. Since the 1985 World Gathering, young Friends and the FWCC have mutually nurtured each other.

Quaker Youth Pilgrimages

A nurturing program for Friends younger than 18 years began in 1959. The possibility of a Quaker Youth Pilgrimage to include an educational and inspirational experience in Northwest England where Quakerism had its beginnings was put forward in 1957 by William Cleveland, a teacher at George School near Philadelphia. The American Section immediately realized that the proposal had merit. From the FWCC office in England, I found British Friends in the Northwest 1652 Committee ready to cooperate, and the European Section willing to recruit participants from their constituency. Participants would be in the age range from 16 to 18 years, with 14 Pilgrims from America and the same number from Europe.

For the first Pilgrimage in 1959, the American Section chose seven boys and seven girls from eight yearly meetings. On arriving in England they met the European contingent, seven from Britain and four from Norway, Switzerland, and West Germany. William and Lorraine Cleveland were the American Adult Leaders. James and Joyce Drummond provided housing at their Friends School in Lancaster, and James Drummond organized the pilgrimages to places of historic Quaker interest, during the two weeks of exploring the Quaker Country, while Elfrida Vipont Foulds' vibrant telling of the story of early Quaker history made it come alive for the 'teenage Pilgrims of 1959.

Daily periods of worship together, climbing Pendle Hill, crossing thè sands of Morecombe Bay, seeing Firbank Fell and other sites important to

Quaker Youth Pilgrims of 1959, rebuilding a burned out youth center in a Welsh village.

Quaker Youth Pilgrims of 1961 crossing sands of Morecambe Bay.

the George Fox period, and getting to know other 'teen-age Friends with diverse Friendly practice and of several nationalities and some differences of language, all made the first two weeks of the Pilgrimage an intense religious experience. Furthermore, the two weeks of work camp which followed, rebuilding a burned out youth center in a Welsh village, helped the Pilgrims to relate spiritual nurture to service where need lies.

Similar Pilgrimages have been arranged in alternate years since 1959. With the 16th Pilgrimage in 1987, nearly 475 'teen-age Friends have experienced the vigorous spiritual exercise of this program. In 1971, 1977, and 1983 the European contingent traveled to America. In those years the group traveled together by bus to Quaker centers, large and small, from Boston to North Carolina, then west to Indiana and Chicago, and once into Canada. The focus has been on the concerns and actions of Friends in modern times, with attention to Quaker history when it had particular relevance to current issues.

In 1984, since relationships with Hispanic Friends had increased, the Section of the Americas planned a cross cultural, bi-lingual Youth Pilgrimage with visits to Friends meetings in New Mexico, Colorado, and Arizona, and to the Rough Rock Friends Mission in Navajo Indian territory. It included a work camp at the Friends Center at Corona de Paz and some wilderness camping. Nine of the Pilgrims were from the United States and three from the Ciudad Victoria Meeting in Mexico.

In terms of the depth of experience for participating during any Pilgrimage, this program is exceptional. It has been the intention of Friends closely related to Pilgrimage arrangements to conduct a survey to discover what individual past Pilgrims may be doing some years after the experience. Although a complete list of Pilgrims' names and addresses was compiled in 1981, the suggested survey has not yet been done.

Concern for spiritual nurture of children

Concerned about children's needs, a New Zealand Friend, Ruby Dowsett, proposed that Friends in different countries write letters which would be printed and distributed to Quaker children in meetings and in families isolated from any meeting. The New Zealand General Meeting endorsed Ruby's proposal and asked Friends in the United States and Britain to support the proposal to the FWCC.

At the same time, in 1947 and 1948, Ruby Dowsett and her husband, Edward, undertook a journey of intervisitation to Friends in America and Europe. Among Friends responsible for work with children, Ruby had

Edward and Ruby Dowsett of New Zealand with A. Ward Applegate,
American Section Chairman 1961-1967.

opportunity to discuss at length her concern for a plan to provide internationally prepared letters for Quaker children.

She presented her concern to the FWCC's Executive Committee in London in September, 1948, giving assurance of interest she had found among Friends in America, Ireland, and the Continent of Europe. She had received offers of cooperation from some Friends, but none had been prepared to take primary responsibility. The Executive Committee welcomed Ruby's offer to coordinate the gathering and editing of letters.

Returning to New Zealand, Ruby arranged for contact persons in many countries, and for help in finding Friends to write and distribute the letters entitled *Round the World Quaker Letters for Children.* The first sets of letters, graded for children aged 6 to 15, were ready to distribute by autumn, 1949.

Printed by FWCC offices in Britain and America the letters were distributed in accordance with orders made by a local meeting or regional group. Children in a local meeting, or in a region, received the appropriate letter by post from a local or regional correspondent who added a personal note. Or, the letters were distributed in children's classes. The parent-meeting-child relationship was an important focus for RWQL, and the first letter in each year was a 'Family Letter' written by the editor and distributed to families of children for whom the letters had been ordered.

In January, 1956, Frank Carpenter, of London Yearly Meeting, became editor. Without the wide contacts among Friends around the world which Ruby Dowsett enjoyed, he had difficulty maintaining a supply of well written letters. Edna Legg, an American Friend with international experience, became editor in January, 1959. For a time, interest in the letters flourished again. But it was not easy to keep both quality and variety in the writing. With reluctance, the FWCC decided in 1964 that publication of Round the World Quaker Letters should come to an end.

The letters were more widely used in some areas than in others, but in 1960 the American Section office distributed 10,000 letters in each of 10 months. The FWCC in Birmingham, England, distributed 2,500. Friends meetings and their children in Australia, New Zealand, and South Africa found the letters well suited to their needs. The English language letters had limited use in Continental Europe, but often selected letters were translated into the appropriate language.

Throughout 14 years of RWQL publication, an editor's assistant arranged 'Pen Friendships' for children who requested them. Many Quaker children were introduced to international friendships in this way, and links were formed between children of meetings in different countries.

European Section and religious education of children

In 1965, perceiving the usefulness of sharing available resources for the religious education of children, the European Section assembled an 'international library' from which convenors of Children's Committees might borrow. Also, they arranged for the borrowing of a parcel of Quaker books for children, sent to a yearly meeting for three months. The Section engaged British Friends gifted in work with children to visit in different European countries, especially with isolated families.

With limited space and equipment, the first Quaker family camp was held in The Netherlands in 1971. Participants were four German, two Norwegian, one British, one Swiss, and five Dutch families – 23 adults and 28 children. The general theme for the camp was, 'How does your Quaker faith permeate and sustain your family life?' In 1978, the Section organized a second family camp at Newtown Friends School in Waterford, Ireland, where 150 could be accommodated. For family camps in 1981 and 1986, each with increased participation, the Section has given financial assistance to families with greatest distance to travel.

The Faith and Life Movement in North America

The World Conference of Friends in Greensboro, in 1967, was an experience of Quaker ecumenicity broader than any known before. Early in its planning, some leading Evangelical Friends had turned down the invitation to serve on the Conference Committee, saying that their deeply held views were too unlikely to be given recognition. As conference plans progressed, several of these Friends observed that their concerns were not pushed aside. A good number of Evangelical Friends then came to Greensboro and took part freely in the conference.

By no means were all barriers to true fellowship removed by the 1967 conference experience. But there was a spirit which prompted six Friends who referred to themselves as 'evangelical' to formally invite each of the yearly meetings in North America to send representatives to a conference. Three members of this group were from the Evangelical Friends Alliance and three from the Friends United Meeting. They met and conferred at a Friends Conference on Evangelism, at Minneapolis, Minnesota, in 1969. David C. LeShana, the President of George Fox College in Oregon, formerly a pastor in California Yearly Meeting, served as their chairman. Calling themselves 'The Committee of Concerned Friends for Renewal', they issued the call for a conference to be held at St. Louis, October 5-7, 1970. The conference theme, 'The Future of Friends', had been the subject of the Interest Group drawing most attention at the Greensboro Conference.

The spirit engendered at Greensboro also influenced response to the conference call. With the exception of three small yearly meetings which had no office or staff, and may have overlooked the invitation, all North American yearly meetings sent representatives to St. Louis. Also represented were the EFA, the FGC, the FUM, and the American Section of the FWCC. Some came fearful that a 'hidden agenda' lay in the call 'to seek, under the guidance of the Holy Spirit, a workable, challenging, and cooperative means whereby the Friends Church can be an active, enthusiastic, Christ-centered, and Spirit-directed force in this day of revolution'. While there were three major speakers, one each from EFA, FGC, and FUM, much time was given to well-mixed small discussion groups where basic beliefs of Friends were considered openly and frankly. Any fear of hidden agenda evaporated as the conference progressed.

Before the close of the conference there came a clear sense that dialogue, barely begun, should be continued in the effort to move toward greater unity among Friends. In one of the later sessions, Everett Cattell, an Evangelical Friend with statesmanlike qualities and fine spirit, proposed that the FWCC's American Section be given responsibility for administering the follow up of the conference. His proposal was approved by the conference and accepted by the American Section whose officers had been consulted in the matter by another leader among the Evangelicals, Milo

Ross, during an intermission a few minutes earlier. The FWCC Section issued the conference report which was published with the title *What Future for Friends?*

Secretaries and Superintendents of the American Yearly Meetings had their annual gathering at St. Louis after the conference closed. They proposed that the policy making body for follow up be formed by EFA, FGC, FUM, and Conservative Friends each appointing two representatives, and that this body of eight would be the Faith and Life Planning Group. Also, each yearly meeting would appoint two persons to a larger Faith and Life Planning Committee, looking ahead to future conferences on Faith and Life concerns. Staff service for these bodies would be provided by the American Section.

At its next meeting the Section's Executive Committee asked Robert Rumsey, in the Midwest Office, to provide those services and to be the Section's link with the Faith and Life Movement.

Over the next three years Faith and Life Conferences were held in eight regions of North America. So far as possible, each region included yearly meetings of the different groupings of Friends. Conference discussions were built around basic beliefs which had been central to the conference at St. Louis.

The Faith and Life Planning Group named a second body called the Faith and Life Panel, nine Friends representing the spectrum of Quaker thought and experience, knowledgeable in the Bible, theology, and Quaker history. The first publication by the Panel was *Quaker Understanding of Christ and of Authority*. This book was widely used in local meetings and for conference preparation by yearly meeting representatives to a continent-wide Faith and Life Conference at Indianapolis in October, 1974.

With every yearly meeting from Alaska to Central America and from Canada to Florida represented at Indianapolis, a remarkable spirit of unity emerged across all lines. According to one participant, 'Friends were listening to each other for the first time'. To another, the experience at St. Louis in 1970 had been 'confrontation' and four years later at Indianapolis 'we experienced consultation'.

From the new spirit which the Faith and Life Movement brought to North American Friends, there came concern for a strengthened peace witness. This concern found expression in the New Call to Peacemaking in which Friends were joined by members of the other peace churches, Mennonite and Church of the Brethren. In continuing nurture of the spirit among Friends, the practice of holding regional conferences and of engaging in other activities regionally is a method whose merits were proven in the exhilirating experience of the Faith and Life Movement.

CHAPTER VII

Friends and the United Nations

AFTER THE 1947 DECISION OF THE FWCC to seek consultative status at the United Nations, the officers very promptly made the appropriate application. At that time, many members of the FWCC viewed this action as an accommodation to the AFSC and its interest in helping to make the United Nations an effective instrument for the social well being of all peoples and for building and maintaining peace among nations. A resolution of the UN Economic and Social Council, on March 3, 1948, granted to FWCC the international non-governmental organization (NGO) consultative status in Category B. To qualify for that category, the FWCC demonstrated that its aims and purposes were compatible with one or more of the purposes of the United Nations.

As the United Nations and its Economic and Social Council became better established, after its Human Rights Commission began to function, and as UNESCO and other UN Specialized Agencies developed their programs, the FWCC cooperated with the AFSC and appropriate committees of London Yearly Meeting to give quiet Quaker witness, sometimes in the formal session of a UN commission, council, or even the General Assembly, but more often in face to face meetings with one or a few national delegates or with members of the UN Secretariat. Rarely advocating specific steps, the Friends Representatives have striven more to awaken UN delegates to the moral dimensions of the issues before them.

Further, the FWCC has opened the way for hundreds of Friends to participate in United Nations-sponsored conferences and seminars on topics which coincide with Quaker concern, in major cities in many countries. Oral and written reports by these participants have helped to bring the United Nations close to a large number of the people called Friends.

Once a scarcely visible appendage of the FWCC's agenda, the Quaker work at the United Nations has become, in the eyes of many Friends, one of the most important functions of their World Committee. And it is valued not less, but more, importantly because it is a program requiring cooperation with Quaker service agencies and other bodies of Friends around the world.

Quaker UN work begins in New York and Geneva

Elmore Jackson, Assistant Executive Secretary of the AFSC, found a number of influential Friends in the New York City area ready to work at establishing a Friends Center close to the international community which would be drawn to New York by the presence of the UN Headquarters. The AFSC named Elmore as Director of the new 'Quaker House', and the FWCC Executive Committee in London appointed him as 'Consultant' at the United Nations. Elmore and Beth Jackson moved into Quaker House in September, 1948. Although for two long periods he was away on important missions of international reconciliation, in Kashmir between Pakistan and India in the late 1940s and between Arab states and Israel in the late 1950s, he was Director of the Quaker UN Program in New York until 1960.

Soon it became apparent that some part of the United Nations operation would be in Geneva as its European Headquarters were established in the offices of the old League of Nations. Friends had an International Center there, with an American Friend, Algie Newlin, serving as Center Director. Because, in the early period, ECOSOC allowed each NGO only one Consultant, the FWCC named Algie Newlin as Alternate to Elmore Jackson. In time, it became the practice of ECOSOC to hold in Geneva the longer of its two sessions each year. Succeeding Algie Newlin, Colin W. Bell became Friends Center Director and FWCC's liaison with ECOSOC in 1950, followed by J. Duncan Wood in 1955. For both, the Friends Center appointment was made by the Friends Service Council, with concurrence by the FWCC to validate their standing at the European Headquarters of the UN.

The 'Quaker Team' during General Assembly Sessions

Largely because of work done by a 'Quaker Team', Friends gradually became aware of the quiet Quaker witness at the United Nations. The concept of an international Quaker Team was initiated by the AFSC which, at first, invited the Friends who would participate and provided the necessary financing. The first 'Team', brought together during the UN General Assembly of 1950, included Gerald Bailey and Agatha Harrison (British), Elsa Cedergren (Swedish), Elmore Jackson and Clarence Pickett (American), and Heberto Sein (Mexican).

Members of the 1950 Team, and of those which followed each year through 1970, had acquaintances within their own national delegations or in the UN Secretariat, and they sought out personal contacts with others. The substance of most conversations and conferences was confidential, but Team members reported to Friends and to the Quaker press the variety of contacts and the issues and concerns they had presented.

Elmore Jackson consulted the Secretary of the FWCC while bringing the Team together, and contacted certain committees of London Yearly Meeting about choice of a British Friend. By 1956, these committees of London Yearly Meeting had formed their United Nations Consultative Committee which nominated the British member of the Team and undertook to contribute financially toward the Team's support. Later, officers of the FWCC and its Sections proposed nominations at the beginning of each annual procedure to select Team members.

The first Friends from outside of North America and Europe to participate in the Team were Kiyoshi Ukaji of Japan, in 1957, and Jotham Standa of Kenya in 1958. More than 50 Friends, of 16 nationalities, gave this kind of service at the United Nations, several of them in two or more General Assembly periods, between 1950 and 1970.

An expanding program at the UN in New York

The need for more staff for the Quaker UN work was evident as the number of UN member states increased and the General Assembly sessions became longer. In 1952, William Fraser, a British Friend, was appointed to assist Elmore, followed late in 1954 by Sydney Bailey, also British. Sydney had served with the Friends Ambulance Unit in China during the Second World War, then briefly with the AFSC in the United States. He had a good knowledge of parliamentary affairs. During Elmore's absences Sydney was Acting Director of the Quaker UN Program.

After a few years, ECOSOC dropped use of the term 'Consultant', and instead an NGO appointee was called 'Representative'. The number of Representatives allowed to an NGO was not specifically limited, and the designation was used for FWCC appointees in both New York and Geneva.

When the United Nations announced a World Youth Assembly to be held in mid-year 1970, the Quaker United Nations Office (QUNO) invited to New York a 'Youth Team' which included four young Friends – Margaret Fay of Northern Ireland, Laban Masimbe of Kenya, Donald McNemar of the United States, and Masaka Yamanouchi of Japan. Later it became regular practice for QUNO to appoint Youth Internes for a one-year term.

United Nations events away from Headquarters

A wide range of conferences, congresses, and seminars, sponsored by one department or another of ECOSOC, and held in different countries, provided opportunity for the FWCC to name observers with FWCC credentials. A few of the UN-sponsored meetings at which there were observers accredited by the FWCC will illustrate the range of Quaker concern and the various national origins among Friends who participated.

Beginning in 1955, for instance, the UN Bureau of Social Affairs sponsored at five-year-intervals Congresses on Prevention of Crime and Treatment of the Offender. At the first Congress in Geneva, the FWCC gave observer credential to Leon Stern, a Friend from Philadelphia, professionally involved in prisoner welfare and prison reform. At the second congress, five years later in London, the FWCC sponsored eight observers, from Britain (3), France (2), The Netherlands (1), and United States (2). Some of these Friends were especially concerned for abolition of the death penalty. The FWCC observers at the congress in Milan, Italy, in 1985, helped to gather support for developing mediation/reconciliation services involving victim and offender.

Playing a critical role at the entire sequence of International Conferences on the Law of the Sea, Samuel and Miriam Levering, experienced lobbyists from North Carolina Yearly Meeting, successfully urged many of the most beneficial clauses of the treaty finally adopted. Recognizing the role of the Leverings and regretting that the United States had withheld its signature from the Law of the Sea Convention, the Section of the Americas in 1982 asked Friends in the United States to urge their Government to reconsider, and to sign, this treaty which 'addresses such practical issues as sea bed mining, water routes, fishing, and whaling, (and is also) an important step forward toward systems of international order and right sharing of the world's resources'.

More than 20 Quaker women, from countries as diverse as Belize, Mexico, Kenya, Britain, and the United States, were FWCC observers at the UN Conference on International Women's Year, in Mexico City in 1975; or the International Conference on the UN Decade for Women, in Copenhagen in 1980; or the United Nations End Decade Women's Forum and Conference, in Nairobi in 1985. Mary Protheroe Eddington of London Yearly Meeting and Clerk of FWCC's Interim Committee, was one of the eight FWCC observers at the Nairobi events, where, among other activities, Friends assisted with a 'peace tent' which was a center for posters, discussions, and questions about work for peace in the world.

The largest role for Friends in any UN-sponsored event was related to the UN Conference on the Human Environment at Stockholm, Sweden, in 1972. Barrett Hollister, at that time Director of the Quaker UN Office in New York, had for three years presided over a committee of NGOs working in support of the conference. He was also a member of the UN Secretary General's advisory panel for NGOs and the Conference-related Forum.

Joseph Haughton, Chairman of FWCC's Interim Committee and Lecturer in Geography at Trinity College in Dublin, Ireland, was FWCC's official observer, and the FWCC Chairman, Heinrich Carstens, of Germany, was an Alternate. Two Kenyan Friends were members of the Kenyan Government's delegation, and other Friends represented certain UN Specialized Agencies or were representatives of the press. Elsa Cedergren, a former Chairman of the FWCC, loaned her Stockholm apartment to Barry and Kay Hollister to use as a 'Quaker House' where quiet talks could be arranged between members of national delegations and representatives of NGOs.

On the recommendation of the Stockholm Conference, the UN General Assembly created the United Nations Environment Program (UNEP), with headquarters at Nairobi, where officers of the FWCC's Africa Section and other Friends have attended UNEP meetings to help keep alive a variety of environmental concerns.

Issues which called for more formal Quaker action

Perceiving their roles as behind-the-scenes counselors, advocates of moral values, facilitators, and informal mediators to be critically needed, Friends at the UN have generally not pursued 'formal' actions. Only occasionally, when they knew that preponderant opinion among Friends and the weight of Quaker testimony would support a particular position, have Quaker Representatives put a formal statement on record at the United Nations, 'officially' advocating specific steps.

Disarmament, the recognition of conscientious objection as an individual right, and the abolition of slavery are among the few issues for which Friends Representatives have advocated certain positions and steps to be taken by the UN.

At some time, and at some place within the United Nations system, *disarmament* must have received the attention of delegates in each year since 1947. Friends Representatives have been alert to those discussions and have tried in many different ways to move the thinking of national delegates, and of committees and sub-committees within the UN, toward even small steps in the reduction of armaments. They have led NGOs in cooperative efforts on disarmament. Because the United Nations Committee on Disarmament, composed of delegates from 40 nations, holds its meetings in Geneva, much of this effort by Friends has been made by the Geneva Representatives.

However, a concentration of activity for disarmament came in New York in 1978, related to the first UN Special General Assembly on Disarmament. Barry Hollister worked closely with the Preparatory Committee for the Special Session and served as Vice-Chairman of the NGO Disarmament Committee. He took the initiative to arrange 'NGO Day' in the Special Session, when 25 selected NGOs had the privilege of making a 12-minutes oral presentation of their case for disarmament.

Barry used every opportunity to learn from Friends around the world the ideas for disarmament they might present in a 12-minutes appearance before the General Assembly. When the NGO Day came, the FWCC's presentation was made by Salome Nolega, a Kenyan woman Friend and educator, serving as part of the Special Session Team along with Miriam Habib of Pakistan and S. K. De of India. Friends emphasized the need to keep alive the goal of general and complete disarmament, speaking of the moral and humanitarian dimensions of the arms race, and of the links between disarmament and development, the environment, and human rights.

Friends made other important efforts related to the Special Session. The Quaker UN Office organized a series of 23 pre-Assembly seminars for delegates from 58 smaller nations, to assist them in giving informed attention to disarmament issues. In another effort, a member of the Quaker UN Committee led in organization of a Disarmament Information Bureau across the street from the UN Building, where delegates, Secretariat people, NGOs, and the public could get information about the Session and a wide range of publications about disarmament.

What did this Special Session on Disarmament achieve? Nothing toward arms reduction in the short run. But the attention of nations was drawn to the need to disarm, and to proposals for steps which must eventually be taken. For the 'Disarmament Times' Barry Hollister was asked to characterize the Special Session. His response: 'Invaluable – and utterly inadequate'.

On another key matter, Friends had hoped that the *right to conscientious objection to military service* would be written into the UN Declaration of Human Rights adopted in December, 1948. They were disappointed. But early in 1956 Friends Representatives in New York found a glimmer of hope in a study undertaken by the UN Sub-Commission on Prevention of Discrimination and Protection of Minorities, on 'discrimination in the matter of religious rights and practices'. The FWCC submitted information which helped to develop the concept of conscientious objection 'in the exercise of freedom to manifest religion or belief'. This concept, however, was excluded from the final report of that study.

Through the 1960s, nevertheless, the FWCC responded every three years to UN inquiries about civil and political rights by updating reports on legislation regarding COs in countries where there are Friends. While these reports never made it onto the agenda of the UN Commission on Human Rights, by 1970 other NGOs were showing interest in the question of conscientious objection; but it still seemed impossible to get it beyond the fringes of an agenda item of any UN body. Finally, Friends persuaded the Netherlands delegate to take an interest in the subject. Delegates from other nations joined him in submitting a resolution, but it timidly asked for an updated report which might prepare the way for substantive discussion at some future meeting of the Commission.

In the 1970s the FWCC Representatives in Geneva and New York took whatever action seemed likely to move the CO question toward more solid consideration in UN circles. Eventually, in 1981, the Human Rights Commission named two 'experts' to prepare a report on the current situation for COs in different countries. The Geneva Friends Representatives saw the experts' report submitted in 1984, recommending that conscientious objection be recognized as a basic human right, along with the right to alternative service and refusal to serve in certain situations.

They worked very hard, along with other NGOs and the co-sponsors (Austria, Costa Rica, France, The Netherlands, Spain, and the United Kingdom) of a positive resolution. After lengthy debate and consideration of amendments as well as two revisions of the original text, the sponsors decided the best course was to defer the question without a vote until 1987.

In 1987, the Commission voted on, and passed, the resolution. The Geneva Friends Center staff joyfully reported, 'This historic resolution is the first (recognizing the right of conscientious objection) by a United Nations body, although the issue has been debated in many forums since the League of Nations'.

Treaties made between nations in the 19th Century *abolishing slavery and the slave trade* were recognized by the League of Nations, and the League fostered the Slavery Convention of 1926 to provide definitions of slavery. Still, in some Arab countries, especially in Saudi Arabia, use of captive Africans and their descendents as slaves persisted, although royal decree forbade that practice. And in parts of Africa and Asia polygamous marriage and the taking of young girls as brides led to practices similar to slavery. Following promptings within the UN, several nations agreed to cover some deficiencies in the 1926 Convention by a Supplementary Slavery Convention of 1956.

During the mid-1950s one Friend, Mary Nuttall, played an active role in the British Anti-Slavery Society which Friends had helped to form more than a century earlier. With support from London Yearly Meeting's Race Relations Committee, Mary Nuttall's concern for action toward world-wide eradication of slavery was endorsed by that yearly meeting and sent forward to the FWCC.

At its Triennial Meeting in 1958 the FWCC asked yearly meetings in countries whose governments had not ratified the Slavery Conventions of 1926 and 1956 to urge this ratification by those governments. It also asked Friends Representatives at the UN to work toward action by the Economic and Social Council to suppress slavery in all its forms wherever in the world such practices might exist. Friends in a number of countries responded to this appeal to yearly meetings.

Friends Representatives in both New York and Geneva created opportunities where they could to bring the slavery question onto agendas of the Human Rights Commission or its Sub-Commissions. The FWCC arranged for Mary Nuttall to join this effort with Duncan Wood in Geneva, once in 1962 and again in 1966. They found some other NGOs ready to press for consideration of the issue.

Eventually, ECOSOC and its Commission on Human Rights appointed a team of 'experts' who would maintain continual surveillance of countries where slavery or practices similar to slavery might exist. The further duty of the experts would be to bring to public knowledge, and therefore to general disfavor, conditions of slavery in any country.

Relationships with UNESCO from 1956

Through FWCC, Friends contributed to, or called upon, UNESCO in several ways. In UNESCO's programs for 'out of school' education and other programs for youth, for instance, Friends and UNESCO found mutual support. British and American Friends were involved in setting up and administering the Coordinating Committee for International Voluntary Work Camps which was given financial support and office space by UNESCO. When American and British Friends, with Friends in Kenya, gathered young participants from Britain, Denmark, Kenya, and the United States to build convalescent cottages for tubercular patients at the Friends Hospital in Kaimosi, from 1955 to 1957, substantial financial support came from UNESCO.

In the decade from 1955 to 1965 many former colonial territories in Africa were gaining independence. Friends had an interest in the educational development of a number of newly independent African countries, and took part in discussion and working groups relevant to Africa at UNESCO. African Friends, too, many of whom were teachers or school administrators, were involved with UNESCO's contribution to education in their countries.

To assist in developing leadership within national Friends groups, the FWCC several times tapped a UNESCO program for Youth Travel Grants which paid interregional airfares for young people who gave promise of future leadership in their local and national groups. For these youths, FWCC arranged for projects and costs to be handled by national Friends groups and service bodies. Between 1957 and 1986, eight young Friends – three from Japan, one from Jordan, one from Kenya, two from New Zealand, and one from Sweden – pursued extensive programs through this resource.

From the mid-1950s, the commitment of Friends service bodies, especially the AFSC, to work at the Paris Friends Center began to decline. Wolf Mendl, a British Friend with experience in America and a period of Quaker service in Japan, was the last appointee to have the responsibility of a Quaker International Affairs Representative (QIAR) in Paris. Wolf arrived there in April, 1958. During four years he managed well the responsibilities of a QIAR appointed by the service bodies and his role as FWCC Representative at UNESCO, without allowing himself to become entangled in the web of UNESCO-NGO activities.

With decline in the use of Paris as a Quaker service base, the fine old house which had been the Friends Center, at 110 Avenue Mozart, was sold by the AFSC. When Louise Wood, a retired service worker living in Rome, came to Paris late in 1962 she was responsible to the Friends Service Council and to French Friends as Secretary of a small French Friends Center at 114 rue de Vaugirard, no longer an 'international' center. In succession, and with gaps between periods of service, Louise Wood, M. C. Morris, and Tony Clay were Representatives at UNESCO until 1968 when Blanche Shaffer made an arrangement with John Kay, a Friend who was teaching at Bootham School in York, England.

John Kay was willing to read selected UNESCO materials, to visit the FWCC office to discuss responsibilities toward UNESCO, to travel to Paris for occasions when a Friends Representative would have special usefulness at UNESCO, and to report to Friends as might seem necessary. This arrangement in some measure fulfilled FWCC's obligations to UNESCO.

When John Kay no longer served as the FWCC link with UNESCO, William Barton asked Sharon Leowald to keep in touch with UNESCO programs and to report to FWCC. Sharon was an American Friend living in Paris, whose husband, Richard, was in the UNESCO Secretariat. Then France Yearly Meeting appointed Richard Leowald as one of their representatives to FWCC. He and Sharon provided information about UNESCO to William Barton and to the European and Near East Section.

By 1976, the FWCC had appointed a Paris Friend, Camille Lataste Dorolle, as Representative to UNESCO. Soon Jane Droutman, another Paris Friend, was also made a Representative. Both gave a great deal of volunteer time to UNESCO 'working groups' on such issues as human rights, the status of women, prospects for youth at a time of unemployment, the fight against illiteracy, adult education, racism and racial prejudice, and the welfare of children in areas of conflict.

FWCC and other UN Specialized Agencies

Through FWCC, Friends have been related to UNICEF and other Specialized Agencies at the UN. When the United Nations Children's Emergency Fund was set up, Friends found the step from Quaker service assignment to field service under this UN agency an easy one. Subsequently, when the proposal to make the Children's Emergency Fund a permanent agency came before the General Assembly in 1953, the 'Quaker Team' vigorously encouraged this action, asking Friends groups around the world to urge their national governments to support the proposal for a United Nations Children's Fund (UNICEF).

As the permanent headquarters for UNICEF was established in New York, a 'UNICEF NGO Committee' was formed. The FWCC has maintained a representative and an alternate on that committee, and often these have been spouses of QUNO staff or members of the Quaker United Nations Committee. When the UNICEF Executive Board meets in New York, and sometimes when its meetings are held elsewhere, an observer for FWCC is present.

In relationship to the United Nations Center for Social Development and Humanitarian Affairs, three members of the small Friends Meeting in Vienna, Austria, have represented FWCC at selected meetings of this body in recent years. Topics considered at these meetings include the status of women, problems of the aged, crime prevention and criminal justice, youth and family issues.

In addition, Friends Representatives in New York and Geneva have followed closely the work of the United Nations Conference on Trade and Development (UNCTAD), and the FWCC has sent an observer to most of its quadrennial conferences, first held in 1964. Unfortunately, the nations with riches and power are reluctant to give ground to the poorer nations which, through the UN have sought a 'New International Economic Order'. The experience of Quaker observers at UNCTAD conferences has been one of frustration.

Broadening Friends' participation; spreading word about the UN

Between 1956 and 1988, the FWCC took several steps to elicit greater Quaker participation in its UN work and to fulfill its NGO responsibility to spread the word about the United Nations. It is an obligation of the Non-Governmental Organization to provide information about the UN to its constituency. In a June 18, 1958, letter Duncan Wood wrote that in the period before 1956 there was a 'tendency to regard the NGO aspect of FWCC as presenting problems too difficult for FWCC to solve. The problems were therefore shelved . . .' At its 1955 meeting, however, the FWCC clearly indicated its intention to provide information from the UN to Friends.

When I came to the General Secretaryship in 1956, I identified such communication as a priority. To achieve it, I worked from the premise that the FWCC must have a good working relationship with the Quaker staff in New York, Geneva, and Paris. I built contacts with them early, developing mutual understanding that consultation and cooperation would be central to our joint efforts. From this base I felt opportunities could then arise through which the United Nations might become meaningful for Friends, touching them in their lives.

To effect this in one region, Ralph Rose reached out from the American Section's Midwest Office to recruit Friends pastors of meetings in Illinois, Indiana, and Ohio for a 'United Nations Seminar' in New York, in April, 1956. Arranged by the Quaker UN staff, this was the beginning of a series of two or more Quaker Leadership Seminars at the UN annually, for more than 20 years, sponsored jointly by FWCC's Midwest Office and the Peace and Social Concerns staff of the Five Years Meeting.

In addition, Marshall Sutton, Ralph Rose's successor, conceived and carried forward plans for United Nations Seminars in the Midwest. At different locations in Indiana and Ohio, usually on a college campus, he organized weekend programs, generally including speakers from the Quaker UN staff and from the United Nations community, along with informed leaders from the Midwest. With 100 to 200 participants in each seminar, held one or two times each year, a considerable number of Midwest Friends gained knowledge of the UN and Quaker work there.

For Friends in Europe the situation was different. In yearly meetings other than London and Ireland the number of Friends was small, and across the European Continent there were several nationalities using different languages. United Nations activity at Geneva was different from, and more limited than, in New York, and there were fewer persons on the Quaker UN staff. Therefore, I began to plan a conference on the United Nations for European Friends.

The result of those plans was a 'Consultative Conference on the Work of Friends at the United Nations and the Specialized Agencies', held during four days (September 29 to October 2) after the FWCC's Seventh Meeting at Bad Pyrmont, Germany, in 1958. Twenty-six European Friends from 10 countries participated, along with one Friend from each of Kenya and Madagascar, India and Japan, and Australia and New Zealand, who had attended the Seventh Meeting. There were also representatives from the AFSC and FSC, and of the Quaker UN Offices in New York and Geneva. The Quaker Representative at UNESCO in Paris and the QIAR in Vienna were there. The FWCC and its Sections were represented by myself, Sigrid Lund, and James Walker.

The 35 Friends at this Bad Pyrmont Conference gave attention to a few concerns which might be pursued in the context of the United Nations. Receiving most consideration, however, were means for relating Friends more closely to the Quaker UN work and the need for increasing support by Friends for that work.

Both the European conference and the American seminars revealed general satisfaction with the increasing involvement of FWCC in work at the United Nations. Expression of appreciation came from the Friends Representatives at the UN and UNESCO, from the AFSC and the FSC, and from Friends in many places who were finding opportunities to take part in a variety of UN sponsored activities.

Two general principles came to determine the FWCC role in Quaker UN work:

1. The FWCC has an obligation to bring small and newer Friends groups, especially those outside North America and the British Isles, into a sense of relationship with Quaker United Nations work, and

2. On substantive matters the FWCC role must remain a consultative one; it cannot be administrative, if by administration is meant deciding on policy to be pursued in any given issue. But FWCC can play an indirect role in policy forming by helping the Society of Friends to clarify its thinking on some issues.

The FWCC convened a 'Consultation on NGO Responsibility', August 21 and 22, 1961, at Limuru, outside of Nairobi, just before its Eighth Meeting at Kaimosi in Kenya. It included 14 Friends representing the AFSC, the FSC, Quaker work in Geneva, Quaker UN Program Committee and staff in New York, the United Nations Consultative Committee (British Friends), the FWCC and its American and European Sections. This consultation recommended specific steps based on the two principles above.

In approving these recommendations, the FWCC agreed to strengthen its participation in the UN work in New York, Geneva, and Paris. It expressed confidence that the Friends appointed to that work 'will represent the highest Quaker ideals in maintaining a Quaker presence at the UN'. It suggested that staff at FWCC's NGO offices be particularly knowledgeable in international affairs. while FWCC staff become especially knowledgeable about the Society of Friends. Because of the added burden these recommendations would place on the FWCC's Central Office, the Eighth Meeting recommended that an assistant for the General Secretary be added to the staff.

In the following year, Blanche Shaffer came to the FWCC Office direct from the Friends Center in Geneva where, as Secretary for the Center, she was familiar with the work of Duncan Wood as NGO Representative. With help from two assistants, each for brief periods, Blanche maintained the FWCC role at the UN near the same level for eight years. Prior to the ninth and final year of her tenure, William Barton became Associate Secretary with an assignment which included strengthening the involvement of Friends in Quaker United Nations work.

It was understood with William Barton's appointment that he would become FWCC's General Secretary when Blanche Shaffer retired at the end of 1970. His experience – as Quaker International Affairs Representative in Vienna, and as General Secretary of Friends Service Council for 12 years – made William better prepared than any previous FWCC Secretary for personal participation in Quaker United Nations work. It became established practice for him to visit within the American Section for two months each autumn, giving two weeks of service with the Quaker UN Office in New York.

In some parts of the world, however, Friends wanted a closer link with the United Nations and Quaker work there. New Zealand Yearly Meeting sent a minute to the FWCC's Twelfth Meeting in Australia in 1973, urging that a plan be devised for ready communication between yearly meetings and Quaker UN Offices. New Zealand Friends supported their request by the promise of a substantial financial contribution toward the salary of a staff person at the New York Office, whose primary responsibility would be the liaison role proposed in their minute.

The FWCC sought to meet this challenge by planning a Consultation on Quaker United Nations work, held in London, May 28 to 30, 1974. Twenty-two participants included representative staff from Quaker offices in New York and Geneva, representatives of the AFSC, the FSC, and the FWCC. Also among the participants were Friends from different regions of the world, including the Clerk of New Zealand Yearly Meeting. This Consultation gave special attention to (1) the spiritual basis for Quaker work at the UN, (2) strengthening the participation by Friends around the world in this program, (3) the role of the FWCC in Quaker UN work, and (4) means of increasing its financial support by Friends. Even before the Consultation, the QUNO in New York had taken onto its staff a young British Friend, Carol Braithwaite Terry, who would give more than half of her time to communication with Friends.

As a result of this Consultation, FWCC took two steps to increase participation and communication. First, it invited yearly meetings to appoint a Correspondent with the Quaker UN Offices, encouraging two-way communication intended, in part, to assist Friends in their own countries to bring concerns related to UN issues before their governments. Several yearly meetings, notably New Zealand, made such an appointment.

Second, to determine a coordinated policy for emphasis on issues dealt with at New York and Geneva, a determination in which the General Secretary of the FWCC would participate on behalf of all Friends, a 'Quaker United Nations Group' was formed. It included two persons each from the programs in New York and Geneva, a member of staff and a member of the program's guiding committee; one representative each from staff or committee of the AFSC and the FSC; and the General Secretary of the FWCC. This 'Group' of seven Friends has met annually in January, alternately in America and Europe. For several years in succession, it has agreed that Quaker UN Offices in both New York and Geneva would emphasize the broad issues of disarmament, human rights, and development or 'the right sharing of the world's resources'.

At the time of the 1974 Consultation, Duncan Wood had served in the Geneva office more than 20 years. Barrett Hollister had been Director of the Office in New York since 1969, and for much longer had been an active member of the FWCC. Duncan and Katharine Wood retired from the Geneva post in 1977, and Barry and Kay Hollister from the work in New York in 1978.

The FWCC asked the Woods and the Hollisters to undertake, soon after retirement, long visiting journeys for interpreting the United Nations work to Friends. During 1978 and 1979, therefore, Duncan and Katharine presented their message in nearly 50 meetings across America, then in New Zealand and Australia. Similarly, in late 1979 and 1980, Barry and Kay met with Friends in different parts of Africa and Europe.

Successors to the Hollisters and the Woods have continued the work of Friends at the United Nations along guidelines determined by the

William E. Barton (left) and Barritt Hollister.

Consultation of 1974. In Geneva, successors to the Woods have been Philip and Janet Martin, Peter and Margaret Whittle, Kevin and Valerie Clements, and Joel McClellan. And in New York, successors to the Hollisters were Stephen and Mildred Thiermann, Roger and Anuk Naumann, and Stephen and Berit Collett.

In the 40 years of the FWCC relationship with the United Nations, Friends Representatives have spoken with hundreds of members of national delegations and of the UN Secretariat, in confidence that seeds of goodwill and of truth will in their time bear fruit. And from some of that planting of seeds there has been harvest.

During the same 40 years, and increasingly in that time, thousands of Friends in all the Continents, through some experience related to the

Duncan and Katharine Wood.

United Nations, have been stirred by the possibilities for human betterment if 'the people of the United Nations' can work together to that end. It is the Friends World Committee for Consultation which has made this possible.

CHAPTER VIII

An Ecumenical Role

IN THE PARLANCE of the Christian ecumenical movement the Friends World Committee for Consultation is a 'communion' and not a 'church'. Similarly, the World Baptist Alliance and the Lutheran World Federation and other world denominational bodies are communions. Since in this sense it is not a church, the FWCC is not eligible for membership in the World Council of Churches (WCC). But, like other world denominational fellowships, the FWCC has been invited to send 'fraternal delegates' or 'consultants' to major meetings of the WCC. FWCC also facilitated information sharing among Friends about the relationship of different Quaker groups with the WCC and with national and local ecumenical organizations.

Besides this showing of interest in the WCC, how else has FWCC played an ecumenical role? Officers of the FWCC have met periodically with principal officers of other world Protestant bodies. 'Observers' have attended sessions of Vatican Council II in Rome. A chairman of the FWCC has initiated colloquia for sharing thought and experience between Christians and Hindus in India, and between Christians and Buddhists in Japan. Cooperative arrangements with other Historic Peace Churches have been made. Relationships with several thousand Christians and persons of other religious faiths have been developed through the Wider Quaker Fellowship. And through participation in the Prague-based Christian Peace Conference, small groups of Friends helped to keep alive a person-to-person contact with Christians of Eastern Europe through the dark days of the Cold War.

The World Council of Churches

Leading up to the formation of the World Council of Churches, some American and British Quaker leaders participated in three strands of the ecumenical movement. These were the International Missionary Council, the Conference on Faith and Order, and the Conference on Life and Work. Through these bodies the tentative constitutional framework for a World Council of Churches was drawn in 1938, just as the FWCC was in its first year. The outbreak of the Second World War in 1939 prevented the WCC from holding its first Assembly in 1941 as planned, but during the war years it was 'in process of formation'. Invitations to appoint delegates to the WCC's First Assembly were sent to London Yearly Meeting, the Five Years Meeting of Friends in America, Philadelphia Yearly Meeting (Orthodox), and the Friends General Conference.

Efforts to identify the views of yearly meetings and inter-yearly meeting bodies about membership in the proposed World Council of Churches constituted one of FWCC's early services for the Society of Friends. At its Second Meeting, in August, 1939, a report of that consultation was at hand. A minute adopted for communication to Friends read in part:

> Without entering ourselves into the question whether or not the World Council is being established on a credal basis, the fact that large numbers of Friends so interpret the matter seems to us to make entry into the World Council difficult for Friends at present.

> On the other hand, we believe there is everything to be said for the closest possible kind of co-operation between Friends on the one hand and the World Council on the other, since the need for fellowship and mutual aid between professing Christians is perhaps greater today than ever before.

At the first Assembly of the WCC in Amsterdam in 1948, there were official delegates from the Five Years Meeting, the Friends General Conference, and Philadelphia Yearly Meeting (Orthodox). London Yearly Meeting had declined the invitation, unwilling to accept as the basis for membership a statement easily interpreted as credal, which defined the World Council of Churches as a 'fellowship of churches which accept Jesus Christ as God and Saviour'. Bliss Forbush, delegate from the Friends General Conference, urged the WCC to accept church bodies which did not require credal confessions of their own members. This was not agreed, but the wording of the basis would remain provisional until the Second Assembly five years later.

The FWCC sent Percy W. Bartlett as fraternal delegate to the Amsterdam Assembly. He had participated on behalf of London Yearly Meeting in the Faith and Order Conference and was well informed about the ecumenical movement. D. Elton Trueblood, at that time Chairman of the FWCC, was part of the press corps at the Assembly, with credentials from *The Friend* (Philadelphia). He helped to arrange a Quaker meeting for worship as one of several worship services held in different churches in Amsterdam. Algie Newlin, delegate of the Five Years Meeting, was appointed by the Assembly to the WCC's Central Committee.

Responding to an invitation to send a fraternal delegate to the WCC's Central Committee meeting in Chichester, England, in 1949, the FWCC named Emilia Fogelklou-Norlind of Sweden Yearly Meeting. As the Central Committee has met in Canada, India, Hungary, Ethiopia, Jamaica, and many other countries, the FWCC has kept contact with the work of the World Council of Churches through the appointment of fraternal delegates, Friends ready to serve as 'consultant' to the WCC and to provide reports to the FWCC and its constituency.

The World Council of Churches Assembly, originally expected to convene at five-year intervals, has met six times but with less regularity. A fraternal delegate of the FWCC has been present on each occasion.

With other Friends who were delegates at WCC Assemblies, and with delegates of the Mennonites and the Church of the Brethren, the FWCC representatives have cooperated to encourage the World Council of Churches in consideration of a religious peace witness. Joint effort in the 1968 Assembly in Sweden resulted in WCC adoption of 'The Martin Luther King Resolution for the Non-Violent Approach to Social Change' as a memorial to the recently assasinated civil rights leader. To implement this resolution, the WCC authorized a 'Study of Violence – Non-Violence'. Together, Friends raised nearly half of the WCC's budget of $25,000 to finance this study program, and they pursued its progress through the WCC Assembly at Nairobi in 1975.

Informal meetings of 'World Confessional Families'

In 1957, the FWCC received an invitation to participate in a meeting of secretaries of 'World Confessional Bodies'. Hesitant in any way to categorize the Religious Society of Friends as a 'confessional body', I consulted my Advisory Committee whose members urged me to take part in the informal meeting with secretaries of world denominational bodies, in Geneva on November 14 and 15, 1957.

Among the seven Protestant bodies represented at this gathering, Friends were by far the smallest in membership. Information about the structure and program of the different world bodies was shared. The main purpose of the meeting was to insure that the encouragement of denominational loyalties world-wide should not inhibit the growth of wider ecumenical interest and commitment. Principal officers of the World Council of Churches were present to press that concern. While no continuing organization was formed, participants at this first meeting agreed to meet again two years later.

At the second meeting, again in Geneva, November 24-25, 1959, participants came from ten denominations ranging from Anglican and Eastern Orthodox to Pentecostals and Friends.

Before she left her post at the Friends Center in Geneva to become the FWCC General Secretary, Blanche Shaffer attended the third meeting of Secretaries of World Confessional Families, the title which this group adopted after some consideration of the role which these organizations should play in the ecumenical movement. An exciting feature of this early April, 1962, meeting was the presence of a representative of the Vatican Secretariat for the Promotion of Christian Unity, who confirmed the Roman Catholic desire that Vatican Council II, to begin in October, be attended by observers from Christian fellowships and churches not in communion with the papal church. Procedures for issuing invitations had not yet been determined.

Through the decade of the 1960s, Blanche Shaffer was the representative of the FWCC and general Quaker interests at annual conferences of the Secretaries of World Confessional Families. She had previous personal acquaintance with some participants whose offices were in Geneva, and with top level staff of the World Council of Churches. When discussions about religious liberty, models of church unity, bi-lateral and multi-lateral dialogues, and formation of united churches became more theologically involved, Blanche was still interested but welcomed the assistance of Friends more experienced in these matters. An American Friend, Dean Freiday, attended these meetings with her in 1968 and 1969. He wrote to Douglas Steere in May, 1970, that 'Blanche Shaffer's concerned and informed participation . . . has earned the respect of all the groups'.

Tayeko Yamanouchi came into the FWCC office as Associate Secretary, with William Barton as General Secretary, at the beginning of 1971. She, too, had assistance from Dean Freiday who attended the World Confessional Families meetings with her in 1972 and 1973. He wrote papers, from a Friends point of view, on subjects under study by the Secretaries of World Confessional Families. Wilmer Cooper, Dean of the Earlham School of Religion in Indiana, who was at that time a member of the Faith and Order Commission of the WCC, also prepared papers relevant to these studies. Moreover, for three years Tayeko was one of the seven-member group which planned these meetings.

The presence of Quaker women as FWCC's Secretaries in these otherwise all-male gatherings was a witness which did not go unnoticed. Beginning in 1962 with Blanche Shaffer, the succession continued with Tayeko Yamanouchi's six-years service. Ingeborg Borgstrom, of Sweden

Yearly Meeting, was the FWCC Associate Secretary from 1977 through 1979, and attended meetings of the World Confessional Families. For ten years prior to her appointment as Associate Secretary in 1980, Val Ferguson was on the staff of the British Council of Churches. Her knowledge of the ecumenical movement, and her keen interest in it, made her a valued member of this informal gathering now identified as Secretaries of Christian World Communions.

An accredited observer at Vatican Council II

Early in 1962, there had been strong rumors that observers from Protestant bodies would be invited to Vatican Council II. I began to poll members of the FWCC Interim Committee for their views on such an invitation.

While the British members felt it would be less than tactful to attend Vatican Council II, since London Yearly Meeting had rejected the invitation to join the World Council of Churches, most members of the Interim Committee were encouraging. Some expressed hesitations about finding a Friend with the expected expertise in theology and church history who could be available at the time and for as long as required, and about the problem of finding funds for the expenses of the observer for the duration of the Council. These hesitations were resolved and the Vatican's invitation to send an observer, received by the FWCC in June, 1962, was promptly accepted.

A Professor of Philosophy at Haverford College, Douglas V. Steere was an obvious choice for Quaker observer at the Vatican Council. He had cultivated relationships with leaders in the Christian Church, both Protestant and Catholic, often through shared spiritual retreats. Through travel and a visiting ministry, he was known among Friends world-wide. But Douglas had made other commitments for the latter part of 1962 and was not available to attend the first session of the Vatican Council.

The fortunate alternative choice was Richard K. Ullmann of London Yearly Meeting. A native German with a degree in Philosophy at Frankfurt University, Richard fled to Britain as a 'refugee from Nazi oppression' shortly before the outbreak of the Second World War. In Britain he was involved in adult education and a variety of Quaker activities with emphasis on the peace witness, and was especially engaged in furthering relationships between Christians in East and West Europe.

In the four weeks Richard Ullmann was able to stay in Rome, he worked hard at understanding the procedure and content of the Council. His ability with several languages, including a working knowledge of Latin, was helpful in making personal contacts with bishops and cardinals to whom Quaker ideas relevant to the Council's agenda might be interpreted. He found that the strong trend toward reform and away from tradition was good ground in which to sow seeds of Quaker simplicity in matters of religious practice. He was successful in circulating, through the Secretariat for Promotion of Christian Unity, a memorandum which used Catholic thought in calling for support by the church for the individual conscientious objector to war.

For the remainder of the Council's first session William Hubben, editor of *Friends Journal*, served as FWCC observer. He, too, was German by birth. He grew up in the Catholic Church, but as a young adult became a member of Germany Yearly Meeting. For two years before the opening of the Council, William Hubben had regularly followed discussion of Council prospects in American and German periodicals. At the Vatican he had daily contact with a number of other observers, and with certain of the bishops who were Council participants.

A brief 'Letter from Rome', which William wrote for the *Friends Journal* as the first session closed on December 8, and a longer report which he prepared for the FWCC, express his cautious optimism about the signs that a huge institutional church might more adequately meet the needs of the poor and other ordinary people.

Pope John XXIII, from whose vision sprang the Second Vatican Council with its promise of renewal, died in mid-year 1963. His successor, Paul VI, carried forward the plans for a second session of the Council, only slightly delayed. His renewal of the invitation to non-Catholic observers was received in July, 1963. When the second session opened in Rome on September 29, Douglas Steere represented the FWCC.

From this second session Douglas sent five long letters to the FWCC. Since he was not available when the third session began in September, 1964, an American Friend, Burns Chalmers, served until Douglas arrived on October 26. Between them, another five report letters were written, and Douglas reported fully on the fourth and final session, from September 13 to December 8, 1965. Because of the Vatican's request that reporting by observers should have limited circulation, very interesting accounts provided by the Quaker observers were given only to FWCC members in all the yearly meetings and to a few of the observers' personal friends. A rich source of information remains in FWCC archives.

Each of the Quaker observers followed up the memorandum on church support for conscientious objection which Richard Ullmann had submitted in the first Council session. In the end, a useful statement was included in the Council's schema on 'The Church in the Modern World'. Other concerns to which the FWCC observers gave attention were the question of a 'just war', the possession and use or threat of use of nuclear weapons, and the role of the laity in the church. Douglas Steere followed the process which led to a Council statement absolving the community of Jews of guilt in the crucifixion of Jesus. He made a proposal, on which the Council took positive action, for establishing a Secretariat for the Non-Christian Religions.

Sponsoring interfaith spiritual encounters

It was possible, during the Vatican Council, for Douglas to confer with Catholic leaders from India and from Japan about his hope to bring together Christians with Hindus and Christians with Buddhists. Before leaving Rome he knew that some of the younger consultants to the Vatican's new

Douglas V. Steere.

Secretariat on Non-Christian Religions would enthusiastically support the kind of 'mutual irradiation' which he hoped for in interfaith encounters.

At its Triennial Meeting in Ireland in 1964, the FWCC made Douglas Steere its chairman. In an address at that meeting, he suggested an experiment in which Friends might serve as host to selected Buddhist and Christian leaders in Japan and to selected Hindu and Christian leaders in India. In a relaxed atmosphere, each group would come together for meals and for discussions and mutual understanding, and for a daily period of worship in some mutually compatible form. The FWCC Interim Committee endorsed this proposal.

Douglas and Dorothy Steere visited both India and Japan in early 1966. With Ranjit Chetsingh they laid the plans which would include Christian and Hindu spiritual leaders and scholars in India. In Japan, with Friend Yukio Irie, they initiated plans for a colloquium of Christians and Zen Buddhists. The two colloquia were held in late March and April of 1967.

A meeting of Zen Buddhists and Christians

Yukio Irie was one of the ten Christian participants in the colloquium in Japan, and served as its chairman. A former Buddhist, he became a Friend soon after the Second World War. He was Professor of English and American Literature at the Tokyo University of Education, and had studied at both Pendle Hill in America and Woodbrooke in England. The 'Quaker Team' which served as host to the colloquium were Tayeko Yamanouchi, who was then in charge of the AFSC's International Youth Seminars in East Asia, and who later became Associate Secretary of the FWCC; DeWitt Barnett, the AFSC's Quaker International Affairs Representative in East Asia; Yoshio Watanabe, Clerk of Japan Yearly Meeting; and Douglas and Dorothy Steere.

Accommodation for the colloquium was at the Oiso Academy House in the small sea coast town of Oiso. The meetings of ten Buddhist and ten Christian leaders and scholars were conducted entirely in Japanese. Each participant made his oral contribution of 15 minutes on each of two topics – The Inward Journey, and Social Responsibility for Ordering Our World. At each session two persons made oral presentations, followed by discussion. The schedule, from March 27 to April 1, gave time for conversations and for personal meditation.

Thanks to the efforts of Yukio Irie and other Japanese Friends, the Zen Buddhist-Christian Colloquium has been carried on, with several new persons added.

Hindu-Christian Colloquium in India

As the site for this colloquium, Ranjit Chetsingh had secured the YWCA Conference Center at Ootacamund, a hill town in the mountains of South India. Nine Christian and seven Hindu leaders and scholars were there, with Ranjit Chetsingh and Douglas Steere included among the Christian leaders. In addition, the Quaker Team of Laurie Baker, Nette Bossert, Doris Chetsingh, Dorothy Steere, and Marjorie Sykes not only acted as hosts, but took an active part in the discussions, which were conducted in English. Except for the Steeres, the members of the Quaker Team all had long experience and current involvement in India. The seven-days meeting began on April 11, 1967.

The schedule and the topics used were much the same as for the colloquium in Japan. But a strong personal element was added with extended self-introductions on the first day. Douglas Steere's report to the FWCC declares that to discuss matters of such 'depth and delicacy with the frankness and sensitiveness that this group found possible in the closing sessions of the meetings . . . showed both the level of mutual confidence that was present, and . . . how much was on the agenda for future meetings!'

On the final evening of the Hindu-Christian Colloquium it was determined that these meetings would be continued in another year, possibly one at a location in the north of India and one in the south. Unfortunately, this expectation was not realized.

As Douglas and Dorothy Steere traveled through Europe after the two Colloquia in 1967, they stopped in Rome. He had kept his friends at the Vatican's Secretariat for Promoting Christian Unity informed about plans for the meetings of Buddhists and Christians and of Hindus and Christians. They arranged an audience with the Pope for Douglas on April 24, when during 20 minutes Douglas described the interfaith encounters which had occurred and participation in them by Catholic Christians. The Pope thanked the Quakers for these initiatives, and said it was not the size of the undertaking but the quality and the initiative which were important. In addition, the Pope asked for suggestions of ways the Vatican might contribute to similar endeavors, and Douglas promised to send a memorandum through the Secretariat for Promoting Christian Unity.

Cooperation with other Historic Peace Churches

In postwar Europe and America, Friends felt uncertain about who should cooperate with the Mennonites and the Church of the Brethren. Those churches, as well as the Friends, had sent American relief workers to wartorn areas in Europe. Friends wondered: When peace church workers in Europe came together to consider their common purposes, should Friends be represented by AFSC staff near at hand, by British Friends relief workers, by other Friends coming directly from Britain, by members of the small Continental yearly meetings, or by persons designated by the FWCC?

The Mennonites and the Brethren strongly desired to build a peace witness within the European churches and in the World Council of Churches. Capable leaders from their American churches gave time to this effort in Europe. American Friends engaged in relief and rehabilitation were sympathetic, but could not give priority to work with European churches. Ultimately, the Peace Committee of London Yearly Meeting accepted representation of Friends in conferring with the other Historic Peace Church representatives in Europe; and Eric Tucker, Secretary of the Friends Peace Committee in London, participated in the first peace churches' conference in Geneva in 1949.

A third meeting of representatives of the peace churches, along with officers of the International Fellowship of Reconciliation whose secretary was a London Friend, Percy Bartlett, was held at the Mennonite Guest House 'Heerewegen' near Zeist, The Netherlands, August 1 and 2, 1950. Responding to a request from the General Secretary of the World Council of Churches, the peace churches' representatives agreed to collect information about attitudes of the different churches toward conscientious objectors, and the legal status for COs within nations. The FWCC and its Sections undertook to gather that information for Friends.

The WCC further requested the peace churches to prepare a statement on the Christian basis of pacifism. The result was two pamphlets – 'War Is Contrary to the Will of God' (1951) and 'Peace Is the Will of God' (1953). The FWCC, especially its American Section, had a major part in distribution of these publications.

Eric Tucker kept the FWCC office and Executive Committee in London informed about meetings of representatives of the peace churches and the activities rising from those meetings. He also was in frequent correspondence with James Walker in the American Section office; and for a meeting at Zeist in the summer of 1951, the American Section appointed D. Robert and Elizabeth Yarnall and Margaret E. Jones as representatives.

I began to urge the European Section to get involved with peace church activities in Europe. Sigrid Lund and others were interested, but limitations of personnel and other resources made that difficult. Instead, the Section asked Eric Tucker to represent them as well as the London Friends Peace Committee, until 1962 when they appointed Dirk Meynen of The Netherlands.

Meanwhile, in America, executive officers of the service bodies of the Historic Peace Churches conferred frequently. When their joint concerns began to extend beyond overseas service to strengthening the peace witness in their respective constituences, each secretary of a service body invited one other person from his denomination to meet with them. In that invited capacity, Errol Elliott joined Lewis Hoskins of the AFSC in meetings of a Historic Peace Churches Continuation Committee which arranged HPC conferences in 1954 and 1956. Although some Section members felt their efforts should be restricted to activities within the Society of Friends, Errol Elliott in 1956 persuaded the Executive Committee that a Friend working with the peace churches Continuation Committee should represent the FWCC's American Section. He was asked to continue to serve.

During the next ten years several different Friends served on the Continuation Committee in America, and further HPC conferences were held in 1959, 1960, and 1962. Then for six years most Continuation Committee activities involved primarily its members. But alarmed at the growing involvement of the United States in the Vietnam War, as well as over a generally deteriorated international situation, the FGC, the FUM, and the American Section helped to arrange still another conference of the Historic Peace Churches at New Windsor, Maryland, in November, 1968. Its purpose was to seek the spiritual undergirding needed to meet the challenges of troubled times.

Meanwhile, in Europe, Mennonites and Brethren workers from America pursued their concern for discussions of the basis of a Christian peace witness with church leaders, especially in Germany and France. One of their efforts took form under the name 'Eirene', first to provide service opportunities for COs, then as sponsor of wider service, and later as a focus for theological studies of a Christian peace witness. Supported by the Peace and International Relations Committee (a new name) of London Yearly Meeting, the FWCC European and Near East Section joined the Eirene Council in 1970, and sent Eva Pinthus, a British Friend and teacher of religious subjects, to several Eirene-sponsored meetings in the early 1970s.

In the late 1970s, the Brethren and Mennonite workers in Europe formed another project called 'Church and Peace' which took over remaining work of the old HPC Continuation Committee and of the Eirene Council. German Friends became interested, and asked the FWCC European and Near East Section to join their participation in Church and Peace. With support from the Friends Peace and International Relations Committee in London, the Section agreed to closer involvement in Church and Peace.

When six Friends from Belgium, Britain, The Netherlands, and Sweden met with representatives of the other Historic Peace Churches in June, 1980, in Amsterdam, their joint declaration said, in part, '. . . the current world situation calls for an unequivocal statement by the Churches that war and violence are incompatible with the spirit of Christ . . . The peace testimony should not only be an expression of our opposition to war and violence, but the outcome of an attitude and way of life that also excludes oppression and injustice'.

The New Call to Peacemaking

In the wake of the Fourth World Conference of Friends, in North Carolina in 1967, Friends in North America experienced a decade of growing unity which was nurtured in the Faith and Life Movement. From that movement came support for a further exercise in unity. A concern for 'a new thrust for peace' by Friends was expressed in the annual gatherings of yearly meeting Superintendents and Secretaries, most strongly by Norval Hadley, Superintendent of Northwest Yearly Meeting. In October, 1974, the Superintendents and Secretaries forwarded that concern to the Faith and Life Planning Committee which appointed a small number of Friends to implement it. That group proposed a series of regional conferences, followed by a continent-wide conference in 1978. A study book prepared for use in that conference was given the title *New Call to Peacemaking*.

At a National Conference of Friends Pastors, in Dallas, Texas, in April, 1976, Russell Myers, Superintendent of the Evangelical Friends Church, Eastern Region, suggested an invitation to the Mennonites and the Church of the Brethren to join in the New Call. Both of these groups gave immediate positive response. A planning meeting on June 30, 1976, with five representatives from each denomination, launched the New Call to Peacemaking.

Conferences were held in 13 regions where substantial Historic Peace Churches involvement was possible, in the autumn of 1977 and spring of 1978. Study papers were prepared, and used in the regional conferences, on three themes: 'Biblical Basis of Peacemaking', 'Christian Peacemaking Lifestyle', and 'Building the Institutions of Peace'. Nearly 1,500 persons took part in the 13 regional conferences.

In a continent-wide conference at Green Lake, Wisconsin, in October, 1978, there were more than 300 representatives from the three peace churches. It was a working conference divided into small groups which presented their concerns to a 'Findings Committee' responsible for bringing a final report and recommendations to the whole conference. Barrett Hollister, Clerk of the Section of the Americas, presided at plenary sessions.

A second New Call Conference with the same basic pattern was held at Green Lake two years later; and a third conference at Elizabethtown, Pennsylvania, in June, 1983, with the theme 'Christians Confronting the Nuclear Arms Race'.

From the inception of the New Call to Peacemaking in 1976 its staff service was provided by Robert Rumsey, until August, 1981, when a Mennonite became the Coordinator for New Call to Peacemaking.

An effort by the New Call to encourage in other American churches a concern for Christian peace witness played some part in the movement of several denominations and many church leaders, both Protestant and Catholic, toward public commitment to ways of peace. In light of this developing witness in American churches, the Friends, Mennonites, and Brethren disbanded formal organization and staff for directing the New Call to Peacemaking. Instead, the appropriate organization in each of the Historic Peace Churches agreed to take in turn a year of responsibility for alerting the other two about any need for joint action.

The Christian Peace Conference

The need for easing of tensions between East and West in Europe became a concern of Friends as soon as those tensions were evident after the Second World War. Seven British Friends visited Russia in 1951. Swedish Friends brought American Friends together with Russian Baptists, in Sweden, in 1954. These were among the earliest of East-West contacts by ordinary citizens.

The Christian Peace Conference, with its base in Prague, in Czechoslovakia, provided venue for church-related persons – 'theologians, pastors, and laymen' – from East and West to meet in the hope of concentrating the energies of Christian believers all over the world in united action for peace. It arose from united faculties of two Czech Protestant seminaries with support from the Protestant churches of Czechoslovakia.

Because its base was in a Communist-dominated country, and since most of its meetings were in one of the Eastern bloc nations where churches were under some degree of government control, it was difficult for the CPC to attract the interest of churches in the West. Its leaders hoped for fair-minded and unprejudiced consideration of world problems. But with the large majority of participants coming from churches in the Communist world, heavily biased statements were made and one-sided resolutions emerged. Too few religious leaders from the West were present for adequate expression of opposing opinion.

Richard Ullmann, out of personal concern and with financial support from British Friends, took an active part in the Christian Peace Conference from its early period. His knowledge of European theology and his linguistic ability made possible his full participation in discussion. At the same time, his familiarity with the West and with the church and the peace movement in the West could be used to correct some of the bias and prejudice which found expression in the CPC. Richard gained the respect of church leaders of the East. He also had some success in getting participation in the CPC by leaders of the church in Western Europe, Britain, and America.

The American Section named Kenneth Boulding and Norman and Mildred Whitney, in Europe for other reasons, as 'observers' at the first All Christian Peace Assembly in Prague, in September, 1960. Sigrid Lund, Chairman of the European Section, was there, having received a personal invitation, and Richard and Lene Ullmann represented committees of London Yearly Meeting. Richard was a member of the CPC's Advisory Committee. When his untimely death occurred in 1963, the CPC invited his widow, Lene Ullmann, to membership on that committee.

The American Section began to look for a Friend who could undertake a continuing role as observer at the CPC. Paul Lacey, a Professor of English Literature at Earlham College, was concerned about developing a continuing relationship with persons in Eastern Europe. In 1959, he was one of a group from the Young Friends of North America to visit Russia. Paul welcomed the opportunity to attend the second All Christian Peace Assembly in Prague in 1964, as an observer on behalf of the American Section.

He found cultural differences between East and West as much a problem as differences in theology or in political viewpoint. There was little or no questioning of draft statements prepared in advance, for instance, and procedure for group decision making was not as open as persons accustomed to Western democracy might expect. But the number of participants from the West had increased significantly, and though positive accomplishment by this gathering of more than 1,000 church men and women was limited, the effort seemed worthwhile and Paul was willing to continue in it. Six other Friends, from America, Britain, and Germany, attended this 1964 Assembly.

The American Section asked Paul to continue to participate, as delegate rather than as observer, in at least one meeting of CPC each year. He was one of six Americans who met with the CPC Advisory Committee at Budapest, Hungary, in October, 1965. The total number of attenders was nearly 200, from 42 countries. Two British Friends were there, Leslie Metcalfe who was Quaker International Affairs Representative in Vienna and Eastern Europe, and Irene Jacoby, member of the British Committee for the CPC. They, with Paul Lacey and a few FOR members from America and Britain, boldly pointed to one-sided and unfair language and positions in draft statements, and brought modification and reasonable balance into at least some of the final statements. For the time being it seemed right to continue to participate as full members.

Paul then helped to organize an American Committee for the CPC and became a member of its small executive body. Journeying to the 1966 meeting of CPC's Advisory Committee, at Sofia, Bulgaria, with the expectation that the worsened situation in the Vietnam War might make it more difficult for any sense of common purpose to be recognized, he was relieved when a greater feeling of trust and mutual respect marked the meeting, along with greater willingness to listen to different points of view. The CPC, for the first time, was acknowledging that there was disagreement within it but that it was important to work together even when common ground could not be found on some very important issues.

One change made by the CPC in response to suggestions by Friends and others from the West was to reduce the number of participants for the Third All Christian Peace Assembly in March of 1968, in Prague. The committees and commissions were smaller, and there was opportunity for exchange of views in real dialogue. Still, there were some 500 delegates from 54 countries and an additional 100 observers. Among these were at least 17 Friends. Paul Lacey represented FWCC's American Section and Helga Bruckner from the German Democratic Republic served as the delegate from the European and Near East Section. Heinrich Carstens, Chairman, and Margaret Gibbins, Secretary, of the European and Near East Section were there, with other Friends from Britain and Germany. It was the time of the 'Prague Spring' and Czechoslovakia was experiencing new freedom.

The Czech freedom could not last. That summer of 1968 Warsaw Pact tanks rolled into Prague. Czech resistance was futile. A harsh regime gradually displaced the country's democratically elected leaders. CPC Secretary Ondra was forced under political pressure to resign. The venerable Dr. Josef Hromadka, President of the CPC from its beginning, also resigned and died soon after. The new leadership of the CPC openly reflected the policies of Communist government. CPC Committees in some Western nations decided against sending representatives to meetings of the CPC, and the British Committee dissolved itself. Sadly, the dialogue between church leaders of East and West quickly declined.

Paul Lacey continued to be active in the American Committee for the CPC for a few years. In 1972 it organized 'Christians Associated for Relations with Eastern Europe' (CAREE), intending to be in touch with both Marxists and Christians. The American Section named Paul their representative to CAREE, but there was little activity by this organization.

At least one British Friend, Irene Jacoby, kept in touch with CPC during its seemingly non-productive years. In 1974, the European and Near East Section asked her to represent them at a CPC-sponsored meeting in West Berlin, for discussion of 'What It Means to Be a Christian'. The CPC made preparations for the Sixth All Christian Peace Assembly, to meet in Prague in 1985, and to some observers in the West there seemed promise of a gathering with more open discussion. The FWCC and the Section of the Americas declined to appoint observers. A few British Friends were there as observers for other organizations.

The Wider Quaker Fellowship

The Wider Quaker Fellowship is a way of reaching out in the ecumenical spirit to persons, rather than to institutions. In his letter of invitation at the formation of the WQF, Rufus Jones wrote:

. . . far from wishing to draw anyone away from the established connection which he may have in a religious communion . . . we are aware that there are persons who without leaving their own church and without coming into full membership, would like to share in this spiritual movement and through that sharing be in closer fellowship with those who call themselves Friends.

That was in 1936, and the Wider Quaker Fellowship was put under the care of the American Friends Fellowship Council. With the merging of the AFFC and the American Section in 1954 the WQF became a program of the FWCC, but only of the American Section.

At various times, the FWCC and the European Section have given interested consideration to the WQF but have not undertaken to sponsor it. On the other hand, some yearly meetings have nurtured a relationship with friends of the Friends in their geographical areas, using the Wider Quaker Fellowship name and pattern of service. In The Netherlands, and in Australia and New Zealand, the yearly meetings have maintained WQF programs over many years, always in communication with the Wider Quaker Fellowship chairman in Philadelphia.

Members have been enrolled in the WQF upon written request affirming sympathy with the Friends' belief in direct human-divine relationship and with one or more of the testimonies for peace and social justice. The major contact made with WQF members has been through periodic mailings from the Philadelphia office, which include a letter from the chairman of the Fellowship along with a few small pieces of literature written by Friends, or about Friends, or on a topic of current Friends' concern. In addition, there has been much personal correspondence between individual members and the WQF chairman or office assistant, often initiated by the member.

Regional gatherings of members of the WQF have sometimes been arranged and personal visits made. The WQF has encouraged contacts between its members and nearby Friends meetings. In an unusual situation, Friends in New York wanted to hold meetings for worship in a state prison where they had visited a number of prisoners. Regulations allowed prisoners to attend worship services only if the prisoner was a member of the sponsoring denomination. Prison authorities, when consulted, agreed that prisoners who joined the WQF might attend meetings for worship arranged in the prison by Friends. In several New York prisons, meetings for worship were arranged in this way, and in one the prisoners organized a monthly meeting.

In its first three years, the WQF enrolled 550 members. The numbers grew rapidly during the World War II years, to more than 3,600 in 1946. Although at one time there was a mailing list of more than 4,000, the number of members stays near 3,600. A WQF 50th Anniversary pamphlet lists 80 countries, other than the United States, in which members live.

The WQF has long wanted to reach out to Spanish speaking persons in the Americas. When the Section of the Americas' work with Latin American Friends expanded in 1977 and later, the need for literature in Spanish became more obvious. Finally, in 1984, a complete mailing in Spanish was prepared, to be followed up annually.

Leslie Shaffer and his small staff guided the work of the WQF in its earliest years. Emma Cadbury, sister-in-law of Rufus Jones, home from Quaker service in Austria in the early 1940s, became the WQF chairman in 1943. She continued in that post for 20 years. Her keen interest in the WQF and its members helped to place her stamp on the service provided. At the memorial service following her death in March, 1965, a Friend spoke of Emma Cadbury as 'pastoral counselor by mail'. The seven Friends who have since served as WQF chairmen, and a succession of able office assistants, have continued this 'ecumenical outreach on behalf of the Religious Society of Friends . . .'

Blanche Shaffer and the FWCC in the 1960s

An important part of the FWCC's involvement in ecumenical affairs came during the tenure of Blanche Shaffer as General Secretary, from 1962 through 1970. As observer for FWCC she took delight in attending meetings of the Central Committee of the World Council of Churches. She could smile inwardly about her position as the only woman in the annual gatherings of secretaries of World Confessional Families. She especially valued her association with FWCC Chairman Douglas Steere when he was an observer at Vatican Council II and during his work with the interfaith colloquia in Japan and India.

At Blanche's first Triennial Meeting, 1964, in Waterford, Ireland, James Walker presided at the end of his three-years term as chairman. Since Guilford College, in Greensboro, North Carolina, had changed its policy and was ready to receive Negro students, the FWCC decided to accept Guilford's invitation, first considered in Kenya in 1961, to hold the Fourth Friends World Conference at that college in 1967.

The conference was at the center of FWCC activities for three years. From it came mandates which called for an expanded role by the FWCC – to bring cohesion into varied international work undertaken by different Friends groups, to enlarge and to implement Friends' concern for the right sharing of the world's resources, and to increase the involvement of the FWCC and of Friends around the world in Quaker work at the United Nations.

To meet these challenges it was essential for the FWCC to have more staff. The Interim Committee arranged for William E. Barton to begin service as Associate Secretary on May 1, 1969. He would begin to work on the three principal tasks mandated by the World Conference.

William Barton was made General Secretary by the FWCC at its Eleventh Meeting, in Sigtuna, Sweden, in 1970, to succeed Blanche Shaffer on her retirement at the end of that year. Tayeko Yamanouchi, a Japanese Friend who had ably carried AFSC assignments in her own country, was named Associate Secretary. As chairman, to succeed Douglas Steere, the FWCC appointed Heinrich Carstens, a German Friend who had served as chairman of the European and Near East Section. While Margaret Gibbins and I continued as Section secretaries, a new team took on major responsibilities for the FWCC world-wide.

The FWCC office had been moved to Birmingham from London in 1956 to give opportunity for this world body with small staff and small budget to establish its own identity away from Friends House and the strong London Yearly Meeting center. After 15 years that identity had been earned, and the way London Yearly Meeting looked at the FWCC had changed. As the year 1971 began, the FWCC office and staff were again in London.

CHAPTER IX

Friends from all the World – Greensboro 1967

By 1967, THE GROWTH OF THE UNITED NATIONS, a greater sense of the world as a global unit, an awareness of Christian ecumenism, the divisiveness and violence of racism, intensifying civil rights movements, the Vietnam and Middle East crises, new problems and promise in Africa – to name but a few factors – called Friends to consult one another and to reason together. But, most significantly, the yearning to be together and to share past and present experience among members of the Quaker world family brought 900 Friends to a Fourth World Conference and nearly 300 more to an overflow Gathering, at Greensboro, North Carolina.

Making an initial rough calculation of cost, before any serious planning for a world conference began, I estimated that the total conference expense, including payment of fares, would exceed a quarter of a million US dollars. In 1962 that was a frightening cost for Friends to contemplate. Could such expenditure 'on themselves' be justified when the world was full of human needs calling for compassionate caring? My anxiety was slightly eased by a news report that the city of Vienna had spent a nearly identical amount preparing for the meeting of only two men – President Kennedy and Party Secretary Khrushchev – and the Vienna meeting ended in almost complete failure.

The Fourth Friends World Conference, at Guilford College in Greensboro, July 24 to August 2, 1967, was a demonstration of the purpose of the Friends World Committee for Consultation and a culmination of FWCC's development until that time. From what transpired then, FWCC developed its service to the Society of Friends after 1967.

Planning the conference

An *ad hoc* world conference committee, appointed by the FWCC, met for two days in July, 1964, in Waterford, Ireland, following the Triennial Meeting of that year. One of its actions requested yearly meetings, according to size, to appoint one or two representatives to a Conference Committee with about 100 members. European members of the committee met twice. American members met three times. A few members from America and a few from Europe met together in The Netherlands in October, 1965. One year later a similar group met in North Carolina. At each of these meetings there were one or more participants from Africa, Asia, Australia, and New Zealand. Planning and preparation for the conference were on an international scale.

Edwin Bronner, at that time a Vice-Chairman of the American Section, was Chairman of the Conference Committee. Lewis Waddilove presided at meetings of the European members. So that he could serve as secretary for the conference, Guilford College agreed to release J. Floyd Moore, a Professor of Religious Studies, from teaching duties for a year. Kathleen (Betty) Taylor left her post in the office of Ireland Yearly Meeting to assist with conference plans, first for a year in the American Section office in Philadelphia, then with Floyd Moore at Guilford.

At the invitation of the FWCC, Friends in several regions suggested subjects of major concern to be the focus of study in preparation for the conference. From the suggestions received, five were selected as topics for the first Conference Study Book, *No Time but This Present*. The topics were The Nature of the Spiritual Life, The Ecumenical Challenge, The Community of Friends, The Community of Peoples, and Peace Making and Peacekeeping. 25 Friends in different parts of world Quakerism agreed to write on sub-topics. With Blanche Shaffer serving as editor, the first Study Book became available late in 1963. It went through three printings for a total of 12,000 copies. An abridged Spanish edition was published, and parts of the book were printed in several languages of Europe.

A second Study Book, *Seek, Find, Share*, was published early in 1967 using responses to *No Time but This Present* from 45 individuals or groups.

The chairman for the Committee on Program was Barrett Hollister, a member of Indiana (General Conference) Yearly Meeting, and later Director of the Quaker UN Office in New York, then chairman of FWCC's Section of the Americas. Program for the conference was developed with emphasis on small group participation, in Worship-Sharing Groups and in Round Table Groups for discussion.

Joyce Blake of London Yearly Meeting and Helen Hole of Indiana (Five Years) Yearly Meeting were co-chairmen for Worship and Ministry, including responsibility for Worship-Sharing Groups. Joseph Haughton of Ireland Yearly Meeting and Lorton Heusel of Indiana (Five Years) Yearly Meeting were co-chairmen for Round Table Groups. Selection of a leader for each of these 82 groups was a time-consuming task requiring a great amount of international correspondence. The Round Table discussion topics closely followed the general themes for *No Time but This Present*, with the addition of 'Friends' Witness in Mission and Service' and 'Developing and Sharing the World's Resources'.

To Clyde Milner, Guilford's president from 1934 to 1965, the convening at Guilford of 900 Friends from around the world was the realization of a dream. He had nurtured that dream since 1960 when the North Carolina Yearly Meeting first considered issuing an invitation to hold a world conference in their state. Only weeks after his retirement in the summer of 1965, Clyde and Ernestine Milner embarked on a 20-months round-the-world journey during which they visited Friends and stimulated interest in the coming conference. Many who came to Guilford in 1967 had met the Milners during that journey.

Succeeding Clyde Milner as president of Guilford College, Grimsley Hobbs opened all the facilities of the college to the conference. It was not an easy thing to do. A summer term closed only a few days before the conference began, and North Carolina Yearly Meeting would be convened at the college five days after the conference closing.

The 900 Friends at Guilford were, in number, about the same as at Oxford in 1952. The large majority still was Anglo-Saxon, or persons for whom English was their first language, although only 79 percent compared with 89 percent in 1952. The increase in numbers from most non-Anglo-Saxon groups was small, with East Africa (from 4 to 14) and Japan (from 4 to 10) having the largest gains. A more striking difference was that in 1952 one quarter of the representatives came from within the United Kingdom; in 1967 the proportion was about one-tenth. And in comparison with 1937, 35 countries were this time represented, against 23; and, from yearly meetings in the Americas, 28 against 15 in 1937.

The Greensboro Gathering

An unofficial 'Greensboro Gathering' was arranged with care by the Conference Planning Committee and staff, with program and activities of a pattern similar to those at Guilford. Participants were spouses of official representatives at the conference, any Friend from outside of the United States who could provide a letter of endorsement from his monthly meeting clerk, and Friends who had a relationship to conference planning but who were not official representatives. From whatever yearly meetings they came, they were an excess of numbers over the quotas prescribed to yearly meetings by the Conference Committee. The University of North Carolina at Greensboro, a few miles along Friendly Road from Guilford, was the site for this Gathering of 280 Friends – 195 Americans, two Canadians, 54

Britons, and 29 from 14 other countries including 13 from Japan. Friends at the Gathering had their own Worship-Sharing and Round Table Groups, and could join in the Special Interest Groups in afternoons at Guilford.

Robert and Patricia Lyon, of New England Yearly Meeting, along with Marshall and Virginia Sutton, were responsible for administration of the Gathering. Marshall was Associate Secretary for FWCC's American Section, in charge of the Midwest Office.

The conference experience

In the opening session, Conference Chairman Lewis Waddilove, said the hope must be that Friends had come wanting to be different and better persons. He continued,

> . . . to be sensitive to another's pain; really to rejoice with those that rejoice and weep with those that weep in the way that Jesus did; and not just talk about it. And after that to be effective in changing attitudes and increasing awareness in all the circles in which (we) move in (our) own home(s) and countr(ies).

> What happens to each one of us in these ways in this conference is of far more importance in this generation than the terms of any pronouncement we may make or the solution we may propose to the complex questions we shall rightly discuss. For the effectiveness of solutions, however rightly devised, depends in the last resort on the response of men and women like ourselves.

If conference participants did become 'different and better persons' this could have occurred under the influence of the Worship-Sharing Groups or the several Round Table Groups considering 'The Nurture of the Spiritual Life'. Or during conversations and shared fellowship outside of formal sessions and in the weekend visiting of North Carolina Friends churches and meetings. Or in the moving meeting for worship following oral presentations by Everett Cattell of the Evangelical Friends Alliance and Maurice Creasey of London Yearly Meeting.

Hugh Doncaster, for 20 years the Lecturer in Quaker history and principles at Woodbrooke College in England, gave the 'Keynote Address' in the second plenary session. First, he recognized wide diversity among the different groups in the world Society of Friends. To illustrate, he pointed to the pastoral system used widely in American meetings and churches, of its apparent advantages in outreach and pastoral care and religious education, but which in Hugh's view was a 'backward-pointing bypath off the main road of essential Quakerism . . .'. Then, of his own London Yearly Meeting, he described a prevalent 'mood of vague permissiveness which affects both matters of belief and social witness and moral testimony . . . which so stresses individual faithfulness and freedom that it undercuts corporate testimony'.

Still, with the great diversities among Friends, there was a unity of purpose, and Hugh believed 'we are all called at this stage to move forward into an attitude which combines tolerance and understanding with faithfulness'. But it was not only to look inwardly that Friends had come to this conference. Friends could not stand aside when in the world around them were so many problems and conflicts. In a phrase most remembered by those who heard the keynote address, Hugh Doncaster told the assembled gathering, '. . . the world as I see it is dying, literally dying, for lack of Quakerism in action'.

In addition to the Worship-Sharing and Round Table Groups, conference participants had opportunity, in five afternoons, to organize groups for considering special interests and concerns. More than 35 topics were discussed in over 60 sessions. David Scull, of Baltimore Yearly Meeting, and Tayeko Yamanouchi, of Japan Yearly Meeting, were co-chairmen for the Special Interests Groups. 'The Future of Quakerism', a topic launched by the Quaker Theological Discussion Group, drew over 200 persons to each of three sessions. It culminated in a fourth session, 'Quakerism *Has* a Future, and Here's How', presented by young Friends.

Unusual for large Friends conferences up to that time, we gave much attention to the arts, under the supervision of Charles Cooper of Pacific Yearly Meeting. Quaker painters, engravers, sculptors, and silversmiths, some who were not at the conference, sent or brought their work. Craft work from East Africa and Jamaica was on hand. Children's art from Friends schools over the world was displayed. A remarkable photographic exhibit showed the variety of Quaker service and missions work. Quaker poets read their poetry to each other, and selected poems were exhibited. Leslie Pratt Spelman, of Pacific Yearly Meeting, an organist of international renown, gave a concert. A large cast from George School's Summer Theater Arts Workshop came from Philadelphia to perform Judson Jerome's *Candle in the Straw*, a play with a Quaker theme – the conflict between George Fox and James Nayler.

The author of an unsigned account of the arts program, which appears in the Conference Report, writes, '. . . of all the music we were able to hear at Guilford I shall remember longest the pure serenity of Klane Robison singing "There Is a Balm in Gilead"; it was a most moving experience and one by which I should like most to remember the whole range of the arts program at the conference'.

Hospitality in the homes of North Carolina Friends was a feature of the weekend during the conference. The Local Arrangements Committee, with Eva Newlin as chairman, had listed 800 beds for the Saturday night. Cars and buses took visitors from the conference and the Greensboro Gathering to nearly all meetings of both North Carolina Yearly Meetings and of Ohio Yearly Meeting's Piedmont Quarter which is in North Carolina. The visitors met with local Friends on Saturday evening, stayed in their homes Saturday night, and joined with them in worship on Sunday. Host groups returned their visitors to Greensboro Sunday afternoon, and many stayed to hear U Thant, the United Nations Secretary-General, address a large public meeting at the Greensboro Coliseum.

The UN Secretary-General's address . . .

Because U Thant was seen and heard on television and radio over a great part of the United States and his address was widely reported in other countries, the conference most impacted the outside world through that public session. The general public, the conference representatives, and Friends from the Greensboro Gathering and from a wide area of North Carolina made up an audience of 8,000 people.

U Thant took as his subject 'The United Nations and the Human Factor'. The UN Charter had not failed the international community, he

U Thant, Secretary-General of the United Nations, addressing a public session of the 1967 Friends World Conference.

said, but the international community had failed to live up to its responsibilities under the Charter. The United Nations could be an effective instrument for keeping the peace if the super powers were willing to cooperate. He emphasized that 'We the peoples of the United Nations', in the language of the Charter, are the primary source of UN operation and the 'people' need to see that governments live up to their responsibilities under the Charter.

U Thant cited the Vietnam War and the Middle East conflict as examples of violations of human rights that inflicted human suffering on a wide scale. He called for steps toward ending the fighting in Vietnam and resolution of the Palestinian refugee problem through 'real and effective international cooperation . . . (This) cooperation can be achieved if there is an awareness at all levels that no man can save himself or his country or his people unless he consciously identifies himself with, and deliberately works for, the whole of mankind'.

. . . and the FWCC Chairman's response

Responding to U Thant's message, Douglas Steere recalled a line in *The Imitation of Christ* – 'All desire peace, but they do not desire the things that lead to true peace'. We are the privileged people and nations may need to pay the price of national humiliation, or of higher costs for primary products, or of dissolving away centuries of domestic neglect of a segment of the population. The tragedy and the breakdown of peace in many world situations was that there was no authentic voice continuously and convincingly putting forth the case for 'the other'. Authentic Quaker witness has a capacity to evoke the human faces behind ideological situations and to quicken our responsibility for each other.

Conference statements and actions

The conference formally adopted three statements brought forward after discussion in Round Tables or Interests and Concerns Groups:

People, Food and the Sharing of Resources. Recognizing the problems of hunger, overpopulation, and their causal relationship to war and violent revolution, the conference called on peoples and governments 'to stop squandering resources on armaments and destruction, to promote family planning and health, to curb population growth, to increase and share food production, and to further economic and social development'. Specific appeals were made to 'our own governments', to Friends organizations and service bodies, and to Friends for personal or local action.

The Vietnam War. On this very timely subject the conference made an urgent plea:

> Our hearts are filled with compassion for the unspeakable suffering of the people of Vietnam. We believe that every effort must be made to furnish them with medical aid in whichever part of Vietnam they may be. Our hearts go out also to the soldiers of all nations involved. The killing and maiming of human beings are contrary to the spirit of Christ and the will of God . . . We appeal to the peoples of the world to demand that their governments both withdraw all support, active and tacit, from this war, and demand an end to it.

In a related action, the conference responded to a message from the Greensboro Gathering suggesting that an international delegation drawn from both the Gathering and the conference should seek an appointment at the United States Department of State. That delegation should present the conference statement on the war in Vietnam and request that steps along the lines of the statement be initiated. On August 7th, six Friends 'spoke this truth to power' at the State Department: Ranjit Chetsingh (India), Dorothy Hutchinson (USA), Kenneth Lee and Lewis Waddilove (UK), Lawrence Wilkinson (Australia), and Raymond Wilson (USA).

A further witness occurred during one lunch period when a considerable number of Friends from the conference stood in silence along one of the campus roads at Guilford, some holding placards, to protest the war in Vietnam and to call for its end.

Friends' Response to Racial Conflict. 'Wherever discrimination, exploitation, and injustice have been kindling hatred over the years, subterranean fires threaten to erupt', the conference statement declared. It cited the United States, South Africa, and Rhodesia whose 'racial issue has become the responsibility of the international community in a special way'. Responding to racial problems was very much a personal matter.

> (We) believe that God is Love and that the seed of that love is implanted in every person. (We) affirm that every society has the basic obligation to nurture this God-given capacity to love and to be loved. Friends must now, with a renewed sense of urgency, ask God's help to understand how our personal attitudes and our political and economic institutions too often destroy the capacity to love, to function fully as human beings, in those exploited and discriminated against. No less surely, when we withhold love our own hearts wither as well.

> (In addition to the spiritual change required in individuals), fundamental changes will be needed in the systems under which

most of us live . . . All of us, even those who may feel the problem remote, carry a share of the responsibility as consumers or investors, as neighbors or fellow employees, as citizens whose representatives determine local, national, and foreign policy . . . It must be our task – and for some it will mean the commitment of a whole life – to work shoulder to shoulder with our fellow men of every race and creed in bringing about constructive social change.

Two statements arising from Round Tables and Special Interest Groups were received by the conference and commended for further study by Friends. Though not issued as statements of the conference, both are printed in the official conference report. The first, on *Peace Testimony and Peace Making*, was a compilation of the results of a number of studies and discussions, both before and during the conference.

The second statement expressed deep concern over the Middle East conflict, the plight of refugees there, and 'an implacable hatred between most Arabs and Israelis made more intense by the recent war . . . Our hearts go out to our Friends of the Near East Yearly Meeting, and to other Friends called to work there'. One Lebanese representative had attended the conference, but the Friend who had expected to come from Ramallah in the old Palestine feared she would not be permitted to return to her home in the Occupied West Bank after travel to Guilford. The conference asked the FWCC to arrange for some Friend to go direct to the Middle East as special visitor to Friends there. Ranjit Chetsingh and Harold Smuck, the latter from the staff of Friends United Meeting, made that visit in September.

Observers from other religious bodies

With the recent valuable experience of having an official observer at Vatican Council II, FWCC happily complied with Douglas Steere's request that other religious bodies be invited to send observers to this World Conference of Friends. It was not at all unusual for Historic Peace Churches to be represented at Friends' conferences, and on this occasion Guy F. Hershberger was the Mennonite representative and William Willoughby came from the Church of the Brethren. In response to the invitation, the World Council of Churches sent Father Robert Stephanopoulos of the Eastern Orthodox Church and Miss Frances Maeda from the staff of the United States Conference for the WCC. It was quite unusual to have Roman Catholic observers, and on this occasion they were the Reverend John B. Sheerin, Editor of *Catholic World*, and Miss Barbara Brunton from the staff of the National Council of Catholic Women. The Jewish observers were Rabbi Balfour Brickner from the Union of American Hebrew Congregations

(Reformed) and Rabbi Myron Fenster of the Rabbinical Assembly (Conservative); and from Islam came Dr. A. H. Abdel Kader, Director of the Islamic Center in Washington, DC.

Clyde Milner chaired the arrangements committee for the observers, and Douglas Steere kept in touch with them throughout the conference. They took part in Worship-Sharing and Round Table Groups and were free to attend plenary sessions of the conference. In the closing session, Father Sheerin expressed in a brief address appreciation on behalf of all the observers for hospitality and fellowship. He also wrote a short article for the World Conference issue of *The Friend* (London) and in it said, 'I seemed to sense a readiness to clarify Quaker beliefs at this conference and to me this is a bright ray of hope. The statement on Vietnam spoke loud and clear. I would hope that the Quakers, under pressure from the Holy Spirit in the ecumenical movement, might eventually clarify their beliefs and speak out loud and clear. If so, they will be able to enter into fruitful dialogue with other faiths in the great cause of religious unity'.

The wider conference influence

A Hospitality Committee was busy for months before the conference, and for several weeks after. Using the special telephone she installed in her Scarsdale, New York, home for this purpose, Ruth Perera and her helpers arranged for most of the 300 overseas Friends to be met as they arrived in America. They provided opportunity for hospitality in more than a thousand Quaker homes, visits to meetings, trips by hired coaches, and Quaker history tours. The contacts made and friendships formed as overseas conference attenders traveled in the United States and Canada led to wider sharing of the world conference experience.

At an early stage of conference preparation the foundation was laid for a good relationship with the press and with radio and television. Releases were prepared with gradually increasing frequency, for both the secular press and Quaker periodicals. Alfred Stefferud, from Baltimore Yearly Meeting, was primarily responsible for this advance publicity. At the conference he had assistance from five Friends working with representatives of the press. No other Quaker-related event has received as much media attention, world-wide, as this conference in 1967.

A Triennial Meeting of the FWCC

The FWCC's Tenth Meeting was held at Guilford College during the four days after the conference. African and Asia-Pacific Area groups were well represented. Thomas Lung'aho, of East Africa Yearly Meeting, told of efforts toward communication and contacts among Friends groups on that large continent. There were plans for a small conference of African Friends in Madagascar in 1969, potentially a further step toward forming an African Section of the FWCC.

The possibility of beginning to develop an Asia-Pacific Area Section was suggested by Richard Meredith of Australia. There was talk of an exchange of news among the groups, to be included in local and regional newsletters. Korean Friends reported that Seoul Meeting had been helped by a number of visiting Friends since monthly meeting status had been granted by the FWCC in 1964. Ranjit Chetsingh spoke to the request of the General Conference of Friends in India (an association of Friends scattered through that large country) for recognition as an official body. That request was granted. A minute of the Tenth Meeting welcomed 'recent efforts which might ultimately lead to the emergence of an Asia-Pacific Section of the FWCC'.

Recalling the great interest among conference participants, including young Friends, in discussions of 'The Future of Quakerism', and the relevance of increased understanding of the diversities among Friends and mutual respect among them, the Tenth Meeting asked that work to this end be given a high priority in the FWCC program.

New vision of FWCC relationship to international work

In a variety of approaches the conference Round Tables and Interest Groups had expressed a need for consultation among Friends agencies involved with international work, in both mission and service. The number of such agencies had increased in recent years. Most represented Friends of only one nationality, and some only part of a single nationality. The conference had proposed that the FWCC (1) find ways of encouraging increased communication and consultation among existing Quaker agencies, (2) seek means for trans-national operations and for fuller use of Quaker personnel resources over the world, and (3) help to develop additional pilot projects featuring inter-agency cooperation.

FWCC sponsorship of Quaker United Nations work vividly illustrated the way regional agencies could work together in this new era. Distinguishing between sponsorship and administration had shown its value. Several agencies could join in sponsorship and assign the administration to a single agency. In the years ahead, such consultation would be needed far more than additional administrative machinery.

After long consideration of many facets of this mandate from the conference, the FWCC in its Tenth Meeting declared itself 'conscious of standing on the threshold of a new era in World Quaker Mission and Service. We know that with divine leading we must respond and move forward together'. But specific action would need to be determined by an executive body and staff. 'We authorize our . . . Interim Committee and representatives of Friends Mission and Service agencies including several Friends interested and experienced in the sharing of world resources . . . to seek and appoint additional staff, subject to our securing funds for these purposes.'

Struggling to meet the new challenges

In the months following the conference and Tenth Meeting, Blanche Shaffer could not find time to pursue the new tasks to which the FWCC was called. The Interim Committee met in late January, 1968. Nothing had been done toward a trans-national Quaker service or to encourage communications between missions and service agencies. The additional member of staff called for by the conference and Tenth Meeting had to be found to implement these concerns.

Joseph Haughton had written to some 40 Friends with expertise relevant to right sharing of world resources, and had received nearly 30 responses which would be circulated to Friends interested in this field. The Interim Committee appointed a 'World Resources Group' of seven members to advise the staff. The American Section created a new committee on Quaker International Affairs and slowly began to develop a program for right sharing of world resources.

Douglas Steere persuaded nearly 50 Friends around the world to write comments on seven themes which had dominated conference thought and discussion. Then, using these comments along with their own thinking, selected writers prepared 'reflective essays' for a post-conference volume with the title *Break the New Ground*. The chapter headings were 'Peaceable Role in World Revolution', 'New Dimensions in Mission and Service', 'Right Sharing of World Resources', 'Friends Work with Youth', 'Friends' Responses to Racial Crises', 'Encounter with Worship-Sharing', and 'Quakerism Looks to the Future'. The book was published in the spring of 1968.

Also in spring, 1968, the FWCC announced that William Barton had accepted appointment to the new post of Associate Secretary. This was good news. Still there was a long wait until the Friends Service Council could release William at the end of April, 1969. At last the FWCC could begin to work on its mandate for new and important tasks.

CHAPTER X

A Role in Friends Mission and Service

WILLIAM BARTON WAS IMMEDIATELY ABSORBED in implementing the mandates of the Greensboro Conference. Correspondence related to Middle East and Vietnam concerns demanded time which he could ill afford to give, but he was determined that the three priority mandates from the Greensboro Conference should receive their due – mission and service, world resources, and Quaker work at the United Nations. Pursuit of these tasks took the FWCC into fields of endeavor beyond the expectation of its founders and expanded the concept of 'consultation' which continued to describe the World Committee's role.

It was part of the agreement in William's appointment that he would not be required to move from London to Birmingham. As Associate Secretary he worked from an office in London.

Concern to bring dialogue between mission and service

On the first day in his FWCC office, May 1, 1969, William addressed a letter to clerks of yearly meetings and to secretaries of mission boards and service agencies, in which he described the programs for which he would be responsible as Associate Secretary. First on his list was the program to provide 'liaison between Quaker mission and service bodies'.

In the American Section, Douglas Steere, Edwin Bronner, and I had been at work to prepare the ground for the FWCC's new program. The Steeres invited principal officers of the AFSC and the FUM to their home on a Sunday in December, 1967. Clearly these Friends were ready to cooperate in arrangements for conferring. But Edwin Bronner, soon to become chairman of the Section, and I knew that the FWCC Associate Secretary would need to build personal acquaintance with, and win the confidence of, yearly meeting superintendents who served also as secretaries of the mission boards within the Evangelical Friends Alliance.

As William was able to turn his attention to this effort, this is exactly what happened. His warm personality and spiritual depth greatly helped him develop the relationships needed. In his annual eight-weeks visits to the North American Continent, his schedule always included at least a one-day visit at the offices of each mission board and the AFSC.

Mission and Service Conferences of the 1970s

Then William focused on organizing a conference, the first of which, at St. Helena Retreat House in London in 1973, gathered together 25 principal officers and staff of mission boards and service agencies, and also Friends indigenous to some areas where there was active mission and service work.

William prepared this conference, and those which followed in 1976 and 1979, with meticulous care. Ample time was allowed for Friends from widely different experience and viewpoint to get to know each other. Together, they considered these questions: What is the spiritual basis of our mission and our service work? What priorities ought we to apply to meeting contemporary spiritual and material needs of our fellow men? How do we strengthen our partnership in Quaker witness? Robert Rumsey, who represented the American Section at the first Mission and Service Conference, described the five unhurried days as 'creative tension between differing points of view'.

Acknowledging that total commitment in mission or service is under the leading of the Holy Spirit, and emphasizing that ministry to the whole person must deal with the inter-related issues of peace, social justice, and race relations, conferees asked that such conferences be held every three years.

In January, 1976, representatives from 16 mission or service agencies gathered in a somewhat larger conference at the Church of the Brethren Service Center in New Windsor, Maryland. In addition, 10 Friends from areas of mission or service work were there, a larger proportion of the whole than in 1973. They made clear their view that no distinction was needed between mission and service, but that both are one undertaking.

In a gentle step forward, William Barton asked the conferees to consider the relevance to mission and service of FWCC's program for Right Sharing of World Resources. Also, the New Windsor conference gave attention to Quaker work at the United Nations.

The Section of the Americas suggested in 1977 that the next conference be held in a country where mission or service agencies had been at work, recommending Guatemala. Late in that year William visited the officers of Central America Yearly Meeting at Chiquimula in Guatemala and, with them, made initial plans for a conference there in January, 1979.

The time was right for involvement of Latin American Friends, following on the efforts of *Comite Organizador de Los Amigos Latinoamericanos* (Organizing Committee of Latin American Friends, or COAL) formed in 1977 with assistance of the Section of the Americas. Among the 23 participants in the conference at Chiquimula were Friends from Costa Rica, Guatemala, Honduras, and Mexico. Other participants came from Botswana, India, Jamaica, Kenya, and Lebanon.

Friends at the Chiquimula conference reiterated points made in the first Mission and Service Conference, and sought for a name which would embody the potential unity, rather than any dichotomy, of the theme 'Mission and Service'. Their tentative suggestion was 'Friends International Witness'.

The Fourth Mission and Service Conference, at Ciudad Victoria, Mexico, in February, 1981, was the first held after William Barton's retirement in mid-1980. Val Ferguson, the new Associate Secretary, was responsible for its planning, with help from Gordon Browne, the new Executive Secretary of the Section of the Americas. Richard Meredith, succeeding William Barton as FWCC General Secretary, attended the Ciudad Victoria conference during travel from Australia to his new work in London.

At the 1982 Triennial Meeting in Kenya, members of FWCC asked that one more Mission and Service Conference be held, to see how well the recommendations of previous conferences had been implemented, and to provide occasion for Friends who had recently come to work in this field to get to know one another. However, new staff did not have the contacts with mission agency personnel which William Barton had cultivated; and, at the 1985 Triennial Meeting, Richard Meredith reported an 'apparent lack of interest among Friends in holding a fifth Mission and Service gathering'. Still, FWCC members asked that 'the Interim Committee and staff of the World Office pursue the possibility of further gatherings as way opens'.

When, eventually, a fifth Mission and Service Conference was held at Woodbrooke College in England, in April, 1988, Val Ferguson was the only Friend present who had been a part of any of the four previous conferences. The 26 participants pointed to the experience of finding unity of spirit and of motivation and, in many ways unity of purpose, as most valuable.

A cautious beginning with Right Sharing of World Resources

The World Conference at Greensboro in 1967 called on Friends to launch 'an all out attack on want', and the FWCC joined that call by pledging 'much more attention to the right development and use of world resources'. A World Resources Committee with seven European and American members was appointed, but the FWCC was unable to finance travel for meetings.

Not until October, 1969, did the Interim Committee seriously consider FWCC responsibility in this field. Its members hoped to stimulate practical action within the Quaker world and efforts by Friends to influence public opinion and policy. FWCC, however, would neither administer projects nor accept contributions in support of projects. Contributions should be sent to Section Treasurers.

The European and Near East Section – early RSWR experience

Before the end of 1967 the Executive Committee of the European and Near East Section carefully considered the Greensboro Conference recommendations. The Section chairman, Heinrich Carstens, circulated a list of 'next steps' toward responsibility in 'the Right Use of World Resources', but the Section did not immediately take action of its own. Instead, certain yearly meetings declared their support of plans calling on members to give a specified percent of income to efforts for economic development in poor nations. Germany Yearly Meeting asked members to give one percent of income. Switzerland Yearly Meeting, along with other Swiss churches, asked members for three percent. And in August, 1968, London Yearly Meeting established a One Percent Fund and appointed a Sharing World Resources Committee to administer it.

The 1969 European Friends Conference adopted a 'Preliminary Statement' on 'Right Sharing of the World's Resources' which called on Friends to seriously and urgently consider 'The gift of One Percent of personal income after tax, in addition to any other giving'. This method of giving, it was felt, would strengthen Friends' appeals to governments to apply 'a further one percent of national income to the development of the poorer nations'.

At its annual meeting in March, 1970, the European and Near East Section heard William Barton describe the Interim Committee's cautious approach to Right Sharing. Deciding to follow its own course and authorizing its treasurer to receive One Percent Fund contributions, it also appointed three Friends to allocate these funds to projects.

Slow start on RSWR in American Section

The International Affairs Committee appointed by the American Section held its first meeting in January, 1968. During two days the committee surveyed the broad field of international activity with which the

Greensboro Conference had challenged the FWCC. Recognizing the urgency of the need for right sharing and for educating Friends about this need, it identified types of projects which might help meet some of the need. It heard with interest a project proposed by its chairman, David Scull, to work with Friends and others in Kenya to provide training and capital for small enterprises – a project later to be called 'Partnership for Productivity'. But the International Affairs Committee, and other Friends, looked toward the central FWCC officers and staff to provide leadership for a program.

After a year passed and there was not a right sharing of resources program of the FWCC, the International Affairs Committee named a small working party which brought recommendations to the American Section's Executive Committee in February, 1969. Action taken at that time was to endorse a 'One Percent Fund' as the vehicle for 'a movement to greatly increase our contributions to and involvement in world economic and social development'. The appeal for participation was made to individual Friends, but the American Section sought the endorsement of yearly meetings to encourage individual participation.

Twenty yearly meetings, including Canada and Jamaica, gave their endorsement to the One Percent Fund during the spring and summer of 1969. Supporting action was taken by the Friends Committee on National Legislation, Friends General Conference, Friends United Meeting, the United Society of Friends Women, and the Young Friends of North America. But endorsement often did not include a plan for implementation, and commitment by individual Friends to make financial contributions, whether or not at the rate of one percent of income, spread very slowly.

To widen the base for forming policy for the One Percent Fund Program, the International Affairs Committee invited yearly meetings and other organizations, which had endorsed the One Percent idea, to send representatives to a consultation in Washington in November, 1969. Eight yearly meetings and eight other organizations were represented. This was the first of such consultations, held usually in the spring and the fall, alternately in Washington and at some place in the Midwest.

In February, 1970, before procedures were established for allocating One Percent Funds, the Section Executive Committee approved a grant of $1,000 to Partnership for Productivity. The Section agreed to accept contributions for PfP and in 1970 received nearly $10,000 for that project.

In September of that year the Section appointed a separate Allocations Committee of seven members, with Harold Cope, then of Kansas Yearly Meeting, as its chairman. Two months later grants were recommended, and approved, for a further $2,000 to PfP; $2,000 to the AFSC's Kafue Self

Help Housing Project in Zambia; $1,000 to the Rasulia Rural Service Program of Friends Service Council and the Canadian Friends Service Committee, in India; $1,000 to the Chorti Indian Resettlement Project of California Yearly Meeting's Mission in Guatemala; and $1,000 for interpretation, coordination, and education (ICE) regarding the One Percent Fund Program. Some yearly meetings earmarked part of their contribution and a Quaker trust fund granted $5,000 to support ICE. Total One Percent Program receipts in 1970 were a little more than $28,000.

The International Affairs Committee in March, 1970, decided that to get the program under way 'there must be significant leadership and coordination provided as support for Yearly Meetings which undertake to implement their own endorsement of One Percent More'. (To emphasize giving for 'right sharing' in addition to other charitable contributions, the term 'One Percent More' was used.) The search for a 'full-time qualified person' brought John Sexton onto the staff of the American Section as Director of the One Percent More Program, beginning in June, 1970. His home in Baltimore was the base from which he assisted Right Sharing Committees in five yearly meetings – Baltimore, Philadelphia, New York, Indiana (FUM), and Western.

One more attempt at world-scale coordination

Early experience proved to the FWCC Interim Committee that a world-scale formal committee on world resources could not serve with satisfaction. In October, 1969, the Interim Committee called for appointment by Triennial Meeting of a broadly representative 'World Resources Group'. Accordingly, at Sigtuna, Sweden, in 1970, the FWCC named 14 Friends among whom were Ranjit Chetsingh of India, Yoon Gu Lee of Korea, Thomas Lung'aho of Kenya, and Juan Pascoe of Mexico, as well as American and European members. Members of the Group would function by correspondence and through conferring as they and the staff might meet during travel for other reasons. It would help to educate and inform Friends about the issues of world poverty and to stimulate attitudes of mind and a sense of commitment to personal involvement.

Seven members of the newly appointed World Resources Group who were at Sigtuna met for two days following the Triennial Meeting, along with 20 other Friends whose interests and experience were relevant to world resources and development. Joseph Haughton presided over this World Resources Gathering of Friends from 13 countries.

The Gathering tried to determine the most important world resources and development issues for Friends and found this very difficult. Certainly education would be an important means toward best use of resources, but where should there be emphasis? Although economic factors were basic in development, Friends could not neglect the human factor. While these and other issues had to be kept in mind, the Gathering agreed on the importance of practical projects, in part because of their educational value.

Heinrich Carstens was named temporary chairman of the World Resources Group. (The 1970 Triennial Meeting had appointed him as FWCC Chairman for the next three years.) Ingeborg Borgstrom, of Sweden, would serve as correspondent for the European and Near East Section, and David Scull for the American Section. Tayeko Yamanouchi, soon to join the FWCC staff as Associate Secretary, would have special responsibility for world resources matters.

When seven members of the World Resources Group, and a few other members of the FWCC, met for a day at Quaker House in New York in March, 1971, there was still optimism about a world resources program for Friends but strong feeling that a world-scale approach to such a program could not prosper.

At the Twelfth Triennial Meeting, in Sydney, Australia, in August, 1973, the FWCC recognized that the World Resources Group had been unable to function effectively. The Interim Committee had already recommended that the Group be laid down. In taking that action, the FWCC reaffirmed its conviction that for Friends the Right Sharing of the World's Resources must remain a major concern, so it asked the organized sections to carry on vigorously and to arrange for communication among the sections about their progress.

European and Near East Section and RSWR in the 1970s

The three Friends appointed to allocate funds contributed to this Section's One Percent Program had no large task immediately. Such money as was at first available was given either to the Friends Schools in Ramallah in the old Palestine, or to a women's cooperative embroidery enterprise in the same area. The Section's Executive Committee continued to encourage contributing through its One Percent Fund, advising yearly meetings who gave support direct to projects to inform the Section.

Danish Friends were giving to the Friends Rural Service Program, a project which encouraged cultivation and use of new vegetable crops in the East Africa Yearly Meeting area of Western Kenya. German Friends became interested in the same program and supported it from their One Percent Fund. German Friends Leo and Lore Englehardt visited Kenya and found East African Friends willing to accept a program for training midwives and an accompanying effort toward family planning. This program, too, had the support of German Friends.

Responding to the FWCC's 1973 Triennial Meeting request, the Section's Executive Committee appointed a group of consultants with Grete Scherer, a Viennese Friend and retired secondary school teacher, as convenor. Roger Naumann, a young British Friend who was serving as Associate with Duncan Wood at the Geneva Quaker UN Office, agreed to serve as World Resources Correspondent.

Members of the consultant group were soon hard at work preparing written materials to stimulate thought and action for right sharing. Grete Scherer gave leadership to this effort and did most of the writing. Roger Naumann provided statistics and other information from sources in Geneva. Before the end of 1975, the European and Near East Section published the writing as the pamphlet *World Resources – Dilemma and Concern*. A printing of 1,500 copies was almost entirely sold in Europe and America during 1976.

Instead of reprinting *Dilemma and Concern*, the Section's Executive Committee asked for a pamphlet to explain the 'New International Economic Order', a program strongly urged within the United Nations by the less developed nations. Sylvain Minault, successor to Roger Naumann at the Geneva Quaker UN Office, agreed to do the writing. This publication, *The New International Economic Order – The Promise and the Reality*, was published in the spring of 1977. It was well received by Friends and by a wider public.

Allocating the modest amount of undesignated One Percent Fund contributions, the Section's committee of three persons favored summer camps for children of refugee families in the West Bank of the Jordan and the purchase of books and other school supplies for children in the Central America Yearly Meeting area of Guatemala.

Since the Quaker UN Offices in Geneva and New York had adopted right sharing of the world's resources as one of three program priorities, and since Friends at Brussels preparing to bring Quaker concern to the European Economic Community also gave high priority to this concern, the Section did not make further appointments to their consultant group. But they endorsed one of the special events in which Friends from around the world might participate as they traveled in Europe toward the 1979 FWCC Triennial Meeting in Switzerland, a seminar led by Grete Scherer, with the title 'An Economy with a Human Face'.

The separate yearly meetings in the European and Near East Section gave generous support to the right sharing projects of their choice. Members of London Yearly Meeting continued to support their One Percent Fund through Quaker Peace and Service which, in recent years, gave top priority to development education. But, most recently, British Friends have phased out their One Percent Fund, deciding that development education can be better served in other ways.

Right Sharing a continuing program of the Section of Americas

In America, the work done by John Sexton as Director of the One Percent Fund Program brought very slow increase in contributions during his first year, 1970-71, not enough for ten percent of the total to pay the cost of interpretation, coordination, and education. Still, the American Section felt it was necessary for the effort of ICE to continue. A Philadelphia Yearly Meeting fund made a second contribution of $5,000 for ICE, and the American Section gave $5,000 from modest reserves, and John Sexton's work continued.

Among the individual Quaker contributors very few were following the one percent of income formula. For this and other reasons, the Section decided to change the name of the program to Right Sharing of World Resources (RSWR).

After two years of John Sexton's leadership of the Right Sharing Program, the annual undesignated contributions were about $34,000, and it was not practical to expect that 10, or even 15, percent of RSWR income would pay the cost of a modest salary and travel expense. Therefore, John returned to teaching in the Baltimore public schools in September, 1972.

At a weekend meeting in Evanston, Illinois, in May, 1973, the American Section's Executive Committee gave Saturday afternoon and evening to a 'Consultation' with the title 'Rich Nations in a Poor World – What Is the Quaker Answer?' The 'Evanston Appeal' issuing from that gathering urged American Friends to support new approaches in development 'at a level reflecting our own general affluence'. Encouraging response to that appeal led the American Section to form a separate standing committee for Right Sharing of World Resources, relieving its International Affairs Committee of that responsibility.

Members of the committee on Right Sharing of World Resources were named in 1974, with Keith Smiley of New York Yearly Meeting as its first chairman. It engaged Jennifer Haines, a young Friend, also from New York Yearly Meeting, as part time staff.

The educating and motivating of Friends toward right sharing continued to be an important part of the RSWR program. It gave attention to articulating the 'spiritual basis of right sharing', with Young Friends of North America taking the lead in formulating relevant 'Queries'. A newsletter of high quality, the semi-annual consultations which brought together members of RSWR committees in the yearly meetings, and the continual visiting of meetings by RSWR staff were principal elements of the educational effort.

After three years Jennifer Haines left the part time assignment with RSWR. Succeeding her in 1977 was Gail Weinstein, a young woman who had recently done volunteer work in a rural village in Guatemala. She organized a Friends study tour in early 1980 to visit projects in Guatemala which had received RSWR support. When Gail went to other employment in mid-1980, her place was taken by Elaine Crauderueff, a young Friend who had lived with her family in Southeast Asia during childhood. Carl Jordan, of Indiana Yearly Meeting, became chairman of the RSWR Committee in 1979 and served for two years. From 1977 to 1981, the RSWR Program made financial grants to 32 projects – 12 were in six countries of Africa, 15 in six countries of Central and South America and the Caribbean Area, four in India, and one in Turkey.

A review committee appointed by the Section of the Americas in 1980 urged increased emphasis on 'development education', making use of projects as an educational tool. Linda Coffin, a member of Iowa (FUM) Yearly Meeting who had done volunteer work in Bolivia, became Clerk of the RSWR Committee in 1981. With Gordon Browne, the new Executive Secretary of the Section, Linda sought to relate the grant-receiving projects more closely with yearly meetings and with contributors to RSWR. The Newsletter, *Right Sharing News*, was used very effectively for these purposes. The RSWR Committee urged traveling Friends to visit one or more projects and to talk about them to their own and other meetings.

Early in 1983, Sharli Powers Land began to serve as staff for RSWR, continuing until 1986 when the American Section passed that responsibility to Johan Maurer, the Section's regional field staff in Richmond, Indiana. In that year, Jane Laesle, of South Central Yearly Meeting, became Clerk of the RSWR Committee.

During 1984, the RSWR contributions exceeded $43,000, and in 1985 were $51,844. There was a dramatic increase to $86,285 in 1986 and, since then, annual contributions have continued at that level. Relationships developed by correspondence between project leaders and RSWR staff often became friendly and personal, and contacts with projects sometimes continued after funding ceased.

Trans-national Quaker Service

In the same minute which urged increased communication and consultation among Quaker agencies the 1967 conference called on the FWCC for help in 'discovering means for trans-national operations and for a fuller use of Quaker personnel resources all over the world'. Responding to that call, the FWCC suggested using 'Quaker Service' or some other name without a national label for interagency operations. Several agencies including the FWCC might sponsor a project while one agency was responsible for the project administration.

This kind of arrangement was made in the early 1970s when the American Friends Service Committee proposed the appointment of a Quaker Representative in the Middle East, a Friend who would maintain contacts with government officials and other leaders in Arab countries and in Israel. This Middle East Representative would endeavor to build bridges of understanding within the region and report to the Quaker agencies who sponsored his work. Sponsors included the AFSC, the Canadian Friends Service Committee (CFSC), Friends Service Council, and the FWCC, with the AFSC serving as the administering agency. The European and Near East Section of FWCC kept close touch with this and all Quaker work in the Middle East. Paul and Jean Johnson, American Friends thoroughly familiar with the Middle East, were the first to be appointed to this service.

As Friends began to look toward relief and reconstruction service in postwar Vietnam, they used a similar arrangement. Invited by the Friends Service Council, representatives of a number of Friends organizations, including FWCC and its Sections, met in London to consider needs for future service in Vietnam. After the AFSC was able to explore needs for service there, William Barton presided over a meeting in Philadelphia where representatives of AFSC, CFSC, FUM, and the Quaker UN Office in New York were present. The name Quaker Service was used when work was undertaken in Vietnam with Friends of several nationalities participating under the administration of the AFSC.

Along with attention to the trans-national service concept came a more ready practice of consultation between the service agencies and the European and Near East Section. At the request of Heinrich Carstens when he was FWCC Chairman, a consultation of staff from the FWCC and its Sections with principal staff of FSC was arranged to develop guidelines for cooperation between FSC and Continental yearly meetings. In the same year, 1971, the European and Near East Section Executive Committee recorded 'growing awareness of AFSC . . . cooperation, (and) their obvious willingness to draw the Section into consultation as opportunity arises'. The

Section was invited to send one or two representatives to the occasional conferences of AFSC and FSC workers in Europe.

European and Near East Section Service Committee

After the Second World War a few Friends in the Continental yearly meetings had worked alongside American and British Friends in postwar service. But members of those yearly meetings longed for some way Continental Friends might cooperate in a project all their own.

That possibility came when Norwegian Friends at the European Section's 1962 annual meeting sought support for opening a service project in Algeria. Discussion in the Section meeting indicated that other yearly meetings would join in support of that project.

Great numbers of Algerian refugees would be returning to their country at the end of the war for independence from French colonial rule. The AFSC and the FSC would work with these refugees just inside Algeria's borders with Morocco and Tunisia. The young Norwegian Quaker couple, Egil and Turid Hovdenak, would open a project in villages of the Kabylia Mountains of central Algeria, where Egil had done volunteer work before the war.

In April, 1963, the Hovdenak family and a Swedish nurse were the first workers to arrive. Other team members followed. Their supporting body was the Kvekerhelp Committee of Norway Yearly Meeting.

The European Section devised a plan for constituting a service committee as part of the Section. Each participating yearly meeting appointed one member of the service committee, someone other than its representatives to the Section. Seven yearly meetings participated – Denmark, France, Germany, Netherlands, Norway, Sweden, and Switzerland; and, in 1964, the Section made their appointees its own Service Committee. Sigrid Lund was its first chairman, and Margaret Gibbins became secretary of both the European Section and its Service Committee.

Each cooperating yearly meeting formed a committee to interpret the work in Algeria, to raise money for its support, and to help find candidates for service. The Kvekerhelp Committee gave supervision to the Algerian project until 1971 when that responsibility was passed along to the Dutch Friends' committee.

An early phase of the project was the construction of a water tower to provide water for a cluster of mountain villages. Project workers developed a model home suitable for the area, then directed villagers in cooperative building of their homes. A health clinic emphasized maternal and child health services, and trained village girls to take over some of that work. Other girls learned practical home skills, while men and boys were introduced to improved agricultural methods and the growing of new food crops. The project provided books for a children's library, and the building constructed as living quarters for project workers was handed over for use as a community center before the end of 1972 as the last of the workers were leaving.

During the ten years that the European Section Service Committee worked in Algeria, 56 persons, of eight nationalities, served on its field staff.

Working with Palestinian refugee children

The European Section was increasingly aware, during the 1960s, of the small Near East Yearly Meeting made up of Friends in Ramallah, West Bank of the Jordan, and in Brummana and Beirut in Lebanon. Struggling at Ramallah were the Friends Boys and the Friends Girls Schools, sponsored by the Friends United Meeting in America, and in Lebanon the Brummana High School which had ties with the Friends Service Council in Britain. The European Section appointed Elsa Cedergren, Hugh Doncaster, Carl Emil Engraf, and Margaret Gibbins to make a group visit to Near East Friends. They visited Ramallah and Brummana during three weeks in September, 1965, and attended the Near East Yearly Meeting held at Brummana.

The following year, when Najib Baz of Brummana and Jean Zaru of Ramallah attended the annual meeting of the Section, they spoke with appreciation for the visit by the four Friends, saying they 'now felt a part of the world family of Friends (and) had gained new knowledge and had been personally strengthened in spirit'. When they voiced the hope that this FWCC Section might have a name which indicated their belonging to it, the name 'European and Near East Section' was adopted.

The 'six-day-war' in June, 1967, between Israel and the Arab countries on its borders, left the West Bank of the Jordan, including Ramallah, occupied by Israeli forces. For the Friends Schools in Ramallah this brought great difficulty since the boys and girls who ordinarily came from other Arab countries to be boarding students could no longer do so. The changed situation made it difficult, sometimes impossible, for Friends in the two parts of Near East Yearly Meeting to meet together.

From their base in Cyprus, Paul and Jean Johnson, the recently appointed Quaker Representatives in the Middle East, carefully maintained contacts with the European and Near East Section as well as with Friends in Ramallah and Brummana, and Section Secretary Margaret Gibbins had frequent correspondence with Near East Friends. At meetings of the Section, Friends sought to find ways to assist Ramallah Friends who had developed small projects to help Palestinian refugees near them. When in 1969 Fuad Zaru, Principal of the Friends Boys School, described needs for which the schools had no funds, the Section immediately asked yearly meetings to respond.

Leo Englehardt, recently named chairman of the Section Service Committee, told the Section in 1972 that, as the Algerian project was soon to close, the Service Committee recommended a new undertaking with concentration in the Middle East. Meanwhile, contributions to the two schools in Ramallah continued, most through One Percent Funds.

Before the 1973 annual meeting of the European and Near East Section, Leo and Lore Englehardt visited the Middle East and talked with Friends in

Am'ary Refugee Camp Play Center.

Brummana and Ramallah, with Quaker workers there, and with officials of government and of the United Nations Relief and Works Agency (UNRWA) for Palestinian refugees. All of these encouraged European Friends to take responsibility for a play center or nursery school for Palestinian refugee children. Later the same year, Margaret Gibbins and Lillian Backer, chairman of the Dutch committee for Quaker Service, visited the Middle East. Margaret's report to the Section Service Committee in April, 1974, urged that action be taken as quickly as possible to prepare for the opening of a play center.

The Section approved a recommendation to proceed. Agreements were made with the regional director of UNRWA and with Ramallah Friends for a play center at the Am'ary Refugee Camp. Teachers would be selected from the local area and trained. An American couple, on assignment from the Church of the Brethren, could undertake supervision of the project. The Ramallah Friends were ready to care for problems which might arise locally, and Sina (Mansur) Hutchinson, one of their own members, agreed to handle a program for education of mothers in the Am'ary Camp. The service committee of Swiss Friends accepted responsibility for 'home administration'. With 57 children enrolled, the Am'ary Camp Play Center opened in the summer of 1975. Through visits by Margaret Gibbins and others the Section Service Committee was assured that both the play center and the program for mothers in Am'ary Camp were doing well.

In the autumn of 1977, Margaret journeyed again to the Middle East, this time accompanied by two Swiss Friends, Amalie Strub who was treasurer of the Swiss Friends committee and John Ward, recently named chairman of the European and Near East Section. Upon their return, they reported that Ramallah Friends wished that use might be made of a building adjacent to their meeting house, known as the Kelsey Annex. The different groups involved agreed that a second play center should be opened. The necessary renovations to the Kelsey Annex were made, and the 'Friends Play Center' opened in Ramallah in September, 1978.

A Ramallah Friend, Violet Zaru, became the supervisor for both centers, and support by the European and Near East Section continued. In the mid-1980s conditions related to the military occupation by Israel made it necessary to discontinue the project at the Am'ary Camp. At the Kelsey Annex, Ramallah Friends carry on with their Play Center although the Palestinian youth uprising of 1987-88 and the increased Israeli military control make regular service impossible.

Section Service Committee disbanded

When the European and Near East Section met in annual meeting in 1988, members recognized that projects for which their Service Committee had been responsible were handed over to local control. They questioned whether the committee might have some new role, perhaps in conjunction with the Section's Peace Consultative Committee which had been formed in the early 1980s. Eventually, they decided to lay down the Service Committee, realizing that a similar entity might some time be necessary if, in the future, new concepts of service should require it.

Friends and the European Economic Community

During the early 1970s, as the European and Near East Section was giving nurture to the small, but thriving, Quaker group in Brussels, members of that group and a few Friends elsewhere in Europe, began to talk about a need to have a Quaker staff in Brussels to carry Friends concerns to the European Economic Community and other international organizations with offices there.

The proposal for a Quaker office and staff raised questions about sponsorship and administration. Brussels Friends sent their memorandum on this subject to the FWCC, giving a copy to the European and Near East Section. Madelaine Jequier, Swiss Friend and chairman of the Section, and Margaret Gibbins were members of FWCC's Interim Committee which considered the proposal in October, 1975, concluding that the matter should be presented to the Triennial Meeting in 1976. But first, the Section had to obtain comments from European yearly meetings and be prepared to bring any consensus view to the FWCC Triennial Meeting in Hamilton, Ontario, Canada.

Marjorie de Hartog, clerk of Belgium Monthly Meeting, presented the proposal at Hamilton, pleading that Brussels had become a center for international affairs extending far beyond its function in the EEC. She said there was need for the voice of ethical and social concern for which Friends stood. But not all European yearly meetings had given their views to the Section which was, therefore, unable to provide a consensus position. Friends from other parts of the world felt poorly informed and, moreover, too little involved in European Community affairs, to respond. The FWCC asked the European and Near East Section to cooperate with Belgium Monthly Meeting in further study of the matter, and to make recommendations to the Interim Committee.

Members of the Section agreed at their annual meeting in 1977 that important Quaker work might be done in Brussels, but there was hesitation about appointment of staff. They arranged a consultation which included two representatives from each European yearly meeting, FWCC staff, and directors of the Quaker United Nations Offices in Geneva and New York.

The consultation asked the Section to appoint an 'Advisory Committee' to work with the 'Brussels QIAR Committee' of Belgium Monthly Meeting. These two committees, jointly, became the body responsible for carrying forward the proposal for a Quaker representative in Brussels.

By 1979, the most concerned Friends had formed the Quaker Council for European Affairs (QCEA) for the purpose of establishing a Quaker office and staff in Brussels. The QCEA appointed Brian and Pat Stapleton, British Friends with experience in economically deprived countries, as 'Quaker Representatives'. QCEA acquired a large four-storey house near the EEC headquarters. As 'Quaker House' it accommodated the Quaker Representatives and was the meeting place for Brussels Friends. QCEA's Governing Council has members from the yearly meetings of France, Germany (Pyrmont), Ireland, The Netherlands, Sweden, Switzerland, and Great Britain (London), and from Belgium Monthly Meeting. It also has an official link with the European and Near East Section.

The Quaker Representative in Brussels regularly reports to the Section and attends its annual meetings. A young member of Quaker House staff acts as coordinator for European and Near East Young Friends. After Margaret Gibbins retired in 1981, the Section named Jonathan Fryer as its Secretary. He was a young British Friend resident in Brussels. When he became ill and found it necessary to resign, Margaret resumed the Secretary's responsibilities until the appointment of Franco Perna in April, 1983. An Italian living in Luxembourg, a short train journey from Brussels, Franco houses the Section office at his home. The small Friends group in Luxembourg is a part of Belgium Monthly Meeting.

International Quaker Aid

From the concern of Dr. Donald Scott, an attender at Radnor Meeting outside of Philadelphia, a different form of Quaker service developed under the aegis of the Friends World Committee for Consultation. When Donald Scott had traveled in Southern Rhodesia (now Zimbabwe), his friend, Douglas Steere, introduced him to Friends in Salisbury (now Harare). The Salisbury Meeting energetically collected funds for modest grants to certain African children for school fees and the purchase of books. Donald Scott decided to give generously to the Salisbury Meeting Scholarship Fund. He asked the AFSC to accept his contributions and send the money to the Salisbury Meeting.

For a year or two the AFSC complied with this request. But its financial officers were uneasy about receiving money to be sent outside the United States to support a project which was not their own. Their tax exempt status with the Internal Revenue Service could be in jeopardy. Hugh Middleton, an AFSC fund-raiser and treasurer of FWCC's American Section, suggested that the American Section handle the Scott contributions. This was the origin, in 1965, of a program to which the American Section gave the name International Quaker Aid. Each year, in advance, the Section named certain countries where local Friends had undertaken work on a problem larger than could be handled with their own resources. Within its legitimate purposes, the American Section could enter into cooperative arrangements with Friends in a country other than the United States. This gave Friends in the American Section opportunity, through financial support and sometimes by providing personnel, to share in significant work of Friends in other parts of the world.

Through International Quaker Aid, the Section of the Americas has assisted the work of fellow Friends in many countries. A few examples provide illustration: IQA paid travel expenses for American young Friends who worked in Northern Ireland with Ulster Quaker Service, directing youth activities in neighborhood centers, alternately in Catholic and Protestant neighborhoods of Belfast. IQA has given to Friends in Bolivia funds for a number of social services, including basic health care for the poor. In Botswana, Friends received assistance to administer a center for refugees from conflicts in nearby countries. Paris Friends have been given modest grants to help meet the expenses of two of their members who maintain the FWCC link with UNESCO.

The International Quaker Aid budget for 1987 was $71,000, to be distributed among 13 projects of Friends in 10 countries. The largest amount designated in that year for a single project was $25,000 to help Friends in Costa Rica purchase and renovate a house in the capital city, San Jose, to serve as a Peace Center. The largest undertaking of IQA has been to provide, over several years, money needed for building a Friends Center and Meeting House for Soweto Friends in South Africa.

World Quaker Aid

At its Triennial Meeting in Mexico in 1985, the FWCC decided to establish a World Quaker Aid Program which would be administered by a committee composed of the FWCC Clerk, General Secretary, and Treasurer, along with the Clerks of the four Sections or alternates nominated by them. This program gives Friends around the world opportunity to participate in the work of meetings in countries other than their own. The first project selected for support through World Quaker Aid was one to assist Cuba Yearly Meeting with the repair of church buildings and homes provided for pastors. World Quaker Aid also undertook to help with the repair of historic Quaker buildings in Kenya.

The Triennial Meeting in Japan in 1988 decided to continue both projects. At the same meeting FWCC approved assistance for other projects: (1) renovations to Quaker Cottage, Belfast, Northern Ireland, a house used to bring together children and youth from Catholic and Protestant communities; (2) support for children in a camp for Vietnamese refugees, in Hong Kong; and (3) the purchase of a transmitter for a radio ministry project of Friends in Guatemala and El Salvador. It was agreed that at future Triennial Meetings each of the four Sections may announce one project which it has selected for support during the next triennium, and that the World Quaker Aid Committee may recommend continuing support for a current project.

Service beyond the intent of FWCC's founders?

The development of functions for the FWCC described in this chapter could not have been imagined by Friends who carried responsibility for the FWCC in its early days. The World Conference at Greensboro provided the lens through which Friends could perceive the need to expand FWCC's role, an expansion which enlarged, but did not violate, the 'for Consultation' modifier in the Friends World Committee's name.

CHAPTER XI

All Continents and Some Islands

WHILE THE AMERICAN SECTION and the European Section of the FWCC developed in strength as each was able, no regional organization was formed by Friends in Africa, Asia, or the South Pacific Area until well after the World Conference at Greensboro.

In 1952, at the behest of the FWCC's Pacific Area Committee, representatives from Japan, India, Australia, and New Zealand, enroute to the World Conference at Oxford, met in conference for the first time – not in the Asia-West Pacific Area, but *at Hampstead Meetinghouse in London*. They agreed that each of their yearly meetings should appoint 'correspondents' who would send information to Ranjit Chetsingh in India, and he would edit some form of communication to be circulated in the entire area. Information came to Ranjit from only one correspondent in the next two years. Friends in the Pacific Area were not ready for such a plan.

Developing relationships among Friends in Africa

During the World Conference at Oxford, representatives from East and South Africa met together. They agreed it might be possible to devise some means for exchanges of information. The FWCC encouraged any initiative by African groups to develop closer contacts.

FWCC took the first initiative as Ranjit Chetsingh arranged the first small conference of African Friends on African soil, at Nairobi in 1956. Financially and in other ways, FWCC facilitated visits among Friends in Kenya, Pemba, and Madagascar during the remainder of the 1950s. It also gave East Africa Yearly Meeting leaders – Benjamin Ngaira, Jotham and Rhoda Standa, Nathan Luvai, and Solomon Adagala – opportunity for acquaintance with Friends and Quaker work in Europe and America.

East African Friends proposed that FWCC's Triennial Meeting be held in Kenya in 1961. Kenya Friends gained self-confidence with the holding of that meeting at Kaimosi, headquarters of the East Africa Yearly Meeting, and stronger relationships developed between them and the rest of the Quaker world.

A proposal to form an African Section of FWCC

Thomas Lung'aho was appointed by East Africa Yearly Meeting to be its Administrative Secretary when Benjamin Ngaira became one of the Commissioners of Civil Service for the East Africa Federation. Friends at work in Kenya under separate sponsorship – the EAYM, the Friends Africa Mission, and Friends Service Council – formed an *ad hoc* Consultative Committee of Friends in East Africa for the sharing of information and concern and to arrange cooperation in some matters. Thomas Lung'aho chaired that committee.

In October 1963, at his suggestion, the Consultative Committee considered the possibility of forming an Africa Section of FWCC. Some 60 members of EAYM, along with Friends from Kampala Meeting in Uganda and Charles Marzuk from Pemba, attended that meeting. Discussion showed concern for closer association of Friends throughout Africa. There was feeling that an Africa Section would enable African Friends to know each other better and to work together on solutions to common problems. The committee named a group to explore next steps.

Need to wait longer for Section to be formed

Thomas Lung'aho wrote letters to appropriate Friends in Burundi, Pemba, Madagascar, and South Africa. The exploratory group noted, early in 1965, that both EAYM and Pemba Yearly Meeting keenly wanted an organized Section of FWCC. Friends in South Africa were interested, but questioned their ability, with so few members, to bear much of the cost. Madagascar Yearly Meeting, much involved in the process of merger with two other denominations in their island country, did not see this as an opportune time for them to give attention to inter-yearly meeting affairs, and Friends in Burundi did not respond.

Again, letters were written to the yearly meetings, with a review of the services which a Section of FWCC might provide. This time there was a friendly reply from Friends in Burundi who had welcomed a recent visit by seven members of the Friends Africa Mission in Kenya. Other visits among the yearly meetings were arranged. Blanche Shaffer encouraged Friends in Kenya and South Africa to believe that visits between their groups would be possible. Will Fox, who was active in the affairs of Southern Africa Yearly Meeting, visited East Africa Yearly Meeting in session in 1966. Two Pemba Friends and Rakotondranosy of Madagascar were also at that yearly meeting.

A second Conference of African Friends

Representatives from African yearly meetings at the 1967 World Conference at Greensboro met together and asked Friends from Madagascar if they would be hosts to a small conference in 1969. Eventually, invitations were issued by the 'Committee for the Friends Center' in Tananarive to a conference to be held August 4 to 12. The Madagascar Yearly Meeting had ceased to exist and those who had once been its members were now a part of the United Church of Jesus Christ of Madagascar. But some of the leaders in the former Madagascar Yearly Meeting were interested in the contribution of the Quaker spirit to the United Church, particularly through the service of a 'Friends Center' recently built in Tananarive with the support of British Friends. The second Conference of Friends in Africa, sponsored by the FWCC, was held at the Center.

There were 30 participants in this conference – from Madagascar 14, Kenya 4, South Africa 5, Rhodesia 2, Malawi 1, and Zambia 1. William Barton was present as Associate Secretary of the FWCC. Conference participants said in their 'Message to All Friends':

> We have valued so much our meeting together, that we wish to continue and extend these relationships. We have considered the possibility of the formation of an African Section of the FWCC and are inviting Yearly Meetings in Africa and other meetings independent of them to join in making this request to FWCC.

Introducing the recommendation for authorizing an Africa Section to the Triennial Meeting at Sigtuna, Sweden, in 1970, Thomas Lung'aho recalled that it had been 14 years since African Friends first requested formation of a Section. Now it was hoped that such a Section could be established, subject to the ratification of the yearly meetings concerned.

As the prospect for an Africa Section came near to reality, problems of financing, great distances and the cost of travel, and other practical considerations gave pause to many Friends in Southern Africa and the groups of Friends in West Africa. They felt unable to ratify the proposal for a Section. In Kenya the establishing of a Friends International Center in Nairobi, with cooperation between East Africa Yearly Meeting and the Friends Service Council, claimed the attention of EAYM leaders at the beginning of the 1970s.

Africa Section is achieved

Early in 1971, however, Friends in Southern Africa felt ready to support the forming of an Africa Section. For the FWCC Interim Committee, Joseph Haughton and William Barton wrote to clerks of yearly meetings and groups in Africa in July that it seemed time for positive steps to be taken, but that the primary action had to be by their own yearly meetings. They suggested that East Africa Yearly Meeting arrange further consultation, designating one of their members to carry out the exploration leading toward forming a Section. The FWCC would provide a subsidy of £500 in each of the first two years.

The new Friends International Center was established on N'gong Road in Nairobi near the middle of 1971, and EAYM appointed Nathan Luvai to be its warden. In September, EAYM asked Nathan to be also the part time secretary of an Africa Section in process of formation under the guidance of a Section Committee at that time made up of EAYM's representatives to the

Nathan Luvai, first Secretary of the FWCC African Section. In background, Friends preparing to depart from EAYM, 1960.

FWCC. In October, 1971, the Africa Section began officially to function, with Filemona Indire as chairman and Nathan Luvai as secretary.

As part of a four-weeks visit to Africa in April, 1972, William Barton conferred with Nathan Luvai and other Section officers in Nairobi. FWCC Chairman, Heinrich Carstens, arrived in Kenya for a visit, expecting to attend the sessions of EAYM in August. Unfortunately, the high altitudes at both Nairobi and Kaimosi created a health problem for Heinrich and he was not able to complete his visit. Nathan Luvai then undertook increasing correspondence with Friends in different parts of Africa, and before the end of 1972 he had produced the first Africa Section Newsletter.

To arrange any visiting between South Africa and Kenya was difficult because of stereotypes which citizens of each country held of citizens of the other, and of immigration regulations reflecting those views. The Southern Africa Yearly Meeting invited EAYM to name one of their members as visitor to the sessions of yearly meeting in South Africa early in 1973. While no Kenyan Friend attended the yearly meeting, later in 1973 Simeon Shitemi stopped in South Africa enroute to the FWCC Triennial Meeting in Australia. Simeon was an assistant to President Kenyatta in Kenya, and this may have made arrangements with immigration authorities easier. Responding to requests from Section officers, Southern Africa Yearly Meeting nominated Scarnell Lean, of Johannesburg, to be the Section Vice-Chairman.

A first Africa Section Conference

Nathan Luvai wrote to constituent groups in the Section that the EAYM had offered to be host to a first conference of the Africa Section just before yearly meeting sessions at Lugulu in August, 1975. Representatives would be urged to stay on for the yearly meeting and for visiting in local meetings.

This first Africa Section Conference was held at the Friends Bible Institute in Kaimosi, Western Kenya, August 16 and 17. The number of representatives, though small, proved satisfactory to the officers – from South Africa two, from Pemba two, one each from Botswana and Nigeria, and 30 from Kenya. William Barton and Simeon Shitemi gave the principal addresses.

The conference approved a recommendation from the Section's Committee that a full time secretary should be employed as soon as finances would permit. Nathan Luvai had been diligent and effective in a part time situation, but he was not available for full time appointment. One of several applicants for the job was David Kikaya, a young member of East Africa Yearly Meeting. He had been one of a 'Young Adult Team' with the Quaker

UN Office in New York in the autumn of 1975. The Section officers appointed David as full time secretary, effective March 1, 1976.

Very little income for the Section was coming from African sources, except for 300 South African Rands annually from Southern Africa Yearly Meeting. The FWCC support had risen from £500 in each of the first two years to £2,000 per year, then to £3,400 when David Kikaya became the first full time secretary.

An endorsement of Non-Violence in Africa

The Triennial Meeting of 1976, held at Hamilton in Ontario, Canada, called on the Africa Section to organize a consultation in which representative Friends might 'examine rigorously both principle and practice of nations, liberation groups, churches and individuals on the issue of violence and to formulate counsel and guidance for all . . .' David Kikaya and other officers of the Africa Section had to deal with this charge by the FWCC while pressing on with further development of the life of the Section.

The seminar was held at Gaberone in Botswana, August 4-11, 1977, with participating Friends coming from Kenya, Rhodesia, South Africa, and Botswana. Fred Moorhouse, a Friend who had lived many years in Southern Africa and had recently taken residence in Britain, was named by the FWCC, the European and Near East Section, and the Friends Service Council as their representative. A Canadian Friend, William McMechan, temporarily in Tanzania, and Eldon Helm from the United States but working in Botswana, were asked by the Section of the Americas to take part in the seminar.

Several carefully prepared background papers were distributed in advance to seminar participants. Re-examination of the nature and efficacy of violence and non-violence and of the peace testimony occupied the first two days. Although recognizing that violence of the social structures frequently leads men and women to the violence of despair, participants re-affirmed their rejection of violence. They affirmed the contemporary relevance of the peace testimony, and undertook to show how Friends can make it a living force on the African scene.

Turning to practical considerations, Friends at the seminar urged more dependence on local initiative and insistence on full decision sharing at all levels of community and national life. They agreed to work toward redistribution of wealth and resources in their nations and in the world.

In an informal report of the seminar experience, Fred Moorhouse said there had been 'a small but very real, growth of understanding and fellowship between our East Africa and Southern Africa Yearly Meetings.

Much credit must be given to those who have pioneered the bridge building despite all the problems over visas' and other barriers to personal contacts. The Africa Section staff and officers had done much to bring this improvement. Following the seminar, Simeon Shitemi made his third visit to South African Friends.

Zablon Malenge comes to Africa Section staff

Early in 1978 David Kikaya was offered an opportunity for graduate study in Britain. He had given energy and talent to the work of the Africa Section, but his ambition pointed toward other fields of labor. He resigned, and left Kenya in pursuit of further education. It was more than a year before Section officers appointed a new secretary, Zablon Malenge.

A product of Kenyan Friends schools, Zablon had some business training and was working in a bank when Section officers gave him the

Zablon Malenge.

secretary's post. He has been a steady and reliable manager of Section affairs. In the midst of turmoil which has divided Kenyan Friends into three, then four, separate groups his quiet manner and firm convictions have helped to keep common goals in view. He has gained the confidence of Friends in all of Africa, and in meetings in America and Europe during his visits there. A good guide for the Africa Section, Zablon Malenge has become a 'world Friend'.

Far-flung groups in Asia-Pacific Area not yet ready for Section

Whatever hopes Ranjit Chetsingh may have felt for an Asian Friends conference, to be followed by the organizing of a section of the FWCC, faded before his return to India after two years in FWCC's London Office. Residing in India from 1956 onward, Ranjit made no further effort toward area arrangements for Asian Friends.

I was convinced by five months visiting in Asia, Australia, and New Zealand in 1959 that to urge any form of area organization would be unwise at that time. Friends in the different countries had no personal knowledge of each other, and tremendous distances separated them geographically. I proceeded to encourage visiting among the groups, which was achieved in part by arrangements for exchange visits by young Friends for whom the FWCC could obtain UNESCO Youth Travel Grants.

Blanche Shaffer, General Secretary from 1962, pursued a similar policy, and made her own extensive visits in Asian countries in 1964.

A latent interest beginning to show life

Late that year Lawrence Wilkinson, as 'Correspondent' for Friends in Australia, circulated a newsletter prematurely titled 'Newsletter No. 1 of the Pacific Section'. This effort was short-lived, but the interest of Australian and New Zealand Friends was wakening.

At the Triennial Meeting at Greensboro in 1967, Richard Meredith of Australia introduced the agenda item 'Asia and the Pacific Area' by saying there was a possibility of beginning the development of the FWCC Section. There were plans for exchange of news to be published in local or national newsletters, and for increased visitation. Representatives from India, Japan, and New Zealand expressed enthusiasm for the proposals and the minute recorded 'support of the recent efforts which might ultimately lead to the emergence of an Asian-Pacific Section of the FWCC'.

Cyril Gare, of Perth Meeting in Western Australia, became intensely interested in relationships with Friends and Quaker work in Asia, and in 1972 he visited meetings and Quaker projects in Asian countries. He wrote to Katherine Knight in New Zealand, with a list of reasons for proposing an Asia-Pacific Section at the FWCC Triennial Meeting in Sydney, Australia, in 1973. She agreed that some of the points made by Cyril Gare deserved consideration but said the suggestion for a Section should come from Friends in more of the countries where there were meetings.

Some small steps forward

In March, 1973, as Associate Secretary in FWCC's World Office, Tayeko Yamanouchi wrote to clerks and correspondents of all yearly meetings and groups in the Asia-Pacific area, suggesting their representatives to the Triennial Meeting at Sydney come prepared to report group thinking about proposals for a Section. Their conclusions were reported by Richard Meredith: (1) Setting up of an Asia-Pacific Section should be reconsidered at the next Triennial Meeting in 1976. (2) Meanwhile, encourage forging of stronger links among Friends in Asia, Australia, and New Zealand, through a center for the exchange of information inaugurated by Cyril and Elsie Gare in Perth, Australia. (3) Cost of this center would be shared by the participating meetings. (4) The value of this service during the next three years would help to make a decision about the need for a Section.

Beginning in 1974, Cyril and Elsie Gare produced each year three numbers of an Asia-Pacific Area Friends Newsletter. Their volunteer service was acknowledged with gratitude at the 1976 Triennial Meeting. FWCC Vice-Chairman, Lawrence Wilkinson, speaking about the area, said they still hoped that some day it might host a fully-fledged Section.

Two Friends conferences in Asia

Before she retired at the end of 1976, Tayeko Yamanouchi helped to set in motion plans for the first Friends conference in Asia. Held in Hong Kong, January 27-29, 1978, the conference brought together 15 Friends from Japan, Korea, The Philippines, and Taiwan. Members of the Hong Kong Meeting were hosts and several took part in one or more conference sessions. FWCC Chairman Edwin Bronner, and his wife Anne, were on a round-the-world Quaker visiting journey which included a Hong Kong visit and participation in this conference.

Along with times for worship, Friends shared their concerns and insights about issues which had been listed in the conference call: disarmament, peacemaking, and nuclear test bans; human rights; right sharing of the world's resources; and the proposed UN Program for A New International Economic Order. Creation of an Asia-Pacific Section was considered, but the group did not feel the time was right to take such a step.

There was a second small conference of Asian-West Pacific Friends in Delhi, India, in August 1982, as representatives traveled toward Kenya for a Triennial Meeting. Ruth Watson, of Australia, told the Triennial Meeting that a strong desire for understanding and mutual support was evident in the conference. Peace work, homelessness, hunger, unemployment, violence in towns, and depletion of natural resources were among the concerns discussed. Again, a proposal for a Section of the FWCC had been circulated – a Section which would start with very modest organization and volunteer personnel.

Richard Meredith's role

With Richard Meredith as General Secretary from 1981, the FWCC again had a Friend from the Asia-West Pacific Area as a principal member of staff. In late 1983 and early 1984, Richard and Bronwen Meredith visited

Richard G. Meredith.

Friends in Japan, Korea, Taiwan, Hong Kong, The Philippines, Port Moresby in Papua New Guinea, Australia, Singapore, and Delhi in India. A primary purpose of these visits was to help Friends carefully consider setting up, at last, a fourth Section of FWCC.

At the end of the journey Richard could report that the Standing Committee of Japan Yearly Meeting had agreed to support the formation of the proposed Section. And that Australia Yearly Meeting was recommending to FWCC that a Section for the Asia-West Pacific Area be set up at the 1985 Triennial Meeting, with promise of specific financial support by Australian Friends. Cyril and Elsie Gare would carry on with a Regional Newsletter.

At long last, Richard Meredith presented the proposal for an Asia-West Pacific Section to the 1985 Triennial Meeting at Oaxtepec in Mexico. He said that during several decades there had been hope that an organization within FWCC might serve to establish links among Friends in this wide region. Now it was time for action to be taken. There would be three recognized geographical areas within the Section – Northeast Asia, South Asia, and Austral-Asia. Assistant Clerks would be responsible for stimulating activities and communication in these areas. He, Richard Meredith, retiring from the post of General Secretary at the end of 1985, had agreed to be the volunteer Secretary for the Section.

The Triennial Meeting adopted the proposal and the Asia-West Pacific Section of FWCC was at last a reality. During the next year Dayal Gour, of the General Conference of Friends in India, and Marian Lyftogt, of New Zealand, were named Assistant Clerks. The first Clerk for the Section was Yoon Gu Lee of the Seoul Meeting in Korea. His successor, named in 1988, was Susumu Ishitani of Japan Yearly Meeting.

Relationships with Friends in Latin America

For nearly 30 years the FWCC had official relationships with Latin American Friends in only Cuba and Mexico. In addition, there was substantial contact with a group of Friends who established a farming community, Monteverde, in Costa Rica, to get away from the claims of conscription for military training in the United States following the Second World War. After the Castro-led revolution came to power in Cuba early in 1959, nearly two-thirds of the Cuban Friends left that country. Most of the Cuban Quaker refugees came to the United States, many settling in Miami, Florida, where they formed their own Friends Church. For several years the FWCC had limited communication and personal contact with Friends who remained in Cuba.

The Latin American contingent at the 1967 World Conference at Greensboro slightly expanded the previous FWCC contact with that part of the world, with three representatives coming from the Central America Mission churches in Guatemala. The Cuban government gave travel permits to only two Friends, although four representatives were requested. From Costa Rica there were four representatives, one from the Bogota Group in Colombia, and seven from the two main groups in Mexico.

The American Section provided nurture to informal groups, at different times, in Buenos Aires, Bogota, Guatemala City, Lima, Rio de Janeiro, San Jose, and Santiago. Most participants in these worship groups were persons of North American or European background.

A conference of Friends in the Americas

Some members of the American Section hoped that the stimulation and inspiration from the 1967 World Conference experience might be maintained through the holding of a large conference of American Friends as soon as 1973. This proposal was examined but rejected as not practical. However, in that year the Friends General Conference offered the assistance of their skilled conference-planning staff, and proposed to forego their own biennial conference in 1977, if the FWCC Section of the Americas would sponsor a conference for Friends in America.

At the invitation of the Section, representatives of the EFA, FGC, FUM, National Quaker Men, the United Society of Friends Women, and the YFNA met in January, 1974, to explore this latest conference proposal. This group recommended a conference which would build on the 'Faith' and 'Life' emphases of the Faith and Life Movement then in progress, an 'open conference' available to more than appointed representatives, and which would include Friends from North, South, and Central America and the Caribbean Area. Thirty-two yearly meetings and six Quaker organizations appointed 46 representatives to a planning committee which met two times. A smaller 'Steering Committee' included two members from Latin American groups and met more frequently, chaired by Donald L. Moon, also Chairman of the Section of the Americas from 1973 to 1978.

To determine whether the conference might be held somewhere in Latin America, the Steering Committee had a three-day meeting in March, 1975, in Mexico City, with invited participants from Mexico, Guatemala, Costa Rica, and Jamaica. The Spanish-speaking Friends said, without hesitation, that the conference should not be held in one of their countries, because their groups did not have the strength to provide local support which a large gathering would require. Instead, the conference was held in Wichita, Kansas, June 23 to July 1, 1977. Friends from Latin America, along with

Donald L. Moon, Chairman of the FWCC Section of the Americas,
1973-1978.

selected bi-lingual Friends from the United States and Canada, had their
own sessions in daytime periods. This small conference focused attention
on 'The role of Friends in Central and South America'.

Latin American Friends to continue in communication

The Spanish-language 'conference within a larger conference' came to
be known as the *Mesa Redonda* (Round Table). Its participants, from
Bolivia, Colombia, Cuba, El Salvador, Guatemala, Honduras, and Mexico
– along with Spanish-speaking North American Friends – started each day
together with listening and waiting in silence, followed by sharing from
their individual and home group experiences. Near the close of the week
they agreed that this communication in depth must be continued.

The most significant result of the 1977 conference was the growth of
acquaintance and cooperation among Spanish-speaking Friends. Before
leaving Wichita they called for formation of a *Comite Organizador de Los*

Amigos Latinoamericanos (Organizing Committee of Latin American Friends, or COAL), with one member from each of the Latin American groups. To give initial direction to COAL they designated three Friends, all resident in Mexico City, as the *Coordinadores Central*, or working core. The three were Loida Fernandez (a member of the long-standing Friends group with Ciudad Victoria as its center, in Northern Mexico), Manuel Guzman (pastor of the Evangelical Friends Mission Church in a Mexico City suburb), and Jorge Hernandez (a member of the Mexico City Friends Meeting). They began immediately to build on the *Mesa Redonda* experience.

In September Alice Shaffer, an Indiana Friend with long experience as a UNICEF administrator in Latin American countries, represented the American Section at the *Reunion General* of Friends in Mexico. She found that the three Friends had already produced the first number of a *Boletin* and plans were developing for other communication and Friendly visiting.

Section of Americas appoints staff for COAL

It soon became obvious that activity stimulated by the increasing interest of Latin American Friends would require the attention of regular staff. Mexican Friends gave high recommendation to Loida Fernandez who would soon complete studies for a degree in theology. They hoped that opportunity for service with Friends might be available to her.

The Section of the Americas appointed an *ad hoc* committee to explore the appointment of staff. Its convenor, Robert Lyon, traveled to Mexico in December, 1977, to confer with Manuel Guzman, Jorge Hernandez and other Friends. In February, 1978, the Executive Committee of the Section of the Americas appointed Loida Fernandez Associate Secretary, approving a job description and budget. The *Comite Organizador de Los Amigos Latinoamericanos* would provide general guidance for her work and she would keep in close touch with the Executive Secretary of the Section in matters of overall policy.

COAL's developing plans

Loida, with Manuel Guzman and Jorge Hernandez, worked to increase personal contacts through visits among Latin American Friends groups. Continued publication of the *Boletin* brought good response. Quaker literature in the Spanish language, already at hand, was distributed, and plans for new publication were set in motion. The possibilities for training in leadership for local groups were discussed. Loida and her advisors began to organize the 'Evaluation Conference' which was held at Monteverde, in Costa Rica, at the beginning of February, 1980.

Loida's resignation a loss for COAL

Unfortunately, Loida resigned from the Associate Secretary post in mid-1981. Jorge Hernandez, with limited available time, tried to care for routine duties in the office of COAL at the Friends Center in Mexico City. Margarita Orozco, a medical doctor living in Tampico, Mexico, was made an Assistant Clerk of the Section of the Americas and a member of the new, smaller Section Executive Committee which met three times a year. She served as a link between the Executive Committee and COAL.

Margarita was also Clerk of the Temporary Committee for Latin American Program which the Section Executive Committee had appointed, with members in Mexico and in the Philadelphia area. This Temporary Committee developed proposals for the composition and program of COAL, and these proposals were approved at Mexico City in February, 1982, by a meeting of representatives from Bolivia, Costa Rica, Mexico, and Latin American Friends living in the United States. While the constituency of COAL thus became formal for the first time, its officers were busy people and COAL could not properly function without staff.

Gordon Browne, the Section's Executive Secretary, tried a variety of means to locate a Friend, bi-lingual and equipped in spirit and experience to work with the different groups of Friends in Latin America. Late in 1983, he found Nelson Salinas, a Chilean living in Austin, Texas, and former Protestant minister who had become a member of the Austin Friends Meeting. Nelson agreed to undertake the duties of staff for COAL for one year.

Renewal of COAL activities

During the year 1984 COAL emphasized intervisitation among the groups in Latin America. It arranged the first of an annual gathering of local meeting pastors. It encouraged support for a 'peace center' in San Jose, Costa Rica. It published its *Boletin* bi-monthly. Nelson Salinas worked effectively with the COAL Executive Committee and was a welcome visitor as he traveled among Latin American Friends.

The Section of the Americas increased its visitation exchanges between North America and Latin America. Molly and Miguel Figuerola of the Monteverde Meeting in Costa Rica, who had already visited other Central American groups, traveled four months in 1984 among meetings in the United States and Canada. Visits were arranged for Javier Tito of Bolivia. Four Friends from the United States went to Cuba in August, to join in the family camp arranged by Cuban Friends and to visit in homes. In October and November, Gordon Browne made a month-long visit which included time with Friends in Bolivia, Colombia, Costa Rica, Guatemala, Honduras, and Mexico.

The Section developed a joint plan with Pendle Hill, the Quaker adult study center near Philadelphia, to bring Jorge Hernandez from Mexico to be 'Friend in Residence' for two terms. He worked on three projects: (1) to strengthen Pendle Hill curriculum appeal and service to Latin American Friends; (2) to assist Pendle Hill with a brief Spanish language course for FWCC members going to the 1985 Triennial Meeting in Mexico; and (3) to prepare for Latin American Friends a Quaker leadership training course which would be distributed through COAL.

Hosting a Triennial Meeting; Andres Carranza becomes Secretary

Preparations for FWCC's Triennial Meeting at Oaxtepec, in Mexico, heavily involved Mexican Friends. With Nelson Salinas' departure in January, 1985, the burden of these preparations fell on Margarita Orozco and others. Andres Carranza, a young member of Honduras Yearly Meeting, was appointed as staff for COAL and was plunged immediately into Triennial Meeting preparations when he took up the work on May 1st. He had also to arrange a meeting of COAL representatives immediately after the Triennial. At that meeting of COAL a new Executive Committee was named, whose Clerk was Manuel Guzman.

The experience of participation in a Triennial Meeting in Spanish-speaking America generated enthusiasm in Latin American Friends for COAL and its program. Andres Carranza visited meetings in Cuba, Bolivia, and Peru. Besides contacting the Central America Yearly Meeting, largely in Guatemala, which was not yet affiliated with COAL, he also arranged a meeting of COAL representatives in La Paz, Bolivia, in January, 1987.

Stronger support from the Section of the Americas

The Section of the Americas recognized the interest developing among Friends in Latin America and determined to make it possible for Spanish-speaking Friends to participate in annual meetings of the Section. To provide assistance needed for the expense of travel was costly, but the additional funds had to be found. Also, agenda and minutes had to be in Spanish as well as in English; and in meetings time had to be taken for interpretation between English and Spanish. In spite of the slower pace required, members of the Section spoke of richer, more joyful meetings with these arrangements.

Late in 1985 the Section of the Americas appointed Alex Morisey to be Associate Secretary, a new staff position in the Philadelphia office. He had gone to the Triennial Meeting in Mexico, representing the American Friends Service Committee. Although not previously well informed about FWCC, he felt a challenge in what he saw at Oaxtepec. Much earlier, he had been a member of a volunteer work camp in Guatemala, and later had operated a business in that country. Soon after his appointment by FWCC, Alex was given responsibility for staff contact with COAL and Friends in Latin America. He continued to have that responsibility when he became the Section's Executive Secretary at Gordon Browne's retirement in August, 1988.

FWCC becomes 'Friends world-wide'

Brief review of the Triennial Meetings from 1973 onward, especially of their venue, demonstrates the achievement of 'Quakers-world-wide' status by the FWCC.

Edwin B. Bronner, with Winifred Bewley of Ireland Yearly Meeting
(1964 photo).

From the ancient Quaker bases of London and Philadelphia the Australian Friends' invitation seemed nearly impossible to accept. But the FWCC was keen on the concept of all Friends as a 'world family', and when one part of a family is ready to be host for a reunion other members of the family respond. A conference on 'Friends and the Changing, Challenging World of Asia' was put into the middle of the Triennial Meeting at Sydney in August, 1973. The extra representatives allowed to Australia and New Zealand, and to Asian yearly meetings and groups, brought the total number of participants to 285.

Tayeko Yamanouchi as Associate Secretary carried a large responsibility in preparation for this meeting, giving it Asian flavor. Heinrich Carstens, for reasons of health, asked not to be reappointed as chairman. His successor, Edwin Bronner of Philadelphia Yearly Meeting, served for the next six years.

Tayeko Yamanouchi (left) and Ingeborg Borgstrom.

Joseph P. Haughton.

Val Ferguson.

1976 Triennial Meeting in Canada

Meeting at Hamilton, Ontario, the FWCC gave to Canadian Quakers assurance of their place in the world family of Friends, alongside larger yearly meetings in the United States. With just over 1,000 members in all of Canada, the yearly meeting was entitled to three representatives. But with special dispensation for the host yearly meeting, the FWCC provided 30 additional places to Canadians. This permitted each local meeting to send at least one member to the Triennial Meeting.

Altogether, 270 Friends came to Hamilton, from 44 yearly meetings in 29 countries. Representatives from East Africa Yearly Meeting played a more prominent role than in any previous Triennial Meeting. Tayeko Yamanouchi had indicated her intention of retiring at the end of 1976, and Ingeborg Borgstrom of Sweden was named as the new Associate Secretary.

A special committee had been at work preparing a written constitution for Friends World Committee for Consultation, adding formal by-laws to the long-standing statement of purpose. One of the paragraphs describing purpose was amended to read, in part: 'To keep under review the Quaker contribution in world affairs *and in the world Christian mission . . .*' The phrase in italics was added to emphasize that FWCC concern included all Friends, especially evangelical Friends who place greater emphasis on missionary endeavor. Because the larger Central and South American groups owe their origin to evangelical Friends' missions, this amendment gave support to their increased involvement with FWCC during the next decade.

Meeting again in Europe, 1979

The Fourteenth Meeting was held at Gwatt, on Lake Thun, in Switzerland. It was the last meeting before the retirement of William Barton in mid-1980, and the first attended by Zablon Malenge, Secretary of the Africa Section. Val Ferguson was named Associate Secretary to succeed Ingeborg Borgstrom. Edwin Bronner had served six years as chairman; to succeed him in January, 1980, the FWCC named Joseph Haughton of Ireland Yearly Meeting, who had been chairman of the Interim Committee since 1970. At the end of 1980 I retired from my post with the Section of the Americas, and Margaret Gibbins from the European and Near East Section in mid-1981.

Midst pending changes of officers and staff, the FWCC proposed to move toward its goals with two areas of focus for the 1980s, namely to facilitate 'loving recognition of diversities among Friends while we discover together, with God's help, our common spiritual ground' and 'full consideration of our Quaker responses to today's issues of social justice'.

Meeting for the second time in Kenya

Richard Meredith had come from Australia to the General Secretary post in London early in 1981. Preparing for the 1982 Triennial Meeting, he and Val Ferguson had to deal with problems arising from division among Friends in Kenya. Then, just as FWCC members began arriving in Nairobi there was an attempted coup against the Kenya government. The coup did not succeed, and arriving Friends could be brought together in Nairobi for transport by bus a further 200 miles to Kaimosi.

An 'International Conference' from August 9 to 13 preceded the Triennial Meeting. Its theme, 'The Transforming Power of the Love of God', had been proposed by the most recent Mission and Service Conference. African Friends constituted about half of the 575 participants. Some 200 FWCC members stayed on at Kaimosi for Triennial Meeting business sessions.

Among concerns arising from the International Conference and acted upon by the Triennial Meeting, three are significant for the continued attention given them by FWCC. First, the young Friends proposed that a World Gathering of Young Friends be held soon. They asked for, and were given, the support of FWCC and the Section offices as arrangements were made for the World Gathering in 1985 at Guilford College in North Carolina.

Second, a concern for continued effort, until all discrimination based on race disappears among peoples of the earth, challenged Friends to work harder at eliminating racism in themselves and in their meetings. From the Triennial Meeting the FWCC issued 'Racial Concerns Queries' for Friends generally and for Friends individually. These Queries were widely distributed and widely used. Third, a Women's Interests Group at the conference prepared a minute of concern which the Triennial Meeting approved for study and appropriate action. This concern has become a long-term program for the achievement of gender equality.

A first meeting of FWCC in Latin America

Margarita Orozco, Jorge Hernandez, and other Mexican Friends were the capable hosts for the 1985 Triennial Meeting at Oaxtepec in Mexico. Among the 300 participants, more than 30 had come direct from the World Gathering of Young Friends in North Carolina. Richard Meredith was retiring from the General Secretary position and would return to his home in Australia. As his successor, the FWCC appointed Val Ferguson who had been Associate Secretary since 1980; and it named Thomas Taylor, of Lake Erie Yearly Meeting in the United States, as the new Associate Secretary.

At this meeting, the FWCC decided that its principal officer would be called 'Clerk' rather than chairman, and the vice-chairmen would become 'Assistant Clerks'. This was a small step toward implementing gender equality concerns, one which the Section of the Americas had taken in 1976. As Clerk for the next triennium the FWCC appointed Simeon Shitemi, a Kenyan Friend.

Simeon Shitemi.

1988 Triennial Meeting in Japan

Appointed a Vice-Chairman of FWCC in 1982, Akio Watanabe worked hard to persuade the 250 members of Japan Yearly Meeting that they had the numbers and the strength to host a Triennial Meeting of the FWCC. In August, 1988, his dream materialized as Friends from 35 countries met at the International Christian University just outside Tokyo, for FWCC's first meeting in Asia.

There, members agreed that Friends should join in a World Council of Churches program to pursue concerns for Justice, Peace and the Integrity of Creation (JPIC). This program is a response to world-wide suffering caused by the absence of peace, the presence of injustice, and the manipulation of the environment.

Important for the future of FWCC was the decision to hold a world conference of Friends in 1991, in three locations. At each of the locations there will be some 300 participants, part coming from the region of that location, the rest from elsewhere in the world. By this arrangement full representation is expected with efficient use of limited travel funds. The proposed locations are Honduras, Kenya, and The Netherlands.

Organized Sections of the Friends World Committee for Consultation now function on all of the world's continents, and on some islands where Friends are living. A very small number of yearly meetings in Africa and Asia, and in North and Central America, do not yet have formal affiliation with FWCC, but with all there are friendly informal contacts.

CHAPTER XII

Inter-Yearly Meeting and International

IN A REPORT OF THE FWCC'S SEVENTH MEETING in 1958, Bertram Pickard wrote that if the Friends World Committee for Consultation had not been organized at an earlier date, Friends would 'find it necessary to form a world committee now'.

Until 1952 the FWCC had not been in reality a *world* committee *for consultation*. Participation in the conference at Oxford in that year came close to representing Friends world wide. The conference program and

The Clerks, 1989 (l to r): Filemona Indire (Africa Section), Harold Smuck (Section of the Americas), Erica Vere (European and Near East Section), Dan Seeger (FWCC Interim Committee), Susumu Ishitani (Asia-West Pacific Section), Simeon Shitemi (FWCC).

arrangements provided a variety of opportunities for consultation for a thousand Friends during ten days. But unadaptability of organization and restrictions in finance prevented the FWCC from sustaining either consultation or a representative quality.

Welcoming the changes in organization proposed by an enlivened Executive Committee in 1955, the editor of *The Friend* (London) was glad that the image of FWCC as a 'rubber-stamp committee' or 'at best a kind of international Quaker post-office, clearing-house, information bureau, or liaison department', might soon be changed. He suggested that the FWCC could become a vehicle for 'communication', a stronger word than consultation.

FWCC finding its identity and its role

Increasingly, in the last half of the 1950s and the decade of the 1960s, the FWCC became a means of communication, expressed in a sharing of experience between the newer groups of Africa, Asia, and Europe and the older-established yearly meetings in the British Isles and North America. Friends who had feared that a 'super yearly meeting' might usurp the prerogatives of yearly meetings became easy with, and accepting of, the FWCC.

It was possible, then, for the FWCC to bring Friends 'from all the world' together in conference at Greensboro in 1967; and at this time Friends were ready to trust their World Committee with new functions within an expanded concept of the modifier 'for consultation'.

With no self consciousness or apology, the FWCC and its Sections have taken on responsibilities for service to the Society of Friends, responding to need for action by an entity larger than any one yearly meeting or national group. Many of the newly undertaken programs are more adaptable to management by one Section or another than by FWCC world-wide.

Some specific tasks in FWCC's expanded role

The FWCC and its European and Near East Section have responded to the special concern of a Friend in Geneva, supported by other Friends in Switzerland, by urging governments and the United Nations to include, under accepted Rights of the Child, assurance that children of 15 years and younger will not be required to perform military service. And beginning in the early 1980s, representatives of peace committees in the yearly meetings of the European and Near East Section have met at least annually as the European Quaker Peace Consultations, now formally linked with the Section.

From 1973 to 1980, the Section of the Americas sponsored a self-administering Friends Committee on Economic Responsibility which provided information and encouragement to Quaker institutions and individuals for socially responsible investment of capital funds. In the same period, a similar sponsorship was given to a group of Friends operating a Quaker Center for Prisoner Support Activities. In both these efforts, Friends from several yearly meetings were involved.

A number of Friends churches and Friends meetings in the United States have under their care Boy or Girl Scout troops. As part of the Scout program, there is training in the religious beliefs and practices of the religious body which is the troop sponsor. At one time the Friends General Conference and the Friends United Meeting had cooperated to prepare a curriculum which could be used by troop leaders. By 1986, need for a more carefully prepared curriculum came to the attention of the Section of the Americas which appointed a committee of Friends with experience of scouting. After two years of work by the committee and communication with persons in the different groups of American Friends, a curriculum which would lead to the religious training award in scouting programs for both boys and girls was approved by the Section in 1988, and presented to the Scout organizations.

Major attention to War Tax Concerns

Payment of the portion of tax which goes for military purposes has been the concern of individual Friends in different countries and different yearly meetings over many years. The FWCC at times assisted with communication among Friends about this concern.

In the early 1980s, Friends in Canada and the United States brought war tax questions to the attention of the Section of the Americas which then arranged a 1984 Conference on War Tax Concerns. This conference of representatives of Quaker organizations called for the formation of a Committee on War Tax Concerns. At that committee's first meeting in January, 1985, it asked for sponsorship by the Section of the Americas.

The Section's representative on the War Tax Concerns Committee, Wallace Collett, served as the committee clerk, and Linda Coffin, also a member of the Section, as secretary. The committee arranged two conferences for Quaker employers, in which there was consideration of appropriate action by an employer when an employee asks that some part of his withholding tax not be paid over to the government. (Some members of the Section's staff took the tax resister's position. As employer, the Section of the Americas had to determine its own policy for handling the money which an employee requested should not be paid to the government; and, at the same time, deal with the government's revenue service which is responsible for collecting the money.)

The War Tax Concerns Committee prepared booklets on nine aspects of the question of non-payment of war taxes, eventually published together as one book. A separate booklet for the guidance of employers in these matters was produced.

In the world, one family of Friends

There has been increasing acceptance of the concept of a Quaker world family in which all parts have equal responsibility and opportunity. Not many years ago, a European or an American officer of FWCC might speak of 'the more distant meetings' when referring to African or Asian or Australasian or Hispanic Friends. Now the 'distant members' are members 'just as we are'. Important gatherings under FWCC arrangement have been held in Africa and Asia and Hispanic America, as well as in North America and Europe.

In the early 1970s the American Section decided to take a new name, realizing that for most people of the world the term American was ambiguous, and that United States citizens had usurped the word 'American' to denote their own nationality. A decision to become the 'Western Hemisphere Section' was not quite final before the FWCC Meeting in Australia in 1973. Officers of the American Section decided to tell the assembled gathering at Sydney that they were near to adopting 'Western Hemisphere Section' as their new name. An unidentified voice from the back of the room, with a definite Australian accent, called out, 'West of what?' The point of the question was clear. The Quaker world has no fixed point from which the position of all Friends is determined. More weeks of thought and communication culminated in the decision to take the name 'Section of the Americas'.

Inter-yearly meeting, international, world-wide

In much of its constituency the international character of FWCC is significant. While international participation is important for Friends in the Section of the Americas, interaction among the 30 yearly meetings in the United States, with differing background and development, requires emphases and program relevant to that Section of FWCC. The FWCC is both inter-yearly meeting and international. Certainly it is world wide.

Among Friends there is recognition of need for a united Quaker body to serve as a voice of international, inter-yearly meeting Quakerism. Friends schooled by participation in the FWCC become aware that it can reflect a unity which only partially exists in Quakerism world wide. But through the broadest interpretation of the 'for consultation' modifier in its name, the Friends World Committee for Consultation is both limited and liberated as spokesman, and as sponsor of cooperative action, for Friends throughout the world.

World Gatherings of Friends

1920 *All Friends Conference*, London, England
1937 *Second World Conference*, Swarthmore and Haverford Colleges, USA – recommended establishing Friends World Committee for Consultation

—— Gatherings arranged by FWCC ——

1938 1st Committee Meeting, Vallekilde, Denmark
1939 2nd Committee Meeting, Geneva, Switzerland
1947 3rd Committee Meeting, Richmond, Indiana, USA
1950 4th Committee Meeting, Oxford, England
1952 *Third World Conference*, Oxford, England
     5th Committee Meeting, Oxford, England
1955 6th Triennial Meeting, Germantown, Ohio, USA
1958 7th Triennial Meeting, Bad Pyrmont, West Germany
1961 8th Triennial Meeting, Kaimosi, Kenya
1964 9th Triennial Meeting, Waterford, Ireland
1967 *Fourth World Conference*, Greensboro, North Carolina, USA
     10th Triennial Meeting, Greensboro, North Carolina, USA
1970 11th Triennial Meeting, Sigtuna, Sweden
1973 12th Triennial Meeting, Sydney, Australia
1976 13th Triennial Meeting, Hamilton, Ontario, Canada
1979 14th Triennial Meeting, Gwatt, Switzerland
1982 *International Conference*, Kaimosi, Kenya
     15th Triennial Meeting, Kaimosi, Kenya
1985 16th Triennial Meeting, Oaxtepec, Mexico
1988 17th Triennial Meeting, Tokyo, Japan
1991 (projected) *Fifth World Conference*, one conference on three sites: The Netherlands, Honduras, and Kenya

Principal Officers of FWCC and its Sections

FWCC Clerks
(until 1985, 'Chairmen')

1938-47	Carl Heath (England)
1948-52	D. Elton Trueblood (USA)
1953-58	Errol Elliott (USA)
1959-61	Elsa Cedergren (Sweden)
1962-64	James F. Walker (USA)
1965-70	Douglas Steere (USA)
1971-73	Heinrich Carstens (West Germany)
1974-79	Edwin B. Bronner (USA)
1980-85	Joseph P. Haughton (Ireland)
1986-	Simeon Shitemi (Kenya)

World Office General Secretaries
(until 1956, 'Secretaries')

1938-46	Frederick Tritton (England)
1947-48	Leslie D. Shaffer (USA)
1948-50	Frederick Tritton (England)
1951-53	Harry T. Silcock (England)
1954-55	Ranjit M. Chetsingh (India)
1956-61	Herbert M. Hadley (USA)
1962-70	Blanche W. Shaffer (USA)
1971-79	William E. Barton (England)
1980	Thomas Bodine, acting (USA)
1981-85	Richard G. Meredith (Australia)
1986-	Val Ferguson (Gt. Britain)

FWCC World Office Associate Secretaries

1969-70	William E. Barton (England)
1971-76	Tayeko Yamanouchi (Japan)
1977-79	Ingeborg Borgstrom (Sweden)
1980-85	Val Ferguson (Great Britain)
1986-	Thomas F. Taylor (USA)

Africa Section

Clerk
(until 1985, 'Chairman')

1971-   Filemona F. Indire

Executive Secretaries
(until 1979, 'Secretaries')

1971-75   Nathan Luvai
1976-78   David Kikaya
1979-   Zablon Malenge

Asia and West Pacific Section

Clerks

1986-87   Yoon-Gu Lee (Korea)
1988-   Susumu Ishitani (Japan)

Secretary

1986-   Richard G. Meredith
           (Australia)

Section of the Americas (until 1954, 'American Section'; from 1954 to 1974, 'American Section and Fellowship Council')
Clerks (until 1976, 'Chairmen')

1938   Alvin T. Coate (Western YM)
1939-42   J. Hoge Ricks (Baltimore YM)
1943-45   Thomas E. Jones (Indiana YM)
1946   William O. Mendenhall (California YM)
1947   D. Elton Trueblood (Indiana YM)
1948-55   Alexander C. Purdy (New England YM)
1956-60   Dorothy Gilbert Thorne (Wilmington YM)
1961-67   A. Ward Applegate (Western YM)
1968-72   Edwin B. Bronner (Philadelphia YM)
1973-78   Donald L. Moon (Western YM)
1979-84   Barrett Hollister (Ohio Valley YM)
1985-88   Heather Moir (Southeastern YM)
1989-   Harold Smuck (Indiana YM)

Executive Secretaries

1938-45   Leslie D. Shaffer
1946   J. Harold Hadley, acting
1947   Allen J. White
1948-49   Leslie D. Shaffer
1950-62   James F. Walker
1963-80   Herbert M. Hadley
1981-88   Gordon M. Browne, Jr
1989-   Alex Morisey

European and Near East Section (until 1966, 'European Section')
Clerks (until 1986, 'Chairmen')

1939-48   Regnar Halfden-Nielsen (Denmark)
1949-52   William H. Marwick (Scotland)
1953-55   Norah Douglas (Northern Ireland)
1956-63   Sigrid H. Lund (Norway)
1964-70   Heinrich Carstens (West Germany)
1971-73   Gunnar Sundberg (Sweden)
1974-76   Madelaine Jequier (Switzerland)
1977-85   John Ward (British, resident in Switzerland)
1986-   Erica Vere (England)

Secretaries

1938   Helen Peach (Brooks) (England)
1939-47   Frederick J. Tritton (England)
1948-52   Elise Thomsen (Denmark)
1953-55   Archer Tongue (British, resident in Switzerland)
1956-63   Sigrid H. Lund, Executive Chairman (Norway)
1964-81   Margaret S. Gibbins (Scotland)
1982   Jonathan Fryer (British, resident in Belgium)
1983-   Franco Perna (Italian, resident in Luxembourg)

Quaker United Nations Offices

Directors, or principal 'Quaker Representatives'

New York Office		*Geneva Office*	
1948-60	Elmore Jackson	1948-49	Algie I. Newlin
1961-62	George Loft	1950-54	Colin W. Bell
1963-69	William Huntington	1955-77	J. Duncan Wood
1970-78	Barrett Hollister	1978-79	Philip L. Martin
1979-82	Stephen Thiermann	1980-82	Peter Whittle
1983-86	Roger Naumann	1983-84	Kevin Clements
1987-	Stephen Collett	1985-	Joel McClellan

Membership Statistics of the Religious Society of Friends 1937-1987

Africa Section	1937	★ 1957	1967	1977	1987
Burundi			1,362	1,396	3,027
East Africa	7,084	28,152	32,155	33,975	45,000
Ghana					17
Madagascar†	5,850	7,700	8,208		
Pemba	100	70	147	200	140
Southern Africa	125	217	142	120	148
Total Africa	13,160	36,140	42,014	35,700	48,300
Asia-West Pacific Section					
Australia	644	808	929	1,000	1,084
China‡	1,350				
India	169	255	508	735	568
Japan	750	200	266	278	258
Korea					12
New Zealand	292	550	668	726	681
Philippines					100
Taiwan			960	2,400	2,500
Total Asia-West Pacific	3,205	1,813	3,330	5,140	5,200
European & Near East Section					
Belgium and Luxembourg					40
Cyprus		10			
Denmark	35	56	53	56	38
France	100	81	83	151	121
Germany (Pyrmont)	212	547	530	413	430
(DDR)				49	50
Ireland	2,108	2,011	1,800	1,747	1,684
Great Britain	19,799	21,563	21,040	20,063	18,076
Near East	131	130	130	100	60
Netherlands	19	100	117	129	150
Norway	70	70	91	117	130
Sweden and Finland	100	124	154	128	129
Switzerland		91	123	150	95
Total Europe & Near East	22,574	24,783	24,121	23,103	21,000

Section of the Americas	1937	* 1957	1967	1977	1987
South America					
Bolivia		1,000	3,000	8,000	20,000
Colombia				6	7
Peru			400	700	3,500
Total South America		1,000	3,400	8,700	23,500
Middle America					
Costa Rica		50	71	65	60
Cuba	1,967	1,073	319	330	300
El Salvador		275**			
Guatemala	3,683	4,112	1,470	2,549	3,386
Honduras	400	900	299	701	1,500
Jamaica	1,136	800	635	679	400
Mexico	56	50	197	125	400
Total Middle America	7,242	7,260	2,991	4,450	6,000
North America					
Alaska	1,317	1,727‡‡			
Canada	1,273	696	792	1,105	1,146
USA — Conservative YM's	3,027	2,140	1,889	1,778	1,671
Friends Gen. Conf.	16,200	20,700	21,272	17,575	17,381
Friends United Mtg.	77,597	62,500	61,076	55,929	43,419
Independent YM's	15,510	24,600	27,702	3,385	6,724
Both FUM & FGC		10,300	10,049	13,842	13,798
Evangelical YM's				25,546	25,593
USA totals	112,334	120,240	121,988	118,055	108,586
Total Americas	122,166	131,000	129,200	132,300	139,200
International membership		59		60	54
Total World membership	161,105	193,800	198,700	196,200	213,800

Notes: The figures ending in one or more '0's are mostly estimates. Hence, the totals are rounded off to reflect a similar degree of accuracy. *1947 statistics not available due to distruption of World War II. †Madagascar YM became part of Church of Jesus Christ in Madagascar in 1968. ‡Chinese Friends became part of Church of Three Selves after cultural revolution. **El Salvador included in Honduras after 1957. ‡‡Alaska became 49th State of Union in 1959.

Sources: *Friends World News*, No. 128, 1987/1.

Bibliographical Notes

THE PRINCIPAL SOURCE OF INFORMATION for this history of the Friends World Committee for Consultation has been the archives of the FWCC. Archives from the central office of FWCC are in the Friends House Library, at Friends House, London. European and Near East Section archives are also at Friends House, although files for 1978 through 1982 were temporarily at Quaker House in Brussels, Belgium, when I examined them in 1983. Archives of the Section of the Americas are deposited in the Friends Historical Library at Swarthmore College, Swarthmore, Pennsylvania.

For the FWCC there are minutes of its meetings which, after the Sixth in 1955, are called Triennial Meetings; also minutes of an Executive Committee, succeeded in 1956 by an Interim Committee. In the European and Near East Section files are minutes of its annual meetings and, after 1955, of an Executive Committee. For the Section of the Americas there are minutes of Annual Meetings and of Executive and Finance Committees; also of a variety of program committees including Intervisitation, New Meetings, Wider Quaker Fellowship and, later, International Affairs, Right Sharing of World Resources, International Quaker Aid, Economic Responsibility, and War Tax Concerns.

The major Quaker periodicals – *The Friend* (London), *The Friend* (Philadelphia), *Friends Intelligencer,* and *Friends Journal* – have particular relevance to the time periods in which world conferences of Friends have occured – 1920, 1937, 1952, and 1967. Also useful are pre- and post-conference study books and the formal reports of each conference.

To better know two early British officers of the FWCC, I read these unpublished manuscripts in the Friends House Library: *Friend Without Frontiers, The Story of Carl Heath, Apostle to Many Lands,* by Roger Smith; and Frederick J. Tritton's autobiography, *My Life and Doings.* A good supplement to these manuscripts is Bernard G. Lawson's pamphlet *The Overseas and International Service of British and Irish Friends in the 20th Century (to 1961).*

Two unpublished student papers were helpful: *The Society of Friends Emerges from Provincialism,* 1963, by David T. Bates at Haverford College; and *Friends World Committee for Consultation,* 1962, by Marjorie E. Nelson at the Earlham School of Religion.

Publications of the FWCC have been an important resource, especially *Friends World News*, beginning with Number 1 in February, 1939, and continuing through Number 129 in 1987. A *Handbook of the Religious Society of Friends* has been published at irregular intervals, usually of five or more years. The recent handbooks have borne the title *Finding Friends Around the World*.

In addition to the published and unpublished written materials mentioned above, individual Friends have agreed to my consulting them by oral interview. Among those in Britain were Dorothy Hogg, Mary G. Lawson, Philip and Myrtle Wright Radley, and Roger C. Wilson; and in the United States, Alice C. Shaffer, Hannah Stapler and Allen J. White. I am especially grateful to these Friends.

General Index

Index of Personal Names

Explanation of Acronyms

Friends organizations and Friends programs:

AFBM   The American Friends Board of Missions was an integral part of the Five Years Meeting of Friends. It was administrator for work in East Africa, the former Palestine, Cuba, Jamaica, Mexico, and in the Tennessee mountains in the USA. The name was changed to Wider Ministries in 1971, and later to World Ministries Commission.

AFFC   The American Friends Fellowship Council was organized within the American Friends Service Committee in the early 1930s. It became independent, with representatives from some yearly meetings in the United States. In 1954 it was merged with the American Section of the FWCC. The AFFC nurtured new groups of Friends and authorized monthly meeting status when a group became strong enough to take that responsibility. It also cared for the Wider Quaker Fellowship (see below).

AFSC   The American Friends Service Committee was organized in 1917 by American Friends to provide young Friends opportunity to give service in relief and reconstruction in war devastated Europe. The AFSC has given similar service during and after more recent wars. It has provided famine relief in many parts of the world. It has developed a variety of programs for international reconciliation. In the United States and abroad the AFSC has worked with disadvantaged people. Peace education receives continuing attention.

AYFC and *AYFF*   American Young Friends Committee was the name used in the early 1950s by young Friends organized across yearly meeting lines in North America. American Young Friends Fellowship was the name used during the 1940s.

CIS   A Council for International Service was formed as a program of London Yearly Meeting in 1919, growing out of increasing concern to be involved in efforts for reconciliation among nations. The CIS and the FFMA (see below) merged in 1927 to form the Friends Service Council.

COAL   Comite Organizador de Los Amigos Latinoamericanos (Organizing Committee of Latin American Friends) was formed by the Spanish-speaking Friends at the Conference of Friends in the Americas, in June, 1977, with one member from each of the Latin American Friends

217

groups. COAL has encouraged communication and visiting among the groups, and has achieved a degree of cooperation in leadership training.

EAYM   East Africa Yearly Meeting was established in Western Kenya in 1946 from the membership and meetings which were the result of missionary work by the AFBM beginning in 1902. Through migration, meetings developed in large towns like Nairobi and Mombasa. There are outposts in Uganda and Tanganyika. Membership grew to about 50,000. The one large yearly meeting is now divided into four: EAYM (Central), EAYM (South), Elgon Religious Society of Friends, and Nairobi Yearly Meeting.

EFA   The Evangelical Friends Alliance began as the Association of Evangelical Friends in the 1940s. The formally organized EFA was established in 1961 by four yearly meetings in the USA. Some other yearly meetings are associate members. Evangelical Friends Mission is a parallel organization which coordinates missionary work of the EFA yearly meetings. In a recent expansion Evangelical Friends International was formed to include yearly meetings outside of the United States.

FFMA   Friends Foreign Mission Association. In 1868 London Yearly Meeting liberated its members with concern and enthusiasm for Christian missionary work to form the autonomous FFMA. It sponsored missions in Central India and West China, in the islands of Madagascar and Pemba, and in the area now known as Lebanon. An action of London Yearly Meeting in 1927 merged the FFMA and the CIS to form the Friends Service Council.

FGC   The yearly meetings of the Hicksite branch completed the formation of Friends General Conference in 1900, combining four associations which had met occasionally to foster specific functions or concerns. For some time General Conferences were held in alternate years, and more recently 'General Gatherings' each year have alternated between eastern and midwest locations. The FGC now provides a variety of services to its eleven member yearly meetings and other Friends.

FSC   The Friends Service Council was formed in 1927 when London Yearly Meeting merged its CIS and the FFMA. The FSC was an agency of London and Ireland Yearly Meetings, responsible for both missions and service work overseas. A reorganization of the yearly meeting structure in 1978 combined the FSC and the former Peace and International Relations Committee into one department called Quaker Peace and Service (QPS).

FUM   The Friends United Meeting, formerly Five Years Meeting of . Friends (see below), is composed of twelve yearly meetings in North America and the yearly meetings in Cuba, East Africa, and Jamaica. A triennial session of FUM is, technically, a representative body, but all

Friends are encouraged to attend and take part in discussions. The work of FUM is done through three commissions: Communication Ministries, Meeting Ministries, and World Ministries.

FWCC Friends World Committee for Consultation.

FYM The Five Years Meeting of Friends, established in 1902, grew out of an effort to provide a common book of discipline and statement of faith for 'orthodox' Friends. This purpose was only partially achieved. Not all orthodox yearly meetings adopted the Richmond Declaration of Faith, and some did not enter into the new organization which met at five year intervals. In 1965 the FYM adopted proposals for restructure which brought the FUM (see above) into being in 1966.

PfP Partnership for Productivity. As Quaker concern for right use and right sharing of the resources of the earth was finding expression in the Fourth Friends World Conference in 1967, a Washington Friend, David Scull, was developing this idea for assisting persons in little developed countries to receive appropriate training and financing for starting small businesses.

QCEA The Quaker Council for European Affairs developed during the 1970s to provide a Quaker presence in Brussels which is a decision-making center for European affairs. The QCEA Governing Council was formed in 1979, representing most of the yearly meetings in Europe and Belgium Monthly Meeting.

QIAR A Quaker International Affairs Representative is a person appointed by AFSC or FSC to be resident in a major capital city, to encourage national and international action for peace and justice, and to report and interpret events to the sponsoring organizations. The term QIAR was used as early as the late 1940s. By 1980 there were few QIARs other than Quaker Representatives at the UN in New York and Geneva.

QPS Quaker Peace and Service has been since 1978 one of the departments of London Yearly Meeting. It also has sponsorship by Ireland Yearly Meeting. QPS administers work for which the Friends Peace and International Relations Committee and the Friends Service Council were formerly responsible.

RSWR Right Sharing of World Resources is a program of the FWCC, especially of its sections in the Americas and in Europe. It developed from a concern endorsed by the Friends World Conference in 1967. It makes modest financial grants to small projects, usually projects known by some Friend or friend of Friends, in poor countries. Preferred projects are those in which local people determine policy and learn to help themselves.

RWQL Round the World Quaker Letters for Children developed from the concern of Ruby Dowsett, a New Zealand Friend. As first editor for RWQL, she solicited letters for different age groups from Friends around the world. The FWCC printed selected letters and provided these to yearly meetings or monthly meetings in accordance with orders made in advance.

WQF The Wider Quaker Fellowship program of the FWCC's Section of the Americas distributes Quaker-oriented literature three times a year in English, and once in Spanish, to persons in over 80 countries. Most are not Friends but have interest in the Quaker approach to life. Some yearly meetings outside the United States have their own WQF programs.

YFCNA and *YFNA* In 1954 American young Friends recognized the participation of Canadians in their activities across yearly meeting lines by forming the Young Friends Committee of North America. Later they adopted the shorter name Young Friends of North America.

Organizations other than those of Friends

CPC Church leaders in Czechoslovakia took initiative during the 1950s to form the Christian Peace Conference, hoping that church-related persons from East and West and all the world would meet in united action for peace. With its base in Prague and its primary leadership coming from countries where Communist control was pervasive, most statements issued by the CPC lacked objectivity and fairness.

EEC Six European nations, by treaty signed in 1957, formed the European Economic Community. Additional European nations have since become members of the EEC. Its purpose was to reduce, and eventually to eliminate, trade tariffs among its members. Other areas of cooperation have developed in parallel with the growth of the EEC.

NGO The Charter of the United Nations provided for a 'consultative status' which might be granted by the UN Economic and Social Council to international non-governmental organizations which meet standards established for Categories A, B, and C. The FWCC has held Category B status since it was granted in March, 1948. Category B NGOs must have 'special competence' in some, but not all or most, of the fields of activity of the UN.

UNRWA is the United Nations Relief and Works Agency, responsible for the UN's work of care for refugees.

WCC By its own definition, the World Council of Churches is 'a fellowship of churches which accept Jesus Christ as God and Saviour'. It developed from three strands of the ecumenical movement in the early years of the 20th century. The First World War delayed its formation which was accomplished at Amsterdam after the war, in 1948.